D1301352

WOMEN, ETHICS AND THE WORKPLACE

WOMEN, ETHICS

AND THE

WORKPLACE

CANDICE FREDRICK

CAMILLE ATKINSON

PRAEGER

Westport, Connecticut
London

Library of Congress Cataloging-in-Publication Data

Fredrick, Candice, 1949–
     Women, ethics and the workplace / by Candice Fredrick and Camille
     Atkinson.
          p.   cm.
     Includes bibliographical references and index.
          ISBN 0–275–95643–1 (alk. paper).—ISBN 0–275–96091–9 (pbk.)
          1. Discrimination in employment.   2. Sex discrimination against
     women.   3. Sexual harassment of women.   4. Business ethics.
     I. Atkinson, Camille, 1960–   .   II. Title.
     HD6060.F73   1997
     331.4'133—dc21   97–8859

British Library Cataloguing in Publication Data is available.

Library of Congress Catalog Card Number: 97–8859
ISBN: 0–275–95643–1
          0–275–96091–9 (pbk.)

First published in 1997

Praeger Publishers, 88 Post Road West, Westport, CT 06881
An imprint of Greenwood Publishing Group, Inc.

Printed in the United States of America

The paper used in this book complies with the
Permanent Paper Standard issued by the National
Information Standards Organization (Z39.48–1984).

10 9 8 7 6 5 4 3 2 1

Copyright Acknowledgments

The author and publisher gratefully acknowledge permission for use of the
following material:

Excerpts from *Women, Family, Future Trends: A Selective Research Overview* by
the National Committee of Pay Equity, Winter 1996. Used by permission of
the National Committee of Pay Equity.

To Fr. Mark Delery for his loving, spiritual presence
and
to Louise A. Barrow for being a model of strength
and for her sustaining love

CONTENTS

Preface   xi
Introduction   xiii

1. ETHICAL THEORY   1
    Introduction   1
    Kantian Ethics   2
    J.S. Mill's Utilitarianism   5
    A Synthesis of Kant and Mill   7
    Aristotelian Ethics   9
    Nussbaum on Aristotle   12
    MacIntyre on Values   16
    Conclusion   17
    Questions for Reflection   17

2. FEMINIST THEORY   19
    Introduction   19
    Modern Feminism and Political Equality   21
    Essentialism and the Construction of Gender   26
    Simone de Beauvoir   27
    Twentieth-Century Thought   32
    Conclusion   44
    Questions for Reflection   45

3. SEXUAL HARASSMENT   47
    Introduction   47

Influence of Advertising   49
What Is Sexual Harassment?   55
Coercive Sexual Harassment   55
Non-Coercive Sexual Harassment   56
Aristotle on Intention   59
Gender Harassment   63
Questions for Reflection   64
Empowerment: Suggestions for How Victims Can
    Protect or Empower Themselves   64

4. COMPARABLE WORTH AND VALUE   67
Introduction   67
Religion and Worth   68
Women and Family Today   73
Karl Marx on Value   79
The Contemporary Workplace   82
Beyond Categories   85
Questions for Reflection   87

5. ADVERTISING   89
Introduction   89
The Nestle Case   91
What They Don't Say   93
What They Do Say   94
The Morality of Gamesmanship   95
Manipulation and Lying   97
Test of Publicity   98
The Whole Truth   100
Media Unrestrained   100
Portrayal of Women in Advertising   103
Questions for Reflection   108

6. LEADERSHIP   111
Introduction   111
The "Glass Ceiling"   112
Breaking the Glass Ceiling   114
Masculine vs. Feminine Styles   116
Masculine vs. Feminine Values   119
Managing Conflict and the Value of Reason   121
A Critical Look   124
Mentoring and Networking   128
Flex Time and Child Care   130
Conclusion   131

Questions for Reflection   132

7. WORKING-CLASS WOMEN   135
    Introduction   135
    A History of the Garment Industry   141
    "The Bridge Called My Back"   144
    Resegregation   146
    The Two Shifts   147
    Pink-Collar Work   148
    Blue-Collar Trades   150
    Women in the Military   154
    Questions for Reflection   156

Conclusion   159
Appendix A: Anita Hill Testimony   163
Appendix B: Women, Family, Future Trends: A Selective Overview 169
Bibliography   171
Index   175

PREFACE

Although our primary interests and teaching experience are in the areas of philosophy and religion, we have often been asked to teach business ethics courses. Apparently, we are considered most able because we possess backgrounds in ethical theory and are relatively well versed in philosophical concepts, the kind of training that most business professors lack. However, when it came to choosing a text for these courses we found little material that we, as women, could relate to or that challenged students to think critically about some of the fundamental assumptions of business in a capitalist economy. More often than not we found that we had to seek out supplementary material in order to address our students' concerns. For instance, women training for business degrees are very concerned about topics such as the "glass ceiling" and sexual harassment and often raise doubts about assumptions that traditional business practices take for granted. Yet, the texts we found almost always begin by framing issues in accordance with a capitalistic model and either do a cursory job of covering problems related to sex and gender or ignore them altogether. Moreover, these texts tend to treat topics only in theory, as abstractions, without considering their concrete applicability; they do not even question whether or not their speculations accurately reflect the experiences of working people.

It is our hope that we can fill this gap and offer some new perspectives and insights for students, professors, and lay people. We envision this book as truly interdisciplinary because we are covering issues important to gender studies, business, ethics, politics, economics, and philosophy. By weaving among these various areas, we hope to show

how they are interrelated and, ultimately, inseparable. It is our belief that in life ethical questions and any attempt to answer them, whether in business or anywhere else, can only be discerned in accordance with certain social, philosophical, and economic principles or traditions. Thus, because we cannot neatly categorize issues as belonging merely to gender theory, business, or philosophy, we do not separate them here. Rather, we try to demonstrate how one question inexorably leads to others and how various directions for further discussion may follow.

We wish to express our gratitude to many people who supported us. First, the idea for this book really began with Maurice Hamington, who saw a need for such work and envisioned its possibility. We cannot thank him enough for his contributions.

Charles Fredrick, Candice's husband, was invaluable in his help, which went well beyond designing its format. In many respects, he really deserves to have his name appear on the cover for sharing so many of the most mundane, technical responsibilities and for being our guide and comfort when we found ourselves nearly overwhelmed by our computer's lack of cooperation. Sharin Elkholy, dear friend of Camille, must be recognized for the proofreading, suggested revision, research materials, conversations, and encouragement. Margo Drallos, close friend and associate of Candice, helped immensely by serving as a sounding board and proofreader. Dr. Bud Watson gave the gift of his discerning eye, especially in Chapters 3 and 4. Mary Kranz and Vicki Morriss made contributions to this project, and we thank them for their efforts. We would also like to express our appreciation for the support of our department chairs: Dr. Ellen Katz, Dr. Rentaro Hashimoto, Dr. Marie Egan, and Camille's dissertation advisor, Dr. Richard Bernstein. And much thanks to Patrick Prendergast for all his help and unlimited patience. Lastly, this book would not have been possible without the mirrors provided by the excited hearts and minds of our students at Mount St. Mary's College in Los Angeles, the New York Institute of Technology, and Manhattan College in New York City.

INTRODUCTION

Not until the second half of the twentieth century have the issues in this book been given a clear voice. Of course, this is not to say that women previously did not face problems like discrimination and sexual harassment. Yet, even to this day, despite the prevalence of such concerns, they have not been examined in detail; nor have most of the underlying cultural assumptions regarding women, work, and family been reflected upon in this context. With women entering the workplace in record numbers and not returning to homemaking as a full-time job, the urgency to address the topics we have raised here is apparent.

We have included theory, practical application, personal narrative, and statistical data in order to ensure both breadth and depth of coverage. In each chapter, we have tried to show how theory relates to life experience and we have critically examined central philosophical concepts because it is our belief that philosophy must have practical value if it is to be meaningful. Philosophy and critical thinking can be useful tools, enabling one to understand the world and one's place in it, and for this reason this should be made available to everyone, not merely left in the hands of scholars and academics. Thus, we have avoided using language that is unnecessarily technical or esoteric wherever possible. When abstract concepts are drawn upon, we have defined their terms and given examples for purposes of clarification, demonstrating how they may be applied. Our objective here is to open up a space for dialogue. Having laid some groundwork for perceiving these issues from a different perspective, we want to challenge others to continue to build from or add to this nucleus. Because many of these topics remain opaque, the best we can do is identify some of the problems working women face and frame the debates surrounding them.

Our position has been informed by both our formal academic training and our own experiences as working students. We have also tried to listen and give voice to women unlike ourselves, who do not possess this same avenue of expression. This has enabled us to step outside the boundaries of traditional scholarship in order to critique it.

This book begins with two theory chapters. The first compares the two most prevalent Modern approaches to ethical questions, namely Immanuel Kant's deontological ethics and John Stuart Mill's utilitarianism. After a brief summary of each and a discussion of their basic positions, we have gone on to show the ways in which their methods for moral deliberation are both illuminating and limiting. We have also shown how a Classical thinker like Aristotle might be of value for mediating contemporary dilemmas. After introducing these thinkers in a theoretical context in order to familiarize readers with them, we have woven their views into the concrete issues addressed throughout each chapter of the text.

In Chapter 2 on feminist theory, we found it necessary to show some historical evolution. Because there is no fundamental agreement as to what constitutes feminist thought and the primary concerns have not remained consistent, thinkers from the eighteenth to the twentieth centuries have been included. From Mary Wollstonecraft's faith in reason and rationality, to Carol Gilligan's "care ethics," to Iris Young's "difference theory," we can see the diversity and dynamic nature of feminism itself. As we have done for ethical theory, so too have we examined the central concepts of feminist thought with a critical eye. And, just as no single philosopher can provide us with a method for ethical deliberation that is satisfactory in all cases, so too is there no simple way of dealing with women's issues.

In Chapter 3 the problem of definition is found to be fundamental to the discussion of sexual harassment. That is, legal definitions shift and change as do social and cultural conceptions regarding what constitutes sexual harassment. After discussing recent court decisions and landmark cases, the topic is broken down into three basic classifications: coercive, non-coercive, and gender harassment. Examples are given for each with the caveat that these categories often overlap. For instance, there is a very fine line between non-coercive and gender harassment. Also, the concept of "intent " is explicated in accordance with a model drawn from Aristotle's ethics. This section ends with an "empowerment" page suggesting how to proceed if one is actually faced with some form of harassment.

Chapter 4, "Comparable Worth and Value," asks the question, What does it mean when we say that women should receive equal compensation for performing the same duties as men in the workplace? From there the problem of defining "worth" within any particular vocation is discussed. For example, is there a systematic method for comparing dissimilar jobs or work responsibilities? And, if there is, what would be the social, economic, and political ramifications of such a system? The problem of which jobs are valued in a capitalist economy, or which work activities have merit, is examined partly through the works of Karl Marx. It is he who reminds us that unfairness and inequality is endemic to capitalism—an economic theory that values profit above people.

Chapter 5, "Advertising," asks the reader to contemplate how the media plays a central role in forming societal attitudes and the dangers of this process if it goes unexamined. Young women are given very clear models of what they should look like through advertisements that portray the "ideal" body type as something few individuals could hope to achieve. This often leads to serious eating disorders and feelings of low self-worth. Perhaps most damaging is the portrayal of women as mere sex objects. We are so inundated with the images of advertising that we fall into the trap of seeing it as innocuous, when, in fact, it is exactly opposite. That is, we are manipulated in an unconscious but insidious way to buy products we do not need or which may even be harmful to us (e.g., cigarettes and diet pills). Young men and women need to become aware of how they are used by business to increase profits.

Chapter 6, "Leadership," examines the problem of the "glass ceiling" that prevents women from advancing to the upper rungs of corporate management. In many respects, this seems to be due to the distinct conceptions that men and women have regarding what leadership involves. We show how a "male" model of power traditionally has dominated the corporate culture, thereby effectively excluding, or limiting, women's advancement. Following this, we examine some of the current claims that there appears to be emerging a woman's style of management that will change the way we look at working relationships and the manner in which business is conducted.

Chapter 7, "Working-Class Women," is a topic that is so under-researched that we not only had to rely on our own experiences as students in the work force, but also on the voices of working women themselves. The feminist movement from the 1960s on has tended to focus on the concerns of the college educated, professional woman for various reasons that are addressed within this chapter. Yet, pink and blue-collar women have distinct concerns and attitudes toward their roles in the workplace, so we must be cautious about painting all women with a broad brush. Much more research needs to be done if we are to include working-class women in any theory of equality and justice, as we barely scratched the surface here.

WOMEN, ETHICS AND THE WORKPLACE

ETHICAL THEORY

The man with a method good for purposes of his dominant interests, is a pathological case in respect to his wider judgment on the coordination of this method with a more complete experience. Priests and scientists, statesmen and men of business, philosophers and mathematicians, are all alike in this respect.
—Alfred North Whitehead, *The Function of Reason*

INTRODUCTION

Why are we beginning a book on business ethics with a chapter on philosophical ethical theory? We do so not in order to introduce a method for ethical deliberation that presumes to have universal validity and application. Rather, we begin from the assumption that any such attempt to do so is misguided. For ethics, belonging to the realm of particularly human affairs, is not conducive to formulaic understanding. Moreover, as Whitehead indicates above, it is likely that when one claims to have found a method that is sufficient for dealing with his or her primary interests (be they science, philosophy or business related), he or she will see it as *the* method and attempt to apply it to all one's endeavors or types of inquiry. In fact, this is precisely what the most influential ethical theorists of the Modern era have done.

Two discernible trends regarding how to approach ethical problems have been dominant since the nineteenth century: specifically, the deontological and utilitarian models. That is, without ever having studied philosophy or even having heard of the two individuals involved, many people's basic moral or ethical intuitions have been shaped or influenced by Immanuel Kant, John Stuart Mill, or both. More specifically, when asked to describe or defend their moral position, most people respond by appealing to some universal "principle" and the motives of the agent (reflecting a Kantian approach)—or to the self-evident intrinsic "good" of happiness and the consequences of an action (a utilitarian perspective). It is therefore worthwhile to take a closer look at these positions in order to understand their vast appeal, examine the presuppositions behind them, and to consider their limits insofar as they attempt to systematize ethical decision making.

KANTIAN ETHICS

Immanuel Kant, speaking as the father of deontological ethics, claims that, "[n]othing in the world—indeed nothing even beyond the world—can possibly be conceived which could be called good without qualification except a *good will*."[1] It is the motive behind an act which serves as the criterion for evaluating its moral worth, and therefore it must be the sole focus of ethical deliberation. In other words, a good will is a dutiful will, and only one who acts on the basis of duty to the exclusion of everything else can be said to have performed a right action. Kant gives no argument as to why a good will must be the highest good. On the contrary, this is taken to be self-evident and the goodness of anything else is determined only by reference to it; that is, without the goodness of the will that wills an act, nothing can be deemed good or morally right. Moreover, what must be left out in any ethical deliberation are the "empirical" elements that are particular or unique to the situation. These include an individual's interests, desires, inclinations, emotional states, relationship to other parties involved, and the intended or possible consequences of the action. The agent possessing a good will must look to the rational concept of duty alone, making it both the motive of (or reason behind) the act as well as the end of (purpose or reason for) the act.

This is Kant's famous "duty for duty's sake" paradigm of moral choice and action. No consideration should be given to any empirical factors; that is, no regard for the context or particulars of the situation should be present in deliberating about what one *ought* to do. Furthermore, Kant points out that the primary function of practical reason is the production of a good will, as well as the discovery of the moral law. That is, contrary to popular belief, human beings possess reason not for the sake of becoming happy or having a satisfying life, but for a strictly moral purpose. We have a more noble aim, he claims, than mere animal contentment because we are first and foremost rational creatures who strive to live and act morally. Reason enables us to discover the moral law, act out of respect for it (duty), and thereby create a good will for ourselves. On the other hand, happiness, for Kant, has no intrinsic moral worth as it is constituted by the satisfaction of desires and interests, which are empirical, subject to change, and differ according to the individual person and context. To consider these factors in moral deliberation, or any other such particulars, would be to render the act and motive relative and contingent, whereas Kant seeks nothing less than universality and necessity. Reason alone, as he conceives it, is the only means by which our motives and actions may be rendered morally valuable in an unqualified sense; that is, it is the only way by which a will that is good in itself may be secured. Thus, happiness must be dispensed with, or, at least, indefinitely postponed. In other words, it must be regarded as something of relative value and secondary importance. In fact, Kant claims that "the good will seems to constitute the indispensable condition even of worthiness to be happy."[2] What this means is that only individuals who possess a good will really deserve to be happy. However, there is no guarantee that they will in fact be happy, for happiness is almost entirely dependent on empirical factors and circumstances, and these are most often beyond one's control. Because Kant seeks an absolute and universalistic ethical system, he not only appeals to "pure practical reason" over and against empirical elements (like desire and inclination), but he also emphasizes the apparent necessity of the moral laws that it discovers as opposed to the relativity of religious values and norms. His is an ethical theory that is designed to work without recourse to *any* particulars, whether individual, cultural, historical, or religious. Moreover, one of the reasons why a religiously based ethics can be so effective and compelling is that it often works on the basis of emotional appeal and requires a set of shared beliefs and experiences which, for Kant, would render it fundamentally empirical and, hence, unreliable as a standard for universality. (For more on this see Chapter 4 on conceptions of values and "family" that are based on religion and the problems therein.) In order to establish an ethics that is capable of making absolutist claims, Kant invokes his "categorical imperative."

Since "[a]n action does not have its moral worth in the purpose which is to be achieved through it but in the maxim by which it is determined," it is important for Kant to provide the means by which such a determination may be effectively made.[3] This is the categorical imperative, which is first formulated like this: "I should never act in such a way that I could not also will that my maxim should be a universal law" (Kant 1959: 18). What this amounts to is that an act cannot be morally correct unless it passes this test for universality. That is, an act is right if and only if the reason behind it is one that the agent would be willing to have everyone act upon in a similar situation. For example, let's consider the case of a male employer who is trying to decide whether to fire a female employee for extending her maternity leave beyond the agreed upon time period. He must ask himself if he would be willing to see the same action taken by every other employer every time an agreement is broken. He can give no regard to the particulars of her situation. For example, it doesn't matter if her child is sickly or if it was an unusually difficult birth and she has not yet regained her strength. Moreover, he must resist any inclination he might have towards sympathy.

What must be adhered to is the "principle" alone: namely, that in this case, an agreement was broken and a remedy must be sought. Whether the agreement was reasonable to begin with, whether she will have the means to support a child if she is dismissed, or whether the business itself will suffer from her absence cannot be considerations. All of what we might ordinarily regard as relevant circumstances cannot be taken into account if the aim is to do what is right according to Kant. Many of us might agree, however, that some of the empirical features should be irrelevant to moral reasoning, such as whether the employer and employee are friends or relatives or how happy the employee is with her position. The decision must be made on the purely abstract basis of what is "dutiful"; and what is so for one must be so for all, regardless of circumstances, as this is what it means to have a "good will" in Kant's eyes. Acting out of respect for the moral law (duty) alone counts as a moral motive. In one interpretation of the case above, the "law" is that agreements should be kept and by failing to do so the woman is in violation of it. The employer would then be remiss if he did not uphold the moral principle by dismissing her. In many ways, this is an unfairly and unnecessarily rigid approach. But still, it is likely that one has encountered individuals like this—those for whom the "principle" takes precedence over everything else, whether that be sympathy and compassion, extenuating circumstances, or detrimental consequences.

On the one hand, there seems to be something quite compelling and consistently fair about a Kantian approach, as it appears to avoid the messiness of emotional responses, individualized conceptions of happiness, and other particular factors. We would all like the security and simplicity that comes with such a system; we would all like to say "what is right is right" no matter what. On the other hand, the Kantian approach sets the stakes very high—by ignoring possible consequences—and also requires that we avoid certain features of life that appear unavoidable—empathic feelings and concerns, the privileging of personal relationships, and a genuine and perhaps legitimate concern with one's own well-being and happiness. Such matters cannot always be clearly separated or removed from deliberation about what is good or right. Kant does not even make clear why we should necessarily want to avoid these aspects of life or why failing to do so would render an act amoral. Is there then another approach we might consider that could address these concerns?

J.S. MILL'S UTILITARIANISM

One alternative that is often contrasted with the Kantian method is John Stuart Mill's utilitarianism. This explicitly looks to consequences in order to evaluate the ethical value of an action and takes human happiness as a self-evident good, thus making it an ethics that claims to be unabashedly empirical. Utilitarianism is "[t]he creed which accepts as the foundation of morals, Utility, or The Greatest Happiness principle, [which] holds that actions are right in proportion as they tend to promote happiness, wrong as they tend to produce the reverse of happiness."[4] Mill's claim, that is simply taken for granted here, is that " pleasure, and freedom from pain, are the only things desirable as ends" (Mill 1962: 257). Therefore, as a moral agent, one is obliged to consider the conse-quences of an act in terms of how much happiness or unhappiness would be produced for all involved. That is, the aim of all ethical action is to bring about the greatest amount of happiness for the greatest number of individuals (without regard to their "worthiness" or "unworthiness" as Kant would insist). Mill maintains that his system is not self-centered or selfish as it is the *general* happiness that is of paramount concern. In other words, it is not simply one's own pleasure that should be the goal of moral deliberation but that of one's family, community, co-workers, or humanity in general. In addition, he insists that he is not advocating a base form of hedonism, which would only take into account simple "animal" pleasures or the satisfaction of crude desires, but one which would aim primarily at maximizing the "higher" pleasures of the intel-lect and deeper human emotions. Given this general framework, how might it be applied to the case described above?

Returning to the case of the employer deciding the fate of an employee on unauthorized maternity leave, he now must consider his options in terms of their probable outcomes. This means that he will need to concern himself with many of the particular elements that Kant insists he leave out—namely, who will be affected by his action, how and to what degree. But, this does not simply mean that he must consider the circumstances and consequences as they pertain to the immediate parties involved—the happiness or welfare of the new mother and child. But rather, he must consider them insofar as they would affect anyone and everyone involved, as there will be several persons who may be affected positively or negatively by what he chooses to do. And this is precisely one of the places where we see the limits of utilitarianism. For Mill does not provide us with any criterion, or set of criteria, to determine just how many people may or may not be affected. For example, how could the employer know what would constitute the "greatest amount" of happiness for the entire company? Perhaps he should also consider the effects on the company's clientele, or the whole community in which the company is situated? In other words, how does he know where to draw the line if my obligation is to maximize happiness to the greatest degree? How can he determine who will be affected (whether directly or indirectly, immediately or remotely), before any action is taken? Furthermore, how is the "greatest amount" to be calculated or measured—that is, in terms of the greatest distribution or highest maximization of pleasure? Is pleasure or happiness even something that allows for an objective standard applicable to all human beings in the same way? That is, do we all share an identical conception of happiness that would allow us to distribute this "good" as we would any other commodity? (These are some of the very questions Kant ponders which leads him to separate happiness and morality.) Finally, can one ever be certain of the consequences of any action ahead of time?

We begin to see already, by this tangle of questions, how an ethics that claims to be empirically self-evident and clear has, in practical application, become increasingly confusing and obscure. Lastly, and perhaps most importantly, we need to ask, aren't there occasions when the rights of an individual should supersede the general good? That is, are there not some occasions when the "part" is more important than the "whole"? The criticism that is most often leveled against utilitarianism is that it sacrifices individual rights for the sake of what is "expedient" or in the "best interests of the whole." Some claim that what is morally good is not a matter to be determined simply by a majority, or a cost-benefit analysis, rather, there are "principles" that should be respected no matter what the conditions (as Kant claims). In fact, this is the fundamental purpose behind the United States Bill of Rights—specifically, that there are individual rights (freedom of speech and assembly, for example) that are "inalienable" and worthy of protection despite the possibility of detrimental social consequences or infringements upon the happiness of others.

Nonetheless, this method of decision and policy-making is not uncommon or unfamiliar to the business world or a capitalist economy. For it is primarily utilitarian principles to which businessmen and women appeal—the "good" being that which is in the company's best interests or that which produces the higher profit margin. Again, the complaint most often heard is that this "end justifies the means approach" ignores the rights of the individual and renders the phrase "business ethics" an oxymoron. Moreover, this is what makes Kant so appealing, as he would assert that what gives an act moral value cannot be determined by something as unreliable as possible, or even probable, consequences, nor by something as transitory as feelings of pleasure, happiness, the interests of a majority, or corporate profit. Where are we to turn now?

A SYNTHESIS OF KANT AND MILL

Some Kantians would like to salvage his deontological ethics by appealing to another formulation of the categorical imperative, one that is designed to have a humanizing effect. For human beings are to be regarded always as "persons," which are objects of respect, and never simply as "things." Thus, Kant says that one should "[a]ct so that you treat humanity, whether in your own person or that of another, always as an end and never as a means only."[5] Some have claimed that this version of the categorical imperative bears a striking resemblance to utilitarian morality, which is supposed to be regarded as the antithesis of the Kantian approach, because it appeals to "ends." However, the "ends" here are individuals themselves—rational beings invested with dignity and inherent value who are capable of determining the good by their will alone (through reason's discovery of the moral law)—not the happiness of some majority. Still, can we find in this the elusive formula that would combine the strengths of both positions while simultaneously avoiding their weaknesses?

The problems that now arise are basically linguistic or conceptual. That is, it is not clear what the key terms might mean if we try to apply them to an actual case like the one we've been discussing. For example, wouldn't the employer above be treating the woman as a mere means if he fired her, as Kant would? In that case, Kant's two formulations seem to conflict: by sacrificing the employee for the sake of upholding the moral law, he would be treating her merely as a means. But, to treat her as an end requires that he see her as a particular person, or unique individual, which would preclude the possibility of achieving the universality that is so essential for Kant's ethics. Mill might say to Kant, "isn't my duty to all my employees? Shouldn't I instead seek to maximize the happiness of the company and respect the interests of my other employees and stockholders?"

What this discloses is that these pivotal concepts of "end" and "means," or "interest" and "happiness," are themselves ambiguous at best, meaningless at worst. These are not univocal terms that could provide some "objective" foundation for resolving complex ethical issues—in fact, the very idea of such a foundation or unambiguous

terminology is in question here.   (Which is perhaps why, out of
frustration, those in business so often turn exclusively to factors that can
be quantitatively measured—such as financial gain or profit—to
determine what course of action should be taken.) The problem with the
utilitarian and Kantian methods is that they both do too much as well as
too little: too little because their key concepts and principles are
ultimately vague, thus allowing for an infinite number of interpretations,
and so give us no real help in coming to an actual decision; and, too
much because they attempt to provide a firm foundation by appealing to
supposedly universal, self-evident, or "objective" concepts and principles capable of covering all possible scenarios.

Whether the ultimate good is happiness or a good will, it still
remains to be explained what this means in terms of actual practice.
Both theories claim to have provided an objective basis for evaluating
ethical action, as well as a universal method of moral deliberation. Yet,
for the sake of this putative universality and objectivity, they have
ignored the subtleties and nuances that are endemic to the human condition and make ethics an inherently "messy" enterprise. In other words,
ethical inquiry is more of an art than a science, with tough decisions most
often being made in the gray areas where neither "white" (supposedly
pure or "abstract") nor "black" (presumably based in experience or
"empirical") criteria are sufficient.

Since the beginning of the twentieth century, the methods of science
and the scientific paradigm of knowledge have been regarded as the only
legitimate model for truth and the standard to which all other kinds of
inquiry must aspire or conform.   That is, methods that emphasize
quantification and dismiss, or seek to remove, all individualized aspects
of experience as well as any emotional elements are seen as the epitome
of rational thought or careful and serious investigation. It is this type of
position that we oppose, as moral deliberation is a distinct species of
inquiry. Moreover, to say that a principle of "empirical" or "rational"
origin is generally true is not to say that it can be rendered universal or
that it remains the same in any and every case of application. (This is a
point that many now claim is the case even in science itself.) For
instance, we may accept that lying is permissible, even moral, under certain circumstances even though honesty is embraced as a general ethical
principle. Cases like this may run from the apparently trivial: for example, saying that one likes a gift when he or she actually does not, to the
serious or life threatening, such as, concealing one's own and one's children's Jewish identities when faced with aggressive anti-Semitism. How
might this apply in business cases? Is lying or withholding information
about the salaries of other employees acceptable? Is lying about the
extent of one's experience on an employment application permissible?

Again, these questions cannot be decided out of context or in the absence of more specific information.

Nevertheless, we would be mistaken if we were to believe that these theories that claim scientific objectivity and universality for themselves are utterly without value. Both point to matters that should at least be part of any careful investigation into what is good or right, and they do characterize the manner in which many of us already think or give voice to many of our implicitly held moral beliefs and ideals. Thus, it is worthwhile to look at the issues that Kant and Mill raise. Still, they do not, and cannot, tell the whole story or disseminate the truth for us as one can only be morally responsible by responding to the concrete demands of the situation with which he or she is faced.

What are we left with then? Is there nothing to which we may appeal with assurance? Is there no method for dealing consistently with these sorts of difficulties? No, if by a consistent method is meant something systematic and formulaic or something akin to mathematics and science. For, as we've seen above, no foundationalist approach that aims at universality and objectivity can meet the demands of a concrete and particular situation. But, there is another version of ethical deliberation that merits attention, one that does not attempt to provide either an ultimate foundation or a definitive method. This can be found in Aristotle's conception of practical wisdom or *phronesis*.

ARISTOTELIAN ETHICS

Before turning to this concept, Aristotle makes some important preliminary points about the study of ethics. First, ethical inquiry is not the kind of investigation in which the primary objective is abstract knowledge of the good (as it was for Plato before him); rather, the aim is to become a good person or develop a moral character (an objective similar to Kant's). Knowledge, therefore, has practical consequences, and it is only this kind of knowledge that ethics should be concerned with. "Will not the knowledge of this good, consequently, be very important to our lives? Would it not better equip us, like archers who have a target to aim at, to hit the proper mark? If so, we must try to comprehend in outline at least what this good is."[6]

Aristotle is something of a pragmatist or realist in two respects: he does not regard knowledge as separate from action (i.e., theory is intimately connected to practice); and "the good" is something that can only be roughly or provisionally given (i.e., comprehended "in outline"). Ethics is not an exact science, nor is it conducive to mathematical formulation and/or demonstration. And, to expect it to be so would be a gross misunderstanding of what it entails. "For precision cannot be expected in the treatment of all subjects alike [and] a well-schooled man is one who searches for that degree of precision in each kind of study which the nature of the subject at hand admits" (Aristotle 1962: 5).

A second claim Aristotle makes early on lends a degree of irony or paradox to the study of ethics. He asserts that before one can even begin to inquire into the nature of the good "one must first have received a proper upbringing in moral conduct" (Aristotle 1962: 7). What does this mean? Is it an indication of Aristotle's elitism, as some would assert? It would appear that in order to become good, it is necessary to be good already. Or, that in order to learn what goodness consists of, one must have already been taught what it is. Doesn't this render any study of ethics superfluous at best, pointless at worst? For if one already possesses knowledge of the good, then there is no need for inquiring further. Or is there?

First, we must remember that an account of the good can only be given "in outline," so any investigation into it can never be complete or exhaustive. We will always need to fill in the blanks, so to speak; thus, our understanding of it will forever be merely provisional. Moreover, Aristotle is really making a much deeper point here: specifically, that the kind of practical wisdom necessary for moral action is not ultimately teachable. It is not simply a matter of learning some basic principles or formulas (like the axioms of geometry) and then applying them consistently in particular cases. If that were true, then why do we not have child prodigies, or geniuses of any age for that matter, in the field of ethics as we do in mathematics, music, or chess? Far from being the mechanical application of universal principles (as Kant, or even Mill, would have us believe), ethical inquiry requires a certain disposition—a desire, tendency, or willingness to do good—as well as a sufficient amount of life "experience" to draw from. This disposition is something that can only be nurtured over time, preferably from childhood on up.

In this sense, Aristotle seems to be validating one of our contemporary assumptions about human psychology; namely, that individuals are affected by their environment and are especially impressionable when they are young. What constitutes a "good upbringing" is certainly a matter of heated debate, and we do not assume that there is only one paradigm for such. But, the idea that it is necessary to instill some moral sensibility and sensitivity in children at an early age and to reinforce this throughout adolescence is rarely a matter of contention. Further, it should be equally clear that if someone has no basic desire to act rightly or avoid wrongdoing, if one does not care to discover what constitutes ethical or unethical action, then no amount of education will ever be sufficient to ensure moral behavior or check immoral behavior. So, what we find in this study of ethics is a blurring of the distinction between feeling and reasoning. Specifically, without the assumption that one cares about morality, we cannot even begin to inquire as to get to what might constitute moral action. Thus, Aristotle's ethics is written for those who at least *want* to know what goodness entails, and this is not something that can be taught in the strict sense.

What about Aristotle's second requirement of "experience"? What does this mean? Aristotle claims that practical wisdom itself is a form of "perception"—that is, the ability to "see" what kind of action is called for under particular circumstances or to discern what the good would consist of when faced with an actual situation in which a choice must be made. "Practical wisdom is concerned with particulars, as well [as with universals], and knowledge of particulars comes from experience. But a young man has no experience, for experience is the product of a long time" (Aristotle 1962: 160). And, once more, this kind of experience cannot be gotten secondhandedly: in other words, it cannot be taught or learned in a formal or academic manner. However, it appears again as if we are stuck in a circle—to be wise requires experience, yet one first needs to be wise in order to reflect upon and understand one's various experiences, making sense of them in such a way that these experiences can provide material for moral deliberation.

Is this an instance of circular reasoning, which one must seek to avoid? Or, is it simply a fundamental and inescapable paradox of human existence? Aristotle suggests the latter, and we would concur. It is one of the essential tragedies of life and, at the same time, one of its cosmic jokes that when we need wisdom the most (when we are young), we are the least likely to have it, although we may think otherwise. When we do seem to have wisdom, we no longer need it as desperately, and can also recognize how elusive it really is. This seems to be life's ultimate paradox—the more we know, the more we know that we know so very little; and the less we know of life, the more certain we are. (Perhaps this is why those who are "experienced" so often try to give their wisdom away by dispensing it to others—again, ironically, to those who need it most but are also the least likely to want or appreciate it!) In sum, practical wisdom is concerned both with "universals" (general principles regarding the good that can only be given roughly or in outline) as well as with "particulars" (those unique and irreducible features of a concrete situation). And, though *phronesis* is required for ethical deliberation, it is not akin to any discipline that can be taught or learned. Thus, we might ask, how does *phronesis* mediate between universals and particulars? And, how does experience allow us to cultivate or develop it, if it is not something we can learn through study. Martha Nussbaum makes some brilliant observations on this point in *The Fragility of Goodness*.

NUSSBAUM ON ARISTOTLE

In Chapter 10 of her book, Nussbaum says that we need to ask "what Aristotelian general rules and accounts are and are not, and how the person of practical wisdom uses them."[7] In the very next paragraph, she states that "[o]ne possibility is that the rules and universal principles are guidelines or rules of thumb: summaries of particular decisions, useful for purposes of economy and aids in identifying the salient features of the particular case." Of course, this is an interpretation that remains faithful to Aristotle's admonition that any general account of the good can only be given in outline and that practical wisdom must ultimately take its cue from, and respond to, the particulars of the case at hand. Aristotle criticizes general rules "both for lack of concreteness and for lack of flexibility" (Nussbaum 1986: 301). Is this not the heart of the criticism of Kant and Mill?—that their theories left both too much room for interpretation and too little room for responding to specific needs or demands. Thus, good deliberation can accommodate the intricacies and messiness of the concrete while simultaneously seeking the universal in the particular—that is, it does not assume that a rule "rules" the particulars; but rather, it allows them "to govern themselves and to be normative for correctness of rule." As Nussbaum states: "[g]ood deliberation accommodates itself to what it finds, responsively and with respect for complexity" (1986: 301).

Another way of putting this is that means (the *how* of moral action) and ends (the objective or aim of morality) are codetermined, that "the end itself is only concretely specified in deliberating about the means appropriate to a particular situation."[8] What this entails is that a general rule for action can only be deemed correct retrospectively, as we cannot know beforehand what will follow from the choices that we make. This does leave us vulnerable to some extent to what Nussbaum calls "moral luck," and we really can't expect much more given the complexities of human actions and relations. For instance, let us say that one is faced with a difficult choice between two jobs. While one may involve a substantial salary increase, it will also require moving her family to another state or city and taking on greater responsibility. The other job by contrast may provide greater security, more pleasant work, and working relationships. How can she say ahead of time with any degree of assurance which will be the right choice? What she cannot do is not choose, for even that is ultimately a passive sort of choice. It may turn out that, after taking one of the positions, new information is revealed that confirms or validates the correctness of the choice made. But, how much of this is merely due to "good" luck? And, if the reverse were to occur—she regrets her decision after having acted upon it—could one really claim that the source of error was simply bad deliberation? How can we make sense of this element of moral luck?

Nussbaum distinguishes three features of choice that show why we will always remain vulnerable to these contingencies to some extent, or why it is the case that practical wisdom or moral deliberation can never be systematic. "First, there is the *mutability* or lack of fixity of the practical" (1986: 302). As much as we may desire and seek the kind of security and stability provided by universal laws, we live in a world of change that is inherently insecure. Thus, practical wisdom must remain responsive, perhaps even creative, in order to meet the demands of a world that is always in process. Second, there is the *indeterminacy* of the practical. To illustrate this point, Nussbaum calls on an example taken from Aristotle himself where he shows that there can be no comprehensive definition of good joke telling.[9] Just as it is clear that there is no science of humor, as it is closer to an art or creative skill, and that what constitutes a good sense of humor is both culturally and personally variable, so too should we regard ethical deliberation in this light. A good comedian, for example, must be responsive to his or her audience in the same manner in which the practically wise person must be capable of responding to the different demands of a particular situation. In a recent *Time* magazine article this point was made with regard to the debate surrounding artificial intelligence: specifically, that "the hardest thing for computers is the 'simple' stuff. Sure they can play great chess, a game of mechanical rules and finite options. But making small talk is another matter. So, too, with recognizing a face or recognizing a joke."[10] In other words, the article claims, "the biggest challenge is giving machines common sense." This "common sense," whether it means the capacity to make or respond to a joke, perceive the tone in which something is said, or recognize which words or actions would be appropriate in a particular situation, is not something mechanical or scientifically objective. Lastly for Nussbaum, there is the feature of *non-repeatability*—namely, that we must recognize the existence of *ultimate* particulars. "This is in part a function of the complexity and variety already mentioned: the occurrence of properties that are, taken singly, repeatable in an endless variety of combinations make the complex whole situation a non-repeatable particular" (Nussbaum 1986: 304).

As in the example given above of the employee on unauthorized maternity leave, there may be many salient or relevant circumstances that must be taken into consideration in any good deliberation. Again, her health and that of the child, her employment history, as well as the original agreement and interests of the company are all relevant features which, taken as a whole, are non-repeatable. Thus, her employer cannot apply general rules in a mechanical fashion—imposing them upon concrete cases without first "seeing" what the relevant issues are or determining whether or not they fit.

In sum, we cannot expect the kind of comfort afforded by the universal application of basic principles when confronted with ethical choices. Rules have only a limited usefulness: they must be regarded as guiding rather than as binding. They point the way, perhaps with a wave of the hand towards some general direction, but cannot function as definitive markers that point directly at something. Nussbaum refers to them as "tentative guides" or "summaries" that enable us "to be flexible, ready for surprise, prepared to see, resourceful at improvisation" (1986: 304–5). For example, one may say that corporate downsizing is generally wrong, but this does not mean that it is so in all cases. As with lying, there may be good reasons for generally refraining from doing so. However, in some particular instances, there may be even more compelling reasons for not telling the truth or taking steps to reduce a company's overhead costs by eliminating jobs. This should then make clear why Aristotle insists that the person of practical wisdom must have a wealth of experience to draw from. People cannot be good at moral deliberation unless they have been able to cultivate their responsiveness, and maintain their composure under the stress of such decision making. It is this life and work history that allows the wise person to "see" what the universal is which is disclosed or revealed in a particular case. Though it is true that, in one sense, the case is non-repeatable, in another sense, such would be "unintelligible without the guiding and sorting power of the universal" (Nussbaum 1986: 306).

We now need to turn to the role of this "universal," as thus far the "particular" has taken precedence. For ultimately, Nussbaum asserts that the relationship goes both ways with each illuminating the other. What then is this universal, and how does it act as a guide? And, how do particulars and universals codetermine each other?

It is the experienced person of practical wisdom who acts as the standard of good deliberation and judgment, according to Aristotle. This is the "thoroughly human being" who "does not attempt to take up a stand outside of the conditions of human life, but bases his or her judgment on long and broad experience of these conditions" (Nussbaum 1986: 290). Moreover, this is not an individual who seeks to escape from or suppress desires and passions (as Kant would have it), but one who has cultivated, and continues to cultivate, these important sources of motivation. However, what the practically wise person desires most of all is to act ethically, and this person will cultivate what is conducive to that. "He or she will be concerned about friendship, justice, courage, moderation, generosity; his desires will be formed in accordance with these concerns; and he will derive from this internalized conception of value many ongoing guidelines for action, pointers as to what to look for in a particular situation" (Nussbaum 1986: 306). For Aristotle, desires and inclinations are not merely animal impulses indicative of our bestial and amoral nature, as Kant would have us believe. Instead, they are "responsive intentional elements, capable of flexible ethical development" (Nussbaum 1986: 307). As choice is defined by Aristotle as "deliberate desire," thus placing it in between appetite and reason;[11] it is only through moral choices that values can be made manifest in the world of human relations. And, just as our intellectual faculties can be developed or cultivated, so too can the affective side of our characters be molded along ethical lines or distorted in various ways. This underscores again Aristotle's concern with bringing up children in such a way that they are sensitized to moral issues as soon as possible. Since, "it is no small matter whether one habit or another is inculcated in us from early childhood; on the contrary, it makes a considerable difference, or, rather, all the difference" (Aristotle 1962: 34).

But, who is this person of practical wisdom that brings the universal element to, or makes it manifest in, the particular situation? Is he or she merely an empty ideal, or a real possibility? If the latter, then what can we do to encourage such character development?

Nussbaum speaks of this individual as one who is rooted in a community and is committed to a conception of the good life, which is expressed in and includes the values mentioned above. But, most specifically, this is a character who seeks moderation in everything. We could say that this is Aristotle's universal principle. However, it is one that is malleable, and its goodness is dependent upon who is interpreting or applying it. "Proper virtuous choice requires, if it is to be virtue, the combination of correct selection with correct passional response" (Nussbaum 1986: 308). And, presumably, it is the practically wise person who will have developed this harmonious relation between her passions and reason, which will allow her to make appropriate choices, or to "see" what the appropriate response would be, in any situation. Is this an unrealistic ideal? Perhaps, if we expect such a person to always and forever respond correctly and leave no room for human frailty, fallibility, or luck. However, what is also problematic in Aristotle is the reliance upon the traditional values of the community. For this is a reliance that seems to preclude the possibility of criticism, which would allow one to determine whether these values had become outmoded, stagnant, or even destructive. And, even if we accept some loose conception of friendship and justice, for example, as moral ideals, isn't it possible that the hardest ethical choice a person might be faced with would be one in which these two values conflict? In other words, to what principle do we appeal when the choice is between benefiting a friend or acting justly?

Or, put more generally, what do we do when we must choose between two universal goods? Is Aristotle's concept of moderation at all helpful, or even relevant, here?

MACINTYRE ON VALUES

This problem is often referred to as the incommensurability of values. That is, there are many goods that we regard as basic and for which no ultimate standard of appeal can be given to determine which should prevail in the case of a conflict. Alasdair MacIntyre discusses this in *After Virtue*. He accepts the Aristotelian claim that it is the practically wise person to whom we must look for moral guidance—an individual with a stable character who listens to and respects passion as well as reason, who belongs to a community, and who lives his or her life as a quest for the good.[12] But there can be no guarantees here—one can never, no matter how virtuous one's character, avoid the possibility of a "tragic confrontation of good with good" (MacIntyre 1984: 224). In such situations, then, there may be better or worse choices, but no truly right choices or correct responses.   And, even the criterion of "better" or "worse" might be subject to infinite variations. This is because

both of the alternative courses of action which confront the individual have to be recognized as leading to some authentic and substantial good. By choosing one I do nothing to diminish or derogate from the claim upon me of the other; and therefore, whatever I do, I shall have left undone what I ought to have done. (MacIntyre 1984: 224)

To return to the case above, let us say that the new mother employee is a dear friend of the employer and that she has acted in bad faith by remaining on unauthorized leave. The employer is then faced with a genuine dilemma. He wants to do what is fair and just for the company and his other employees, yet he also values this woman's friendship and knows that she would be harmed by a decision to let her go. Ultimately, there can be no "right" answer here, for he must choose between the two basic goods of friendship and justice. Either way, he acts rightly *and* wrongly—devaluing or preferring friendship for the sake of justice or justice for the sake of friendship. What this case shows is that there are personal consequences at stake in addition to the practical affairs of doing business. For how he decides will not only determine the fate of his employee, it will also affect this particular friendship. So, we seem to be right back where we started with no firm ground on which to stand when making moral choices. Have we learned nothing then from this exercise?

CONCLUSION

We maintain that we can learn something here. Once again, although there can be no systematic method for moral deliberation, we can become more thoughtful, careful, and self-conscious in the choices we make. Still, as human beings we wear many hats, and thus we face many responsibilities that may come into conflict. We are employees and employers, friends, lovers, parents, children, brothers, sisters, and public citizens; so we have personal, professional, and social or political responsibilities that cannot be denied. How to negotiate this network of possible moral dilemmas is something that clearly will require time and experience, and even then one will often be forced to compromise something of value. Perhaps recognizing this one thing above all will be what is most beneficial to us. For true wisdom consists in knowing one's weaknesses and limits as well as one's strengths, knowing what aspects of our lives we can and cannot control. As Socrates would say, the wise person is one who is aware of his or her own ignorance. Also, we can draw something from the lessons of the philosophers above, even if this merely involves the discovery of what we *ought not do*. That is, we should not ignore our desires and passions or suppress them as if they are necessarily detrimental to moral reasoning and deliberation; nor should we appeal strictly to pleasure and happiness or to duty and good will as "ultimates," pretending that these are things that are clearly definable, measurable, or quantifiable. As Aristotle indicates, we need to remain sufficiently open in order to "see" what the good might be, and how it may be realized, in each and every particular situation.

Some cases will, of course, be harder to evaluate than others. That is why a practically wise person must have some sense of what is of universal value, or what his or her ends and objectives in life are. The problem is that these can be quite elusive, since they are manifold and subject to change for any thoughtful individual. Moreover, the contingencies of human history and culture preclude the possibility of giving any stable interpretation to concepts of justice, friendship, generosity, or any other basic goods. We are left, then, with doing the best that we can in a world that refuses to make this a simple enterprise. Thus, we hope that what this book will provide are some basic guidelines for discussion—that is, that we can stimulate or encourage dialogue among men and women who share a concern for ethics and who are seeking to establish a working environment that is productive and satisfying for all.

QUESTIONS FOR REFLECTION

1. Can ethical theory adequately respond to the specific needs and demands of the workplace?

2. Is "business ethics" an oxymoron due to a fundamental concern with profit?
3. Do moral concepts, such as duty and happiness, have a place in business?
4. In what ways is practical wisdom (*phronesis*) helpful in moral reasoning?
5. Do all vocations speak a common "ethical language"?
6. What is the relationship between universal principles and particular moral issues?
7. Is ethics inherently situational?
8. Why can't rational thought alone give us answers to moral questions?
9. To whom is one ultimately responsible?—family, friends, the company, oneself? And, how is this to be determined?

NOTES

1. Immanuel Kant, *Foundations of the Metaphysics of Morals*, trans. by Lewis White Beck (Indianapolis: The Bobbs-Merrill Company, Inc., 1959), p. 9.

2. Ibid., p. 9.

3. Ibid., p. 16. Also note that the "maxim" Kant refers to is essentially the motive of the action or the "principle of volition."

4. John Stuart Mill, *Utilitarianism and Other Writings*, ed. by Mary Warnock (New York: New American Library, Inc., 1962), p. 257.

5. *Foundations*, p. 47.

6. Aristotle, *Nicomachean Ethics*, trans. by Martin Ostwald (New York: Macmillan Publishing Co., 1962), p. 4.

7. Martha Nussbaum, *The Fragility of Goodness* (New York: Cambridge University Press, 1986), p. 299.

8. Richard Bernstein, *Beyond Objectivism and Relativism* (Philadelphia: University of Pennsylvania Press, 1983), p. 147.

9. *Nicomachean Ethics*, p. 108.

10. *Time* 147, 13, March 25, 1996, p. 148.

11. Ibid., p. 148.

12. See, in particular Chapter 15 from Alasdair MacIntyre, *After Virtue: A Study in Moral Theory* (Notre Dame, Ind.: University of Notre Dame Press, 1984).

2

FEMINIST THEORY

Contemporary feminists have done much to puncture stereotypes, to encourage the re-thinking of sex roles, to work for change in the education of girls, and to open up questions of women's work by insisting on equal pay and equal opportunity. At present, we insist that a woman be treated just the same as a man. Are we sure we want to be treated as most men are in our society? Or do both sexes deserve something better?

—Kay Keeshan Hamad

INTRODUCTION

Feminism should be counted as a basic movement for human emancipation, along with the abolitionist, civil rights, and labor movements. To trivialize it as the "Women's Lib" of White, middle-class American women in the 1960s and 1970s is to remain ignorant of its rich and varied history. Moreover, such belittling denies the depth of suffering experienced by so many women throughout world history as well as the seriousness of feminist claims and ultimate concerns for the entire human population—for if women suffer, so, too, do men and children. So, why has this history been overlooked? Whether or not there was any intent to deny the significance of women's roles is not something we wish to consider here. The facts show that women were very much involved in both the French and American revolutions as well as in abolitionist, labor, and antiwar movements, all of which were central events in the Western world from the seventeenth century to the 1970s. Many of the women who fought for the rights of workers or against such forms of oppression as slavery recognized important connections between these injustices and those perpetrated against themselves. In the United States, for example, the feminist movement for women's suffrage largely grew out of the abolitionist movement. Once African Americans had won their emancipation and the vote had been extended to African-American males (in the 14th Constitutional Amendment of 1868), it was inevitable that the women who had been so instrumental in this process would seek enfranchisement for themselves.

Since this is a text in business ethics that focuses on contemporary women's issues on the North American continent, we must limit our emphasis to what is most directly relevant to the tradition we have inherited. Thus, it should be understood that we are concerned here with problems of discrimination and women's subordination that have occurred in the context of democratic and capitalistic societies situated within the Anglo-American and Western European traditions.

It seems reasonable to assume that if one has been subject to centuries of servitude and oppression (sometimes in the name of upholding religious values) and denied an education, there will be little space available for cultivating thought or finding the means for political expression. Nonetheless, it is important to note that over one hundred years before Mary Wollstonecraft's *A Vindication of the Rights of Women* was published in 1792, women had been writing about discrimination and arguing for recognition and redress.

Because theory is a prerequisite for critical thinking in ethics and because equality in the workplace is a central issue for feminists, it may be worthwhile to take a look at the history of feminism and feminist theory particularly in light of this pivotal concept. Also, as there is no single paradigm for what constitutes a "feminist perspective," we need to consider some of the different thinkers who have been traditionally identified as feminist theorists (whether or not they used this term to describe themselves) and to examine the evolution of the discourse. As in ethical theory, there is no overarching or singular method for dealing with women's issues or with questions concerning the subordination of, and discrimination against, women. So, too, are there no easy answers to the questions, What is feminism? or What constitutes a feminist position? Thus, the aims of this chapter are as follows: To look at some of the individual feminist thinkers who have shaped the development of the discourse and explore the nature of their claims; to trace the historical evolution of feminist thought and consider some of the disputes within feminist theory itself, especially with regard to the different interpretations of basic concepts and philosophical assumptions; and, lastly, to examine the pivotal concept of equality itself and see how it can be used to encapsulate the history of feminism when we consider its diverse incarnations throughout the Western tradition. Because this is a theory section, we will not be able to explore the many practical and political contributions women activists have made. However, were it not for them and their struggles, it would be unlikely that we would be writing this book today.

For purposes of clarity we will delineate three basic epochs and consider the general themes and objectives of each. Modern or Early Feminism of the eighteenth and nineteenth centuries traces its beginnings to Wollstonecraft, who regarded the treatment of women as being contradictory to the democratic ideals of self-determination and equal opportunity. Twentieth century feminism, which may be characterized more as a critique of society and culture than as being oriented towards changing policies (particularly since women had already made many political gains by this time), begins with Simone de Beauvoir. She is unique insofar as she acts as a kind of bridge between Modernism and the feminism of the 1960s and 1970s, sharing certain features of both, yet making many revolutionary contributions of her own. Finally, there is Contemporary Feminism with its emphasis on the differences among women (class, race, sexuality, ethnicity) and the philosophical assumptions and problems that are internal to feminist theory; at the present time, equality itself, among other concepts, is problematized and addressed accordingly by feminist theorists.

MODERN FEMINISM AND POLITICAL EQUALITY

The nascent feminism of the Modern age followed closely on the heels of the Enlightenment and accepts many of its basic presuppositions and ideals: namely, that human beings are fundamentally rational creatures capable of understanding universal truths and who have an inherent potential for virtuous action:

In what does man's pre-eminence over the brute creation consist? The answer is as clear as that a half is less than the whole, in Reason. What acquirement exalts one being above another? Virtue, we spontaneously reply. For what purpose were the passions implanted? That man by struggling with them might attain a degree of knowledge denied to the brutes, whispers Experience.[1]

Thus, individual human beings should be recognized as autonomous subjects, endowed with inherent dignity due to a moral consciousness, who are the bearers of certain inalienable rights.

However, since Aristotle, women had rarely been regarded as truly or fully human because they were said to possess a defective rational faculty that rendered them incapable of virtuous action. Rousseau, who was otherwise admired by Wollstonecraft for espousing egalitarian and democratic principles, merely perpetuated this position in his description of "Sophie" over 2,000 years after Aristotle. He, too, saw women as "naturally" inferior. Sophie was a fictional character conceived of as the appropriate and complementary partner to "Emile," who represented Rousseau's ideal man. And, he argued that she should serve as a proper paradigm for women to emulate. Women, he claimed, should "learn many things but only those that are suitable for them to know."[2] They ought to have "little freedom [as] they tend to excess in the freedom that is left to them. And, they possess a "natural" talent for "guile" in addition to "gentleness" (Rousseau 1979: 370). In essence, women should remain dependent and relegated to the domestic sphere, thereby allowing only men to busy themselves with public affairs; women should concentrate primarily on what "pleases" them and on keeping themselves physically attractive to men. In contradistinction to this, liberal feminists of the time, whether women like Wollstonecraft or men like John Stuart Mill, argued for the inclusion of women into the political arena, which had historically been an exclusively male province. They based their position on egalitarian and democratic ideals and pointed out the injustice and illegitimacy of any philosophical position denying that women possessed reason. According to Mill, "the legal subordination of one sex to the other—is wrong in itself, and now one of the chief hindrances to human improvement."[3] Specifically, they flatly denied the claim of natural inferiority and irrationality attributed to women, arguing that women were, in fact, as capable of rational thought and virtue as men and, therefore, should be afforded the same rights and privileges as men through political legislation. In other words, based upon the democratic principle of "perfect equality" for all human beings, women, too, should be regarded as autonomous rational and moral agents who possessed the same capacities as men and granted the same legal status. For women are no less human (i.e., rational) than men. These Modern feminists did not question whether "rationality" accurately characterizes most men, or if it alone is adequate as a more general definition of "human nature." The working assumption was that all human beings were essentially rational and moral creatures who would act accordingly if given the opportunity. But this meant that women had to work doubly hard to "prove" that they, too, were endowed with the kind of reason that had previously been seen as belonging only to men.

Because of their unshakable faith in the power of reason (both their own as well as that of others), these feminists believed that everyone would inevitably come around to accepting the apparently irrefutable truths of their position and support their call for equal treatment under the law. Some have referred to Wollstonecraft as the "female John Locke" due to this very faith and because she appears to be so firmly entrenched in the ideals of liberal democracy. She consistently held to the "simple principles" that every individual has a natural right to political and social self-determination and that moral relations can flourish only among equals. Wollstonecraft saw feminism as simply the logical extension of humanistic and democratic principles. She took pains to point out the prejudice of denying women what was automatically granted to men (the voting rights of inheritance and education, for example) by simply claiming women lacked faculties of judgment necessary to being good citizens without giving them a chance to prove otherwise. However, she also recognized that women and men were socialized differently and that this often accounted for what had been traditionally considered the "natural" distinctions between the sexes.

Wollstonecraft argued that Rousseau, due to his own prejudices, had falsely and maliciously depicted women as being incapable of certain kinds of rational thought as well as virtuous activity and had attributed qualities to them that would serve merely to justify their subordination. Against Rousseau, Wollstonecraft claimed that if women and men appeared distinct or acted differently, this was simply because women had not been allowed the opportunity to exercise their rational and moral faculties of judgment. This exercise would enable them to function as responsible citizens and contributing members of society, as it was assumed men had before them. If, for example, women were denied the vote, it was because they were thought to be guided more by their passionate nature than by reason. Although she agreed that this was true to some extent, she did not believe women's reliance on passion was a natural or inborn trait. Rather, women were all too often taught to cultivate those very qualities, identified by Rousseau (among others), that would only serve to perpetuate their subjection and that were, paradoxically, the source of both their exaltation and degradation.

Pleasure is the business of woman's life, according to the present modification of society; and while it continues to be so, little can be expected from such weak beings. [Being designated the beautiful sex]—they have, to maintain their power, resigned the natural rights which the exercise of reason might have procured them, and chosen rather to be short-lived queens than labor to obtain the sober pleasures that arise from equality. [T]hey constantly demand homage as women, though experience should teach them that the men who pride themselves upon paying this arbitrary insolent respect to the sex are most inclined to tyrannize over, and despise the very weakness they cherish. (p. 59)

This neatly sums up Wollstonecraft's fundamental position—that is, despite the fact that women possess the basic human capacities for reason and virtue, society has encouraged them to cultivate their roles as beautiful and passive objects, instead of as rational and active subjects.

Women have then faithfully followed this recipe and become their own worst enemies, thereby colluding with those who would keep them in "their place." For they too have been taught to participate in their own degradation (see chapter 6, "Advertising," for further examples of this collusion). Thus, Wollstonecraft places the responsibility for change not only on men and political legislation but on women themselves, calling upon them to find the courage to buck tradition and follow a different path (as she herself had done).

It is easy to see why this rationalist position was so seductive to feminism in its earliest stages. First, the Enlightenment's ideals of reason and scientific objectivity dominated all philosophical inquiry at that time (late eighteenth and early nineteenth centuries)—though the idea of feminine equality was still a radical notion; and, there was pervasive optimism about, and faith in, the moral progress of human history. Secondly, in a society in which male domination had rarely even been questioned, the only open avenue for female inclusion would be to buy into this ideal of rationality. And thirdly, and perhaps more significantly, feminists like Wollstonecraft needed to believe in the independent power of reason and objective nature of truth. For otherwise, "[i]f there is no objective basis for distinguishing between true and false beliefs, then it seems that power alone will determine the outcome of competing truth claims. This is a frightening prospect to those who lack (or are oppressed by) the power of others."[4] Thus, the acceptance of a conception of the human being as fundamentally rational and possessing an inherent capacity for virtue, as well as the call for the inclusion or recognition of women as full-fledged members of the human race, served as an important first step in the feminist revolution. In this context, the clarion call was for the democratic revolutions to make good on their ideal of political equality and universal human rights through the inclusion of women. However, the concept of equality itself was not critically examined. What kind of equality, or what particular conception of it, was being assumed here? This is a question that did not arise for the Modern feminists, but that is now being explored by many Contemporary thinkers (as we will demonstrate below).

What is also notable, in retrospect, is that the psychological effects of discrimination and male domination on women had not been explored. (This, too, was to come later, beginning with Simone de Beauvoir, though she was no fan of the prevailing Freudian psychoanalytic methods of her day.) It wasn't until the twentieth century that the liberation of female consciousness was called for in addition to political and social equality. Feminists of the Modern period were concerned primarily with the reformation of laws that were unfair to women. They did not strike at the heart of male domination, nor should we have expected them to.

Their attacks on laws relating to the marital union and divorce—as well as their arguments that the institution of marriage itself was inherently oppressive and unequal on several levels (sexually, socially, and economically)—were radical enough without their taking on men themselves and questions of male supremacy more directly. Still, many women pointed out that not only are women not paid for housework and child rearing but they are not fairly compensated when they do work outside of the home (a problem that persists today; see chapter 4, "Comparable Worth and Value"). And, almost all feminists, regardless of their place in history, have agreed that financial independence, or economic self-sufficiency, is a basic prerequisite for political equality as well as self-determination and personal autonomy. Many Early feminists also argued that until equality in the private realm of the home and personal relations were achieved, any political gains that might be won would continue to rest on shaky ground. Thus, the distinction between public and private spheres, which had previously been taken for granted, was becoming increasingly blurred. And it is the feminist movement that can be credited with continuing to raise questions about the traditional separation of the two.

Another primary characteristic of nineteenth century feminism, besides its faith in reason, scientific objectivity, and the virtuous subject, is the lack of any critical distinction between the categories of sex and gender. It was simply taken for granted that one's gender identification was continuous and consistent with one's sexual organs—that one was either a man or a woman, and, thus, either masculine or feminine but never both. Again, since Aristotle, the anatomical differences between male and female were seen as a fundamental biological fact accounting for the "opposite natures" of the two sexes. The ways in which the male and female in the human species are strikingly similar were overlooked. Even biologically, male and female are much more alike than unlike. This latter point was the focus of feminists like Mill and Wollstonecraft who denied that physical differences affected our capacity for rational thought and moral action. However, they did not separate or offer any critique of the concepts of sex and gender themselves. They did not ask themselves the philosophical question, What is woman? Nor did they concern themselves with whether there is a distinct "feminine" essence that might not be reducible to a "masculine" conception of human nature. Rather, they accepted the prevailing view of humankind as essentially rational creatures, arguing that this included women as well as men. It would thus be left to the next wave of feminism, which took gender as a central category and utilized it in the analysis of social and cultural practices, to critique the concept of a human essence as male biased. So begins the shift to the feminist theory that was typical of the twentieth century, with de Beauvoir bridging the gap between the rationalism of the Early feminists and the "essentialism" of twentieth century feminists.

ESSENTIALISM AND THE CONSTRUCTION OF GENDER

In most respects, the history of twentieth century feminism began by emphasizing the ways in which men and women are fundamentally different. Basically, the assumption is that there are differences between the gender categories of man and woman. The underlying idea here is that of "essentialism"—that is, that men and women experience the world differently, have distinct interests, opportunities, and affinities as well as certain capacities, with the result being that some things are considered characteristically masculine while others are regarded as inherently feminine. However, these gender distinctions may or may not be consistent with one's sex, as is evident in the case of the proverbial "tomboy" or the "butch" lesbian, individuals who are anatomically female but male identified (some even going so far as to live as men).[5] There is also the reverse case of "sissy" boys or male "queens," those who are anatomically male yet are said to possess "feminine" mannerisms and identify more with girls, women, or their mothers than with other males. What this indicates is that gender may be something that is socially or culturally "constructed" according to traditional values and unexamined assumptions. In other words, whether it is due to biological distinctions, the division of labor, entrenched social structures, cultural norms, or asymmetrical relations of power, "man" and "woman" are conceptual constructs, not facts of nature. The assumption, then, is that gender is to sex as culture is to biology and anatomy, or, that one may be born male or female, but one *becomes* a man or woman by cultivating the traditionally accepted characteristics of one or the other. This is expressed in the famous quote with which Simone de Beauvoir's *The Second Sex* is neatly summed up: "one is not born, but rather becomes a woman." (Such a view was also manifest in Wollstonecraft's work when she claimed that women could be educated or taught to think and act differently—specifically, as men presumably thought and acted. Still, as noted above, she did not explicitly problematize the concepts of gender and sex themselves, or question this "masculinist" concept of humanity.)

The main issue for most essentialist feminists is that what has traditionally been seen as masculine has been privileged or valorized over the so-called feminine qualities. (Perhaps this is a clue as to why "sissies" are more likely to be victims of harassment than are "tomboys" and gay men are more often victims of violence than their female counterparts.) The aim, then, is to show how this privileging is grounded in fallacious assumptions and to question the hierarchy of male dominance. Simone de Beauvoir is among the first to explicitly examine the relationship between sex and gender. However, whether or not she sufficiently criticizes the traditional male role model, or the ways in which gender is constructed, is a matter of debate. In some respects her thought is quite radical, while in others it appears quite traditional. Therefore, as mentioned above, she functions as a bridge or link between Modern Feminism and the twentieth century paradigms of feminist thought found in theorists such as Carol Gilligan and Nancy Hartsock, who do critique "masculinist" models of community, power, morality, and the "male bias" implicit in traditional conceptions of human nature.

SIMONE DE BEAUVOIR

When *The Second Sex* was first published in 1949, women in most parts of the Western world had made many political gains, including the vote and the extension of property rights and inheritance. Thus, de Beauvoir's criticisms tend to be more cultural and social. Unlike Wollstonecraft and other Modern feminists, her primary aim was not to lobby for political changes or argue on behalf of equal rights. However, like her predecessors, she was critical of discriminatory social and cultural practices, and accepted many traditional assumptions. At the same time, her writings display a much finer understanding of the role played by gender identification and construction and a greater concern for issues of freedom and women's psychological emancipation.

When de Beauvoir asks, What is woman?, she immediately notes the oddness of such a question. On the one hand, we all recognize that human females exist; yet, at the same time, "we are told that femininity is in danger; we are exhorted to be women, remain women, become women."[6] Nearly one hundred years before de Beauvoir explored this question on a theoretical level, Sojourner Truth (a former slave who could neither read nor write) raised it in a powerful, compelling, and very personal speech at a women's rights convention:

That man over there says that women need to be helped into carriages, and lifted over ditches, and to have the best place everywhere. Nobody ever helps me into carriages, or over mud-puddles, or gives me any best place! And ain't I a woman? Look at me! Look at my arm! I have ploughed, and planted, and gathered into barns, and no man could head me! And ain't I a woman? I could work as much and eat as much as a man—when I could get it—and bear the lash as well! And ain't I a woman? I have borne thirteen children, and seen them most all sold off to slavery, and when I cried out with my mother's grief, none but Jesus heard me! And ain't I a woman?[7]

In addition, de Beauvoir notes that even to ask such a question is indicative of something significant, for a man would never think to ask, what is man? "A man never begins by presenting himself as an individual of a certain sex as is indicated by the common use of *man* to designate human beings in general " (de Beauvoir 1989: xxvii). Therefore, men do not in any way distinguish themselves from what is properly said to be human. Their humanity is not in question, for it is never at stake. On the contrary, it is simply taken for granted or given; whereas women's humanity is in question or must somehow be proven. Women are thus defined as "Other," and this is made manifest in the various philosophical dichotomies that are more often assumed than critically examined. For example, if man is reason, woman is passion; if man actualizes himself in culture, woman is represented by the world of "nature." As rational culture is designed to dominate and control the natural realm of the senses, so, too, is rational man meant to dominate and subdue passionate woman. If man is the substantial soul or consciousness who possesses a free will and is capable of transcending himself, woman is the insubstantial body who is limited and determined by her concrete circumstances and, thus, "doomed to immanence." In sum, man constitutes the truly human, while woman is the human being who is not quite human. Woman is not seen as a free being capable of standing alone, but must be defined in relation to man. De Beauvoir notes that this has also been said of anyone who is not white, Anglo, or of European descent— for instance, Jews and Blacks of both sexes. Women's situation is, she implies, analogous to that of other minorities or victims of discrimination and oppression who have traditionally been understood as "Other."

Furthermore, why is it that only womanhood and femininity are in question? Why is it that functioning as a female and possessing a particular kind of anatomy are not enough to make one truly a woman? Is there some universal and immutable, though evidently fragile (for apparently it can be "lost") essence of womanhood? For the most part, this has already been answered in de Beauvoir's conception of "Otherness": it is always what is "Other" or exceptional that must be explained. If being a man represents the "rule" for what it means to be human, then woman as "Other" manifests the exception to it. If the masculine is the "absolute human type," constituting the human per se, then what is opposed to or derived from it must be analyzed and explicated. "Woman" is thus the eternal mystery for mankind and requires interpretation. Moreover, otherness almost always implies inferiority and subordination, for no group ever establishes itself as "the One" without simultaneously constituting "the Other" in contradistinction to it. This is true not only for women but for all who have been oppressed in one way or another: "Jews are 'different' for the anti-Semite, Negroes are 'inferior' for American racists, aborigines are 'natives' for colonialists, proletarians are the 'lower-class' for the privileged" (de Beauvoir 1989: xxix).

As previously indicated, Aristotle had long ago sharply distinguished men from women by defining the latter through their lack of certain essential "human" qualities. Specifically, he claimed that women lacked the kind of reason necessary for moral discourse and virtue, which would thereby deny them full-fledged membership in the human race. Such claims of sexual difference are obviously not value-free. The analogy that is often cited by feminists is that of the mirror, whereby women exist only as relative beings in opposition to men: they are what men are not, or are considered as human in merely a derivative sense. However, this mirroring is in no way faithful to its subject or accurately representative of its object (i.e., man). As Virginia Woolf puts it, "[w]omen have served all these centuries as looking-glasses possessing the magic and delicious power of reflecting the figure of man at twice its natural size."[8] What this means is that although the category of womanhood is derivative, it nevertheless plays a necessary role in man's understanding of himself. "[M]irrors are essential to all violent and heroic action. That is why Napoleon and Mussolini both insist so emphatically upon the inferiority of women, for if they were not inferior, they would cease to enlarge. That serves to explain in part the necessity that women so often are to men. And it serves to explain how restless they are under her criticism" (Woolf 1929: 36). De Beauvoir says something remarkably similar when she claims that

History has shown us that men have always kept in their hands all concrete powers; since the earliest days of the patriarchate they have thought to keep woman in a state of dependence; their codes of law have been set up against her; and thus she has been definitely established as the Other. This arrangement suited the economic interests of the males; but it conformed also to their ontological and moral pretensions. Once the subject seeks to assert himself, the Other, who limits and denies him, is none the less a necessity to him: he attains himself only through that reality *which he is not*, which is something other than himself. (de Beauvoir 1989: p. 139, italics mine)

Women thus appear to be the essential inessential—that is, without their acting as mirrors for men, men could never effectively "see" themselves. In this way, one can also begin to understand how and why particular women, as well as the "feminine" qualities in general, have been devalued or regarded as having only a secondary importance. For if reason, consciousness, culture, and autonomy are all equated with masculinity and what is essential to one's humanity, then the passions, physical body, nature, and dependency will be on the side of what is peculiarly feminine and inessential to being human, yet nonetheless necessary for distinguishing the One from the Other. Still, what is not clear is how and why this situation is historically reproduced or perpetuated. Thus, de Beauvoir asks, Why do women, who do not represent a minority in the population, unlike Jews and Black Americans, accept this state of affairs? In responding to this question, she considers the effects of male dominance but does not let women entirely off the hook. "If women continue to be seen as the inessential which never becomes essential, then it is because they themselves have failed to effect such a change"(de Beauvoir 1989: xxxi). Specifically, she maintains that this is because women have never properly organized or seen themselves in terms of a "we" or community. They have no sense of solidarity, she says, for they lack a collective history or common interest—as presumably Jews, workers, and slaves had. Moreover, women are more dependent upon the men in their lives (husbands and fathers) and attached to their children than they are to one another. Despite the apparent fact that men have made women subordinate through political legislation and cultural practices, it is women who are primarily at fault for having colluded with this situation.

When man makes of woman the *Other*, he may, then, expect her to manifest deep-seated tendencies toward complicity. Thus, women may fail to lay claim to the status of [substantial] subject because she lacks definite resources, because she feels the necessary bond that ties her to man regardless of reciprocity, and because she is often very well pleased with her role as the *Other*. (de Beauvoir 1989: p. xxxiii)

So, although de Beauvoir blames men for initiating this state of dependency and subordination, she holds women responsible for its perpetuation. She also notes the vicious cycle that prevails "when an individual (or group of individuals) is kept in a situation of inferiority, the fact is that he *is* inferior" (de Beauvoir 1989: p. xxxvi). Rousseau made the same claim about slavery—that is, that anyone born into slavery was clearly born *for* slavery, having the opportunity for little else—though he denied that this was a "natural" condition, arguing that nature cannot be the origin of inequalities as it alone cannot confer rightful authority or grant superiority of one man over another. (Note the inconsistency of Rousseau's liberalism and egalitarian principles when it comes to women, as he insisted upon their "natural" inferiority.) Is de Beauvoir then blaming the victim here, as some would assert? Is it fair for her to place the burden of change upon women despite the fact that they seem to be caught in a vicious circle?

If women wanted to be treated as equal to men whether in public or in private, then they should act accordingly. But again, this implies acting like men had purportedly always acted. Like Wollstonecraft before her, de Beauvoir does not question the concept of masculinity itself (in her case, this is constituted by transcendence and autonomy, which can be seen as analogous to reason and virtue). Nor does she explicitly ask whether these ideals actually apply to most men. For instance, how often do men transcend or break free from entrenched social and cultural practices and ideals and independently forge their own destinies? Lastly, de Beauvoir accepts nearly all of the basic dichotomies that have characterized philosophy from the seventeenth century onward—namely, reason vs. passion, transcendence vs. immanence, freedom vs. Determinism, culture vs. nature, and conscious-ness vs. body, with man being characterized by the former and woman, the latter. As transcendence refers to the possibility of choice and going beyond limitations, yet women are doomed to immanence or what is factual and circumscribed by given conditions, it would seem that there is no way out! De Beauvoir simply assumes that these dualisms are fundamental and ineradicable and that women remain on the side of what is lacking. So, how can there be a solution to the de facto inferiority of women? How can women transcend their situation if they are, in fact, incapable of doing so? Her response is ultimately unsatisfying on this count, for she virtually reiterates Wollstonecraft's claims—that is, because men have made the world, women must learn to adopt their values if they wish to live as men's equals. Perhaps her position is even a bit more extreme than Wollstonecraft's, for women's emancipation is left almost exclusively to them, with men bearing very little of the burden. Given the changes in the political state and public realm, women must now work to change their social standing and personal relations. How then, according to her, are they to do this?

According to de Beauvoir, women must ultimately reject the "femi-nine" virtues that are central to the roles of wife and mother. Only in this way can they define themselves as individuals, not as relative to others or as the instrumental mirrors of man's self-knowledge and self-aggran-dizement. De Beauvoir recommends that women enter the public sphere of intellectual discourse and political activity, leaving behind the duties of domesticity. But then, one cannot help asking, who fills this gap? Do we simply hire professionals to raise children and perform household tasks? De Beauvoir says nothing about men having to choose between family life and political activity. Is it even fair to expect women to conform to these putative ideals of the man's world, and what makes autonomy so much more valuable than interdependency? She claims to be showing women the way towards greater freedom and independence, yet she denies the legitimacy of certain choices. By placing these kinds of limitations on women, she seems to be fettering them further, not allowing for their emancipation. The criticism most often leveled at de

Beauvoir is that she, too, is guilty not only of uncritically accepting the dichotomization of man vs. woman but of privileging or valorizing what has traditionally been considered masculine. For instance, she does not consider the sustenance of life via nurturing and care, or the traditional feminine virtues, to be essential to what makes us human. Rather, these are the very activities that women should seek to transcend, or move beyond, in order to be seen as men's equals. From this critical basis arises the transition to the feminists of the twentieth century who attempt to respond to some of the questions and assumptions that de Beauvoir evaded or left unexamined.

TWENTIETH-CENTURY THOUGHT

Carol Gilligan's work began as a criticism of Lawrence Kohlberg's theory of moral development, which itself owes much to the influences of Kant and Freud. Kohlberg composed several hypothetical cases involving moral dilemmas, presented them to his subjects seeking responses, and then rated them according to the standards he had developed. What bothered Gilligan was that women habitually scored lower than men and were therefore incapable of reaching the higher levels of his ethical scale. Rather than assume that this was due to some defect in the women themselves, as Kohlberg had, she began to question Kohlberg's standards as well as his method. When she did her own study, she noticed that two distinctive "voices" emerged, "two ways of speaking about moral problems, two modes of describing the relationship between other and self."[9] She also noted that these voices were almost always distinguished by sex and that women, instead of being morally underdeveloped as Kohlberg had concluded, were perhaps appealing to criteria of judgment that were not the traditionally masculine ideals. So, what were the evaluative criteria that Kohlberg applied? And, what specific differences characterized the distinctive feminine voice?

Kohlberg's standards reflect the tradition of Western thought, which had begun to be criticized as male biased, namely, individual autonomy, objectivity or impartiality, universality, and duty were all assumed to be essential to moral reasoning and the capacity to make ethical decisions. In contrast, Gilligan found that women tended to regard themselves less individualistically than men, recognizing and accepting an inherent interdependence among themselves and others—perhaps due to their traditional roles of wife and mother, which are by nature relational or "relative," as de Beauvoir, and others, had maintained. Thus, they do not regard themselves as independent or autonomous as men tend to do. Gilligan chose to see this trait as a strength rather than a weakness as many before her had, including de Beauvoir. Secondly, women often considered "objectivity" to be identical with the dismissal or repression of emotional factors (which is, of course, exactly what Kant himself meant by objectivity). To most women this impartiality appears as indifference or as indicating a lack of care and concern for relationships and the feelings of others. Gilligan saw this, too, as a positive characteristic, whereas Kohlberg and his predecessors had evaluated this apparent lack of objectivity as a failing. Thirdly, the ideal of universality fails to consider moral problems in their specific context and assumes that an ethical dilemma can be examined abstractly or as divorced from all particular circumstances (again, the very essence of what Kant maintained constituted moral reasoning). And, lastly, the concept of duty remains too rationalistic and apparently separate from the caring, affective, or emotional elements that are not only not irrelevant or contrary to moral reasoning, as the women subjects claimed, but are necessary for it to proceed effectively.

These discoveries did not lead Gilligan to conclude that men and women possess entirely distinct or mutually exclusive ethical positions, but rather that they manifest different orientations: with women as oriented primarily towards "care" and men, towards "justice." The justice orientation is characterized by the standards appealed to by Kohlberg, with the emphasis on rights and duties; while the care orientation focuses on one's concern for, and responsibilities to, others. The moral example Gilligan used for her study was abortion, a case which, she argues, is not accurately described as an instance of conflicting "rights" (though that is how it has traditionally been framed in moral discourse). Rather, she says, abortion involves a question of how one can respond to the situation with care and avoid harm as much as possible—and that this, in essence, is a question of how to act responsibly. The language of rights and justice has historically tended to be very individualistic, with the individual asserting his or her right to some specific thing (speech, property, privacy, and the like) over and against a community of other human beings. Thus, a tension between oneself and others is necessarily presupposed in this form of moral reasoning. On the other hand, being responsible means taking responsibility for myself in how I treat others, thereby mitigating any competition or conflict over whose rights should prevail. Acting responsibly presupposes some shared interests or sense of community—that is, others to whom I am, or should be, responsible besides myself. Still, Gilligan wants to make clear that she is not privileging one orientation over the other. Instead, she is claiming that both need to be used and are called for at different times depending upon the circumstances and context of the problem. Also, she argues that women who have traditionally acted in self-denying ways and, hence, irresponsibly towards themselves, need to learn from men how to be more autonomous (a claim not unlike Wollstonecrafts's and de Beauvoir's). And, that men should look to the examples set by women in order to become more nurturing and accepting of their own dependencies and interdependencies.

Along these same lines of criticism, Gilligan claims that moral problems should be reformulated, not in terms of either/or propositions (as traditional dilemmas have been constructed), but more in terms of "how to" or "how much." That is, in the case of abortion, it is not a question of either respecting the rights of the fetus or the rights of the woman, but a matter of how to act responsibly towards oneself as well as towards another and how much privacy is at stake here. Gilligan's conclusion is that both orientations are valid for different contexts and situations and that we need these distinctive methods (along with many more perhaps) for resolving different kinds of moral issues. This is not to say that there are no right answers to ethical questions, but that such can only be discerned concretely in relation to a particular set of variables and conditions, and that one's moral choices are not subject to abstract universalization (as Aristotle has already indicated in his conception of *phronesis*, which is discussed in the preceding chapter).

The centrality of community and care for others is typical of other feminist theorists, such as Nancy Hartsock, whose positions are also designated as "essentialist" or "standpoint." Whether "natural" or due to socialization and entrenched cultural practices, the basic idea here is that women and men possess certain essential qualities that make them what they are, or, that there is some singular and basic standpoint from which one makes judgments or reflects, and that this differs between men and women because each experiences the world differently. According to Gilligan and many others, these differences are most likely due to women's experiences as mothers and daughters. Specifically, Gilligan draws on Nancy Chodorow's account of male and female development and gender identity formation whereby male children typically identify themselves as "masculine" by separating from and rejecting their mothers (thereby experiencing problems later, as adults, with intimacy and empathy), while female children tend to develop their sense of gender by identifying with and relating to their mothers (often facing difficulties as women with separation and valuing themselves as individuals).[10] The net result of all this, according to Chodorow (and Gilligan and Hartsock by extension), is that women have apparently developed a keener sense of interdependence and "communitarian" values, while men have a greater sense of their own independence and celebrate individuality. Furthermore, Hartsock begins from the position that labor is divided along sexual lines as well, leading to different world views for men and women. What she envisions are possibilities for a rethinking of power and community from a feminist perspective, or women's standpoint, which would stand in contrast to the traditionally male interpretations.

According to Hartsock, it is not consciousness that determines activity but activity that determines consciousness. In other words, it is not our thoughts that cause us to act in certain ways but particular kinds of activities and practices that determine how we think. Put differently, how we see ourselves and others is conditioned by what we do. Thus, if men and women appear to think differently, we must ask what kinds of activities are typically feminine or specifically masculine. That is, what kinds of activities do men and women typically engage in? From the beginning, Hartsock presupposes a collective standpoint—namely, "women"—which she considers as analogous to Marx's working class or "proletariat." Like workers, women are in a subordinate position, with men functioning as the "bourgeoisie" or "capitalists"—that is, those who, in Marxist terminology, typically own the means of production, or, more basically, those in whose hands power is concentrated. Men are therefore the dominant gender in society, with women generally holding a subordinate status. So, we can see already how the experiences and activities of men and women will be said to differ if we assume these fundamental sexual distinctions that are conceptualized by Hartsock as a class.

Women's labor or housework, according to Hartsock, is focused on the domestic sphere. It tends to be concrete and immediate, bound up with individual personalities and the unique relationship between mother and child. It is repetitious or cyclical: as bathing the children and washing the clothes, for example, are tasks that must be repeated again and again. And, this kind of work is diffuse, as the distribution of tasks and the order in which they are done varies from day to day and from person to person. On the other hand, work done outside the home tends to be abstract in the sense that one is replaceable and the activities are not dependent upon individual personalities or one-of-a-kind personal relationships. It is linear, with beginnings and ends more clearly defined, as opposed to cyclical. And, it is more structured and regulated, with consistent rules and expectations made explicit. For Hartsock, there is, thus, a sharp distinction between the public and private spheres, between the workplace and the home. And, as long as this separation is maintained, tensions will remain between the woman's and the man's worlds. However, these tensions can provide a space for criticism (which is the objective of Hartsock's work), for the logic of the marketplace can be criticized from the standpoint of the domestic realm.[11] It is the market model of community, she argues, which abstracts from life by denying the values of the home and worth of housework. In order to render her position more explicit, we must look at her analysis of power and its relationship to class and gender.

Hartsock says that our traditional understanding of power, and what it means, needs to be rethought and, moreover, that we must not equate it with domination. That is, the problem for feminism is not power itself, but a particular conception of it that renders it tantamount to male domination and the subordination of women. She argues that "the form taken by the exercise of power in a community structures human interaction within that community, and so, in a community where the exercise of power takes the form of structured and systematic domination of some over others, the community itself is formed by domination. It follows that to change the practice of power is to change the structure and nature of the community" (Hartsock 1983: 3–4). Thus, a change in our understanding of what constitutes, or should constitute, a community will entail a rethinking of power relations and their effects, just as the kind of community one lives in will determine one's understanding of power.

As noted above, Hartsock, like any orthodox Marxist, distinguishes between the bourgeoisie and the proletariat. The former "tend to privilege activities having to do with money—using it to buy things, investing it in order to increase it, banking it," while the latter looks to "the activity of production as the paradigm for power relations" (Hartsock 1983: 4). What corresponds to the bourgeois conception of power is the "market model" of community in which a "fundamental gulf between buyer and seller (and, in the analogy, the parties to a power relation) persists." It is in this context that

participants have conflicting interests and therefore can be expected to distrust each other. In addition, the community established in this way can be only partial, since it is on the one hand constituted by the common interests of the participants and on the other limited by their conflict. They are engaged in a contest to determine which one of them will be the dominant party to an exchange; they need in principle have only enough in common to actually engage in a competition or exchange. (Hartsock 1983: 4)

The feminist twist that Hartsock adds to this is to maintain that the bourgeois market model of community is typically male (a correlation Marx himself did not make, believing that his position was gender-neutral). What Hartsock intends to do in her analysis is to explore the possibilities of substituting this masculine model with a proletariat or female paradigm. She sees the former as perpetuating inequalities, and as ultimately inadequate for insuring a genuine sense of community, while the latter apparently is fertile ground for constructing a more truly humanistic conception of community and a more just economic system. Thus, she argues, we should seek a means of replacing the presumably destructive masculine model of power with a female one, which is assumed to be more humane and productive. (For more on this topic see chapter 6, which deals with women and leadership.) Moreover, the gender bias inherent in our conception of community is also present in our understanding of sexual power. That is, power involves questions of sexuality, she claims, for "[b]oth the exchange of things and the erotic fusion of sexuality bring human beings together" (Hartsock 1983: 6). Hence, a connection between sex, power, and money is inevitably at the root of all human relations; and, if these relations are distorted or unequal in any way, this will be reflected in the economy and our sense of community.

Again, Hartsock brings to light the fact that our understanding of power in a capitalist, male dominated society is not gender-neutral. Rather, the ways in which power and male virility are linked indicate a gender bias that privileges men and perpetuates women's subordination on a sexual level as well. This is nothing new, she argues; it is a fact often brought out by feminist activists who have shaped the debates surrounding rape and pornography. Their point is that the control and domination of women by men, often to the point of violence, is eroticized. And, that rape is better understood as an act of aggression than as an expression of one's sexual needs. Historically speaking, "[m]asculine sexuality was central to the construction of [a] community structured fundamentally by rivalry and competition" (Hartsock 1983: 7). For example, the Homeric heroes and Athenian citizens, who were considered ideals of masculinity, were characterized by their warrior virtues of courage, honor, and physical strength. Hartsock concludes that the notion of community and power that pervades the Western world is, at root, both capitalistic and masculine. She questions whether an alternative vision is possible, one based on *women's* lives and experiences rather than men's. Thus, she looks to the activities of women, as described above, and considers their implications in order to critique the traditional masculine paradigms of power and community that have been handed down and reproduced in our culture since ancient times. What, then, would a feminist conception of power or community look like? Does Hartsock offer any positive constructions or viable alternatives of her own?

The short answer to this latter question is, no. Hartsock's objective here is to criticize the existing notions of power and community and show how they serve to reinforce one another in a way that perpetuates inequalities and male domination. Hers is a call for a "re-theorization of power on the basis of women's as well as men's life activity [which] could be important in re-evaluating our understanding and practice of

politics. It could perhaps lead toward the constitution of a more complete and thoroughgoing human community" (Hartsock 1983:   12).
Between the economy, which is male dominated, and the domestic
sphere, in which women maintain some primacy and control, lies the
realm of the social/political/cultural, which can function as a site of
mediation. In other words, some means must be found that will enable
us to bring the values of the household into the public arena of the
workplace and economy, thus allowing for the establishment of a
community based on truly humanistic principles, as opposed to merely
masculinist or even feminist ones. This is the ultimate conclusion of
Twentieth Century feminists like those discussed above. Their intention
is to offer some hope of a new direction by criticizing existing social
structures, without dogmatically asserting what that might entail.

Iris Young, Jane Flax, Nancy Fraser, and Linda Nicholson are all
contemporary feminists who take a critical stance towards Modern feminism and "essentialist" twentieth century theories. Their aim is primarily the "deconstructing," or critical analysis of, the categories, dichotomies, norms, and fundamental assumptions that have been central to
the Western tradition, which these earlier forms of feminism seem to
have taken for granted. Thus, this contemporary period in feminist
thought is characterized more by its internal debates than by its emphasis on political action and social change or social and cultural criticism.
No longer is there a generally agreed upon and common "enemy." And,
some of the concepts themselves (e.g., equality, gender), as well as many
traditional dichotomies (e.g., masculine and feminine, community and
individuality, cooperation and competition) and philosophical assumptions, are now the subjects of controversy. Moreover, in some circles,
there is presently an increasing resistance to theory itself and an even
greater reluctance to providing a foundation for, or systematic understanding of the causes of, discrimination and oppression. Additionally,
any constructing of new or alternative paradigms of power, community,
and so forth is regarded by these thinkers as necessarily exclusionary and
limiting. Thus, contemporary feminist theories may best be summed up
as "anti-theory" or as those in which "criticism floats free of any universalistic theoretical ground."[12] On the one hand, contemporary feminism
is very careful to avoid making any general claims or arriving at
definitive conclusions, by concentrating instead on issues of "difference."
Yet, on the other hand, feminists of this period remain at a very abstract
level of understanding, criticizing concepts as opposed to social structures or cultural practices, which leaves many to doubt whether such
thought is in any way practically applicable.

In their introduction and essay, Fraser and Nicholson's basic
complaint about feminists like Gilligan, Hartsock, and Chodorow is that

they are "insufficiently attentive to historical and cultural diversity, and they falsely universalize features of the theorist's own era, society, culture, class, sexual orientation, and ethnic, or racial group" (Fraser 1990: 27). Thus, they charge earlier forms of feminism with being inclined towards an essentialism that obscures or denies differences among women. Moreover, they argue, these twentieth century thinkers were preoccupied with seeking a singular "cause" of women's oppression by appealing to "women's labor, to women's sexuality, and to women's primary responsibility for child bearing" (Fraser and Nicholson 1990: 5–6). And that all of these cases are guilty of projecting Western culture and values upon all, or almost all, areas of human history. They are thus assuming a falsely universalistic perspective, which is not unlike the male philosophers whom they have criticized. For both Nicholson and Fraser, then, the rallying cry is for feminism to be more attentive to historical factors, "attuned to the cultural specificity of different societies and periods and to that of different groups within societies and periods." Thus, "postmodern-feminist theory would be nonuniversalist [and] comparativist attuned to changes and contrasts instead of to covering laws" (Fraser and Nicholson 1990: 34).

In this same text (*Feminism/Postmodernism*), Iris Young's essay takes on Gilligan directly, and Hartsock and Chodorow indirectly. She is critical of these standpoint theorists for privileging "unity over difference" and the "relational over the competitive," thereby implicitly accepting a whole host of dichotomies—community vs. individuality, care vs. justice (which can be reduced to sentiment vs. reason), and the masculine vs. the feminine.[13] By identifying women with the first side of these oppositions and valorizing them, Twentieth Century feminists are merely inverting the traditional hierarchies of Modernity and failing to criticize the foundations on which such dichotomies are based. This results in leaving intact many of the implicit assumptions and presuppositions of Modern dualism—the position that all human thought and activity can be reduced either to reason or passion, autonomy or dependency, transcendence or immanence, and so forth. For example, Young argues that both individualistic as well as communitarian ideals deny "difference," the former by presuming the self-sufficiency and autonomy of the subject, and the latter by positing "fusion rather than separation as the social ideal" (Fraser and Nicholson 1990: 307). Moreover, she, along with others who call themselves postmodernists, argues that all dichotomies are reductionistic—that is, they assume that all experience can be explained by reference to one of the two sides of these binary oppositions, and that this precludes any possibility of radical change.

Jane Flax also criticizes the essentialism of early twentieth-century feminism on some of the same grounds as those above. She notes that feminist theorists like Hartsock, Chodorow, and Gilligan "have offered a variety of causal explanations including the sex/gender system, the organization of production or sexual division of labor, [and] child rearing practices" and that these may function as useful hypotheses for the study of gender relations in a particular society, time, and place. But, that each model of explanation is "deeply flawed, inadequate, and overly deterministic."[14] Flax gives some examples of what she means by this when she asks why would a feminist thinker (like Hartsock) merely attempt to extend the Marxist categories of work and production to include "women's work" without questioning the gender bias of the concept itself. Another problem arises when one merely identifies child rearing practices as the root of gender relations without asking why women have this as their primary responsibility in the first place. If one were to appeal to the fact that because only women have the capacity to bear children it naturally follows that they would rear them, then one is falling back into a "biology is destiny" position. The assumption here is that "nature" is what determines our social structure and cultural practices when perhaps, instead, it is the latter that conditions our understanding of the former. In other words, Flax contends that it is more likely that socio-cultural factors determine one's understanding of what is or is not "natural," rather than the other way around. Once again, it becomes apparent that what is most problematic for post-modern feminists are the concepts themselves (e.g., nature, culture, and so forth). And, that before one can employ such to make sense of gender relations, they must be deconstructed along critical lines.

Gender, too, is a category about which there is no general agreement as to what specifically it entails; yet it is still intended to serve as a category for social and cultural analysis and criticism for so many feminist thinkers. Flax considers one of the most significant advances in feminist theory to be the questioning of this concept and its relationship to sex. To separate the two, regarding sex as reflecting natural anatomical differences and gender as a matter of cultural identity, is ultimately inadequate and overly simplistic. For although no one would deny the existence of anatomical differences, this is merely a descriptive fact and it is the meaning of those differences that needs to be explained. Moreover, little attention is paid to the ways in which men and women are physically similar. "So why ought the anatomical differences between male and female humans assume such significance in our sense of our selves as persons?" (Fraser and Nicholson 1990: 51). Flax finds this kind of reasoning to be circular, as she did in her critique of the Marxist model of production. That is, what is being assumed here is precisely what requires explanation—whether that be our concept of gender or notions of sex, production, or community. For, she claims, gender itself is relational, both as a category of cultural analysis and criticism as well as a social process of personal identity formation or one's self-understanding. This means that it cannot be conceived as something fixed and static; rather it must be construed as always in process or problematized to some degree.

We live in a world in which gender is a constituting social relation and in which gender is also a relation of domination. Therefore, both men's and women's understanding of anatomy, biology, embodiedness, sexuality, and reproduction is partially rooted in, reflects, and must justify (or challenge) preexisting gender relations. In turn, the existence of gender relations helps us to order and understand the facts of human existence. (Fraser and Nicholson 1990: pp. 51–52)

If there is nothing "outside" of human understanding—and the way in which we understand something is always conditioned by our experiences—then there is no means of effectively separating things like nature and culture. For how we interpret one determines, to some degree at least, our interpretation of the other. Thus, there is a dynamic relation between concepts like sex and gender (nature and culture) with each functioning as a means for understanding the other. Flax and her contemporaries maintain that it is these relations and processes which are always in motion, so to speak, that should now be the focus of feminist thought. For these kinds of critical approaches, though perhaps providing no new or alternative visions of their own, can avoid the kinds of limitations and simplifications that are endemic to earlier forms of feminism that have uncritically adopted static and implicitly biased categories borrowed from Modernity or nonfeminist thinkers.

But, can feminism proceed without theory? How can one act effectively without some grounding or theoretical basis to spring from? If we are to take postmodern or contemporary feminism seriously, then even the concept of "difference" requires unpacking. What does it mean to be different, or which kinds of differences count? Differences of class and race presumably have significance, but what about differences in eye or hair color? Do women with blond hair and blue eyes experience the world differently from those with dark hair and eyes? Underlying all of these seemingly trivial questions is a real concern, namely, how can we account for differences without some corresponding synthesis or means of making generalizations? To claim something is distinct inevitably implies something to which it is opposed or contrasted. Is it thus possible to focus exclusively on what is particular without any recourse to a "universal"? Can one be "attuned to changes" without positing some fixed point? Finally, how can one be "comparativist" without referring to some principle of comparison? These are the types of questions currently being posed in response to the claims of postmodernism—and about which the debate rages on.

Some contemporary feminists have attempted to bridge the gap between abstract conceptual criticism, which leaves us little room for action, and naive social or cultural criticism, which proceeds from too many unexamined assumptions to overly simplistic conclusions.   In order to consider some of their claims, let us concentrate on one particular but very basic and problematic concept for feminism, namely, the principle of "equality." It is by no means clear, nor is there any consensus, as to what this principle entails in theory, let alone in actual practice. We thus need to ask what is meant by this term, or what kinds of equality are feminists calling for? And, what are the presumptions that underlie our understanding of this fundamental concept?

Alison M. Jaggar and Christine A. Littleton have each illuminated this problem in helpful ways. There is no doubt that the concept of equality is a central issue for feminists, but how is this to be understood? Does it mean treating all people identically regardless of their different circumstances? Or, does it require accommodating differences? Jaggar argues, that an affirmative answer to either question will only serve to perpetuate women's subordination:

When women are treated identically to men, as some feminists have recommended, we are penalized for our differences because we are measured against a male norm. When we are treated differently from men, as recommended by other feminists, even the provision of so-called special benefits, rights, or protections may often have damaging consequences insofar as it reifies currently perceived sex differences, confirms stereotypes, obliterates differences between women, and reinforces the status quo.[15]

Still, one is compelled to ask, to what extent must we reflect before we can act or move ahead in any direction? This rethinking cannot proceed indefinitely, for we live in a world that constantly calls upon us to act whether we possess sufficient knowledge or not. Moreover, it is not even clear to us what would constitute sufficient knowledge. For Jaggar, both the "sex-blind" and the "sex-responsive" approaches are inadequate for feminism because neither can effectively account for differences (Jaggar 1994: 22). Rather, "a more deeply feminist understanding of sexual difference must be dynamic." That is, "it must reflect the continually expanding feminist awareness of the ways in which the history of women's subordination, especially as this intersects with the history of other subordinated groups, has shaped and continues to shape both existing differences between the sexes and the ways in which we perceive and evaluate those differences."[16] What this means, however, is not that we must immediately abandon both of these approaches and begin anew (if that is even possible). But rather, her claim is that sometimes a sex-blind approach may be suitable for achieving the goal of social justice, and sometimes sex-responsiveness would be more appropriate, while at other times factors other than sex would take precedence. Jaggar's point is simply that there can be no one method for dealing with questions of equality and justice. Just as there can be no singular model of moral reasoning, with both deontological and utilitarian positions making valid claims in different contexts, questions of equality are also only meaningful situationally.

Littleton makes virtually the same claim when she distinguishes between "symmetrical" and "asymmetrical" approaches to equality.[17] Those who respond to questions of sexual equality according to a symmetrical model "attempt to equate legal treatment of sex with that of race and deny that there are in fact any significant natural differences between women and men; in other words, to consider the two symmetrically located with regard to *any* issue, norm, or rule" (Littleton 1987: 1287). A contrary position, which Littleton calls asymmetrical, "rejects this analogy, accepting that women and men are or may be 'different' [and] rejects the notion that all gender differences are likely to disappear, or even that they should."[18] Again, it is evident that the former approach has resonances with thinkers like Wollstonecraft and de Beauvoir, who encouraged women to transcend the mere cultural practices that distinguished them from men; while the latter is more reminiscent of feminists like Hartsock and Gilligan who imply that women's differences from men should be accepted as valid and possibly celebrated for their own sake.

Even within these two positions, one finds variations of interpretation, as Littleton is clear to point out. On the one hand, there is the "assimilation" model of symmetry, which is based on the idea that women are or, given the chance, could be exactly like men. On the other side, the "androgynous" model argues that some intermediate position should be found that would treat all cases as androgynous persons would be, entirely doing away with masculine/feminine distinctions (Littleton 1987: 1292). Asymmetrical approaches include "special rights" (like those afforded to individuals with physical disabilities); "accommodation" (which allows for strictly biological differences to be accounted for); "empowerment" (which argues that we should focus exclusively on issues of subordination and domination forgetting about the academic question of difference); and "acceptance," which is how Littleton characterizes her own position (Littleton 1987: 1295). Acceptance "asserts that eliminating the unequal consequences of sex differences is more important than debating whether such differences are 'real,' or even trying to eliminate them altogether" (Littleton 1987: 1312).

This position would challenge the valorization of "male" qualities and skills, but not to the extent of merely reversing the hierarchy and replacing these with so-called female qualities and skills. It also acknowledges that women and men do not stand in symmetrical positions within an institution or society at large. Littleton appeals to the case of athletics to illustrate her position:

[E]quality as acceptance would support an argument that equal resources be allocated to male and female sports programs regardless of whether the sports themselves are 'similar.' In this way, women's equality in athletics would not depend on the ability of individual women to assimilate themselves to the particular sports activities traditionally engaged in by men. [And it] would support an equal division of resources between male and female programs rather than dividing up the available sports budget per capita. Since . . . per capita distribution would simple serve to perpetuate the asymmetry, diverting more resources to male programs, where the participation rate has traditionally been high.[19]

In this way, differences between men and women, as well as among women themselves, are accepted while their negative consequences are mitigated. Still, the question may be raised as to the ultimate sources of these differences and what these differences mean on a deeper level. However, Littleton is more of a pragmatist and thus limits her focus to the legal and political aspects of difference and inequality, and she offers two reasons for this. First, that such speculation only brings us back to the question of nature vs. nurture, or the distinction between biology and culture, which she agrees is, itself, culturally based and upon which there is no consensus (as most postmodern feminists claim). But more importantly, she says, if in fact women "choose" to enter certain professions rather than others (nursing, for example, over real estate appraising), they still do not "choose" to be paid less. For her the causes are less significant than the consequences. "It is the *consequences* of gendered differences, and not its sources, that equal acceptance addresses" (Littleton 1987: 1312). Littleton thus leaves the ultimate ontological or metaphysical questions to the feminist philosophers, choosing instead to concentrate on the practical aspects, or what will be most conducive to real social change.

CONCLUSION

In sum, it should be clear that there can be no singular paradigm for what constitutes a feminist position or feminist theory. While some general observations may be made, and must be made if we are to understand our world at all, they will always be subject to criticism or revision.   Thus, we believe that examining the history of feminist discourse will have been worthwhile in order to better situate ourselves today and identify our present concerns, values, beliefs, and assumptions when approaching questions of business, work, and ethics.   If nothing else, we hope that others have become more aware as to just how elusive "answers" in the realm of human relations are and, ideally, have become more sensitive, thoughtful, and critical in how they examine gender issues.

QUESTIONS FOR REFLECTION

1. How can feminist theorists help us in thinking about women's issues in the workplace?
2. How are contemporary women's problems similar to or distinct from past concerns?
3. Are there any "natural" distinctions between the sexes? If so, what does this imply?
4. In what ways might concepts of human nature be gender-biased?
5. Is the criticism of systematic thinking, or "reason," a strength or weakness in twentieth century feminist theory?
6. How have feminist thinkers borrowed from or criticized their male predecessors?
7. Does one's gender identification determine one's perspective (socially, politically, philosophically)?
8. What is meant by "equality"? And why is this such an important issue for women?

NOTES

1. Mary Wollstonecraft, *A Vindication of the Rights of Women* (New York: Alfred A. Knopf, 1992), p. 13.

2. Jean Jacques Rousseau, *Emile,* trans. by Allan Bloom (New York: Basic Books, Inc., 1979), Book V, p. 367. All subsequent page numbers refer to this edition.

3. J.S. Mill, *The Subjection of Women* (Indianapolis, Ind.: Hackett Publishing Co.,1988), p. 1.

4. Jane Flax, "Postmodernism and Gender Relations," *Feminism/Postmodernism,* ed. by Linda Nicholson (New York: Routledge, 1990), p. 42.

5. Feinberg, Leslie, *Stone Butch Blues* (Ithaca, N.Y.: Firebrand Books, 1993).

6. Simone de Beauvoir, *The Second Sex* (New York: Vintage Books-Random House, Inc.,1989), p. xxv.

7. See Patricia Hill Collins, *Black Feminist Thought* (New York: Routledge, 1991), p. 14.

8. Virginia Woolf, *A Room of One's Own* (New York: Harcourt, Brace, and Jovanovich, 1929), p. 35.

9.   Carol Gilligan, *In a Different Voice* (Cambridge, Mass.:   Harvard University Press, 1982), p. 1.

10.   Ibid., pp. 7–8. See also Nancy Chodorow, *The Reproduction of Mothering* (Berkeley: University of California Press, 1978).

11.   Nancy Hartsock, *Money, Sex, and Power* (New York: Longman, 1983).

12.   Nancy Fraser and Linda J. Nicholson, "Social Criticism without Philosophy: An   Encounter   between   Feminism   and   Postmodernism," *Feminism/Postmodernism*, ed. by Linda J. Nicholson (New York: Routledge, 1990), p. 21.

13.   Iris Young, "The Ideal of Community and the Politics of Difference," Ibid., p. 300 and 307, respectively.

14.   Jane Flax, "Postmodernism and Gender Relations in Feminist Theory," Ibid., p. 46.

15.   *Living with Contradictions: Controversies in Feminist Social Ethics*, ed. by Alison M. Jaggar (San Francisco: Westview Press, 1994), p. 14.

16.   Alison M. Jaggar, "Sexual Difference and Sexual Equality," Ibid., p. 23.

17.   Christine A. Littleton, "Reconstructing Sexual Equality," *California Law Review* 1279: 75, 4 (Berkeley: University of California Press, 1987), pp. 1279–1337.

18.   Ibid., see section beginning p. 1287 and following.

19.   Ibid., p. 1312.

3

SEXUAL HARASSMENT

As I said, I may have used poor judgment. Perhaps I should have taken angry or even militant steps, both when I was at the agency or after I left. But I confess to the world that the course that I took seemed the better as well as the easier approach.

—Anita Hill

INTRODUCTION

We live in a strange dichotomy: while we are encouraged by the media to see specific gender stereotypes in order to sell products, we later have to dismiss these same stereotypes in order to work together in a professional manner. The way both men and women in our society are portrayed, most explicitly through the media, mirrors the prevailing norm that we are bombarded with daily, whether we are conscious of it or not. Billboards, magazines, music videos, and computer games provide endless examples of how the media tells us what we must do to fulfill the gender "ideal." This flood of advertising leads to certain stereotypical or biased views of women and men that cannot help but influence attitudes and behavior in the workplace and, unfortunately, can lead to sexual harassment. The good news is that cultural biases are learned behavior and can be changed with time and commitment. We can begin to alter attitudes and insensitivity to gender issues in the workplace by reeducating men and women about their sometimes unconscious learned behavior and its consequences.

Dr. Jean Kilbourne, in her moving documentaries *Still Killing Us Softly* and its popular sequel *Slim Hopes*, offers a visual presentation of her research on how our society constructs the "ideal" man and woman and how this is destructive to all of us.[1] Women are portrayed in advertising as sex objects, even when shown in the workplace. They are passive, painted, sprayed, toned, starved, high-heeled, and forever young, aspiring to an image that attracts men. This, of course, is a game in which all women ultimately lose. For, obviously, we cannot keep up this image, even if we managed in youth to approximate this supposed "ideal." Not only are women degraded in advertising by the characteristics that our society labels as "feminine"—intuition, selflessness, vulnerability, and cooperative skills—but these traits are devalued when found in men as well.[2] Most disturbing is the link many researchers feel exists between the popular societal views of women and violence against women. The statistical reality is that many women are victims of violence, sexual or otherwise, and they are most likely to be victimized by someone they know. Music videos and ads often come close—dangerously close—to glorifying violence against women. In her video presentations, Dr. Kilbourne gives us a wake-up call. We are inundated daily by these images and they permeate all aspects of our lives. Further, as most of us spend the bulk of our waking time in the workplace, we bring societal attitudes about sexuality to this environment where they can prove destructive when they lead to sexual harassment.

Another serious concern voiced by scholars who research gender issues in advertising is the recent practice of showing children in suggestive or pornographic positions in order to promote products. Although it is risky to depict children in this way in a society that is clearly offended by such tactics, it appears that even negative publicity can lead to increased sales. The challenge is how to stop this cycle, especially ads that influence the young and impressionable in a climate where they are often victims of sexual exploitation and abuse. There has been a marked increase, for example, of ads showing very young girls dressed and made up to look like sexually provocative adult women, making an erotic connection between youth, innocence, and sexuality that may be carried over to the real world. There are times when even the most liberal among us must agree that paternalism is necessary. Paternalism—that is, making decisions for, or in order to protect, others—is appropriate when it involves children. This is, obviously, a hotly debated issue and one that will be addressed later in this book (see chapter 5).

INFLUENCE OF ADVERTISING

Andy Rooney, in a recent *60 Minutes* segment, noted with awe the number of professional women who bought out the latest issue of *Cosmopolitan* at a newsstand in his building. This was not the *New York Times*, *The New Yorker* or *Time* magazine, but *Cosmopolitan*, one of the biggest offenders of the type of advertising/stereotyping we have been discussing. What's worse, in his view, is that the women purchasing these magazines were professional women, obviously educated and aware of the issues of the nineties. Rooney concluded that women are their own worst enemies and their complaints about sexism in the workplace must start with themselves, not the newsstand. This indictment of women is nothing new and has even been voiced by some feminists. However, if we agree that the media is a powerful influence in determining sex roles, then its importance in forming attitudes that seep into the workplace cannot be underestimated. Perhaps we have become so desensitized through the saturation of advertising that the issue has become banal. One often does not realize, on a conscious level, how influential the media is despite sex or educational background.

While this issue of advertising will be dealt with in greater depth in a later chapter, it is introduced here briefly to illustrate the issue of sexual harassment as one that is deeply entrenched in societal stereotypes, deeply influenced by advertising, and perpetuated in both personal and professional relations. How we have come to accept these stereotypes and the realization that these attitudes can be changed is our challenge as women enter the workplace in greater numbers. The woman working next to you is not the air-brushed, silicone-breasted model from the cover of *Cosmopolitan* or the "bitch" or "whore" portrayed in rap music, but a coworker who deserves to be treated with dignity and a sense of professionalism. She is there, data tells us, to support or give critical supplemental support to her family, not to have a place "in which to wear her sweaters," as a recent magazine advertisement proclaims.[3] How to treat one another professionally is not something we are usually taught, and old ways of relating to women are not working in the business setting. Sexual tensions aside, the workplace is not a dating bar and we should be able to train and enlighten most people to treat coworkers appropriately. This has to be a priority because the number of harassment court suits and grievances is alarming. It is a dangerous game we are playing if we do not recognize this problem and begin to deal with addressing and modeling professional behavior. On the job harassment needs to be confronted before it turns into a grievance.

We occasionally see examples of professional behavior in the face of highly charged political issues. A female colonel taking questions on a CNN talk show was asked about the potential dangers of her lesbianism when commanding young nurses in the field. What should be noted is that no one is surprised when a question like this is asked of a gay person who is working with members of the same sex, but that many would be shocked if it were routinely posed to straight men who will be working with women. "No, this is not and has never been an issue," the colonel protests, for when she was in Vietnam commanding nurses she was a trained professional who knew what that meant in terms of doing her job well. In other words, she did not see a danger of mixing the personal with the professional. She was a professional first, and she knew what that entailed. The words "trained professional" are key here; how we lead our personal lives need not necessarily influence or spill over into our working relationships. If we train workers at all levels as to what professional relationships involve, we should make some headway. Abuses, of course, are inevitable, as they probably were in the combat circumstances of Vietnam for heterosexuals and homosexuals alike, but they are not insurmountable.

One of the difficulties in dealing with such a socially saturated problem is that many men have not often had to deal with women on both levels, the personal and the professional; therefore, they often use the personal model, since that is the one with which they are most familiar. They are ill equipped to deal with the professional side, for there is no previous guide, map, or blueprint showing the way. More-over, we all live in the realm of the personal before we move into a professional world. Many men are honestly astounded when confronted with an indictment of sexism. They often think they were simply acting as they always have, or that they were just being friendly and are genuinely unaware of what might be taken as unwelcome or threatening behavior. Therefore, we need knowledge, education, and sensitivity as tools to help us to understand the "other." Because we are fighting the weight of culture, on the job training may be needed to begin unraveling the complexity of sexual harassment. Just as many psychologists urge us to learn to build cooperative romantic relationships built on trust and friendship as well as sexual gratification, so, too, can we begin to learn what it means to have professional work relationships despite sexual tensions. However, before we attempt to resolve this complicated issue we must start with the most basic question: what is sexual harassment?

Despite being an issue of growing importance, considered by many to be *the* issue in business ethics, there is much confusion about just what sexual harassment is and what can be done to stop it. As growing numbers of women enter the business world, especially in traditionally male occupations, it is important that sexual harassment be carefully examined and defined. The confusion surrounding sexual harassment can be seen in all areas of society, public and private. As was demonstrated in the Clarence Thomas/Anita Hill case, the senators involved in the questioning, as well as the media pundits commenting on and watching the proceedings, had only a vague notion of the issue and manifested confusion about how seriously the charges should be taken. We will examine not only what sexual harassment is, but also how it affects the lives of those involved. Can education in the workplace help curtail this problem? What stopgaps can we institute in the organizational structure than can short circuit sexual harassment problems before they begin? Should coercive sexual harassment be the domain of the courts and litigated as a tort targeted only at the harasser? Is it fair to hold businesses legally culpable for the actions of certain employees; if the answer is "yes" then under what conditions? These questions will be the foundation around which this chapter will revolve.

Part of the difficulty in finding a common definition is the question of just how prevalent sexual harassment is. In the absence of long-term studies, data is unreliable and "in process," and no common vocabulary exists to aid in the communication of research. A further complication may be found in the methodological flaws that social scientists often face in obtaining data on subjects that people tend to see as politically sensitive. Women often feel ashamed or reluctant to admit to being victimized in this way, and are uncomfortable discussing it. Many have indicated that they simply quit their jobs when they felt uneasy, as they did not want to face the time consuming, and sometimes humiliating, process of reporting grievances. This issue is further clouded by the use of polls that do not make clear what they are polling or define issues so loosely as to be deceptive. Surveys and polls can be a powerful source of misinformation. The Merit Systems Protection Board determined that 42 percent of the women (and 14 percent of men) working for the federal government had experienced some form of unwanted sexual attention between 1985 and 1987. The United Methodist Church established that 7 percent of its clergywomen experienced incidents of sexual harassment, with 41 percent of these naming a pastor or colleague as the perpetrator and 31 percent naming church social functions as the setting.[4] Looking below the surface, we find that the United Methodists' survey defines sexual harassment as any sexually related behavior that is unwelcome, offensive, or that fails to respect the rights of others. Obviously, this definition is too broad in that it could include everything from an off-color joke to outright assault.

The very process of gaining reliable information about a highly sensitive issue that may involve emotional scars is difficult at best. In order to be accurate in finding material that can be used in examining sexual harassment, researchers have to take pains to make sure they know what is generally accepted as categories of sexual harassment and that their respondents have a common understanding. Currently, we have no such common language in dealing with this issue. In fact, the linguist Deborah Tannen has shown that the very words, phrases, and conceptual frameworks we rely on are distinguishable along gender lines.[5] That is, how sexual harassment is understood depends upon whether a man or a woman is doing the talking. What we do know, however, is that this issue is of growing concern and frustration for both men and women in the workplace. And, that there is a significant lack of understanding as to exactly how it is constituted and how it might be stopped.

It should be noted that when speaking of harassers in this chapter, the authors' references are to men. Although men can certainly be victims of sexual harassment, it is generally considered a woman's problem because of the politics of the economic power structure (see chapters 4 and 7) and the stereotypical images of both men and women that pervade our culture and affect how we interact. In other words, because women are more economically as well as physically vulnerable, they are less likely to leave a job or confront their harassers directly. Statistics on its prevalence suggest that anywhere from 15 to 65 percent of working women encounter *some form* of sexual harassment. Again, the wide range between percentages is attributable to the difficulty researchers face when collecting data on sensitive issues that people often deny and in an area that is so loosely defined. Studies also reveal that there was a constant increase in cases during a five-year period from 1986 to 1991—a time when women were entering the marketplace in record numbers, further indicating that this problem is a product of changing sex roles and power dynamics not of sexual interest or relations.[6]

Although limited in size, one of the most interesting studies available is a self-selected survey of 92 women conducted by Peggy Crull in order to obtain data on the relationship between harasser and victim. Not surprisingly, her study shows that victims of harassment are likely to hold low status or low paying positions that make them particularly vulnerable. Fifty-three percent of the victims considered themselves to be clerical workers, and 15 percent occupied service positions. While verbal harassment was the most common complaint, over half of Crull's subjects said they were routinely physically harassed. Seventy-nine percent claimed that they reported the incidents to someone in authority but that the situation was remedied in only 9 percent of the cases. Half of the respondents felt their claims were not taken seriously; further, 26 percent experienced retaliation, and 24 percent were soon fired. Most disturbing and frustrating is Crull's finding that 79 percent of the men involved had the power to fire or promote their victim.[7]

However, there is much anecdotal evidence to show that the above is not always the case. That is, while sexual harassment always involves relations of power, this does not necessarily mean that it must be the man who holds the position of authority. For example, in 1995, Angela Dodson filed a lawsuit against the *New York Times* alleging, among other things, gender harassment (*Village Voice*, January 23, 1996). In her case, there were no specific allegations of explicitly sexual misconduct; nonetheless, she claimed that acts of insubordination were committed in an attempt to sabotage her position as senior editor. When such behavior does take on a sexual dimension, it can be even more effective in putting women on the defensive and creating a hostile or threatening environment. Patients who proposition their doctors, or interns who grope fellow interns, are no less guilty of sexual harassment than those who hold superior positions.

In all of these situations, an attempt is being made to undermine the woman's power or to diminish her accomplishments by "reminding" her of her vulnerability to sexual assault. Some feminists say this is indicative of the fact that many men resent women in positions of authority and so attempt to get the "upper hand" by asserting their sexual prowess. The reason this is often so effective, they say, is that many women have a latent, if not conscious, fear of sexual violence, seeing it on a continuum with sexual assertiveness, whether in word or deed. Women tend to see sexual harassment as threatening in a way that men do not, as women are more likely to be victims of rape or sexual assault. Moreover, as already mentioned, media images portraying women in this manner (sometimes even for the purpose of titillation) abound in our society, thus making the threat of violence appear more real than it actually is. Even without this specter of physical assault, women feel humiliated or degraded as human beings when they are reduced to nothing more than a sexual being instead of receiving the kind of treatment they deserve as professionals.

Another small but fascinating anthropological study comes to us from England and the researcher Helen Watson. Watson studied sixty people with the aim of soliciting personal accounts of their experiences. She worked with a group of thirty males accused of harassment and thirty women who had made formal accusations of harassment. Hopefully this study will be the beginning of many more, for her results show a clear and disturbing difference in perspective between the accused and the victim. Most of the males she interviewed saw sexual harassment in terms of a potential sexual relationship "gone wrong," while the women who were victims did not see the harassment in relational/romantic terms at all: they saw the unwanted overtures as a power/control issue. Besides looking at the responses in this study as the age-old problem of "talking apples to oranges," a deeper explanation uncovers something much more insidious. By using the language of "sex gone wrong," these harassers are keying-in to an explanatory device that has dominant societal appeal. As Helen Watson summarized:

It is my suggestion that the greater the emphasis on harassment as a consequence of sexual attraction gone wrong, the greater the dominate appeal of an
explanatory model. It is useful to examine representations of harassment in
relation to the pattern of language used and the style of explanation offered,
particularly in relation to that realm of power defined as the capacity to set an
agenda, to say and thereby to establish what is or isn't relevant. A typical
harassment case involves a rival account which consists of mutually incompatible explanations. In such a contested situation, the advantage of credibility for
the individuals concerned as well as a wider "audience" may be gained by a
narrative which explains behavior in terms of familiar or dominant norms and
values.[8]

In other words, the men in this study see sexual harassment as an inevitable by-product of pursuing a relationship and having it fall short because of variables such as bad timing or lack of interest. When equat-ing sexual harassment with the courting ritual, any offense this ritual causes is construed simply as miscommunication. In addition, it obscures the fact that charges of sexual harassment may still be valid even if there has been a prior relationship that has subsequently "gone wrong." This scenario puts an amoral spin on an act that victims clearly see as destructive and criminal. We used to use similar excuses in cases of rape at a time when there was a resistance to viewing it as an issue of power or control; rather, rape was interpreted and seen as a sexual issue. This often led to seeing the victim as provoking the rape, or "asking for it," by dressing or acting in a certain way. It also prevented women from bringing charges against their husbands or lovers, as sexual contact was seen as a male prerogative in such relations. Watson's study brings us full circle to our beginning discussion regarding the distinction between personal and professional relationships. The narratives of the accused harassers in her study are denying the professional and excusing harass-ing behavior in terms of the personal. By use of terms and language typically known as the natural "sexual dance" between men and women, the harassed are left feeling that they were somehow responsible for the harasser's behavior. They gave the wrong clues or brought on harass-ment by being too nice, too friendly, or by not recognizing the pursuer's intention. Yet, even if this were the case and the harasser felt provoked or seduced, it would not entirely absolve him of the responsibility to behave professionally in the workplace. This difference in perspective is an obvious area in which we need to do further, much more extensive research.

WHAT IS SEXUAL HARASSMENT?

The U.S. government's definition is the widely accepted legal definition. The Equal Employment Opportunity Commission guidelines which are part of Title VII of the Amended Civil Rights Act of 1964, define sexual harassment as follows:

Unwelcome sexual advances, requests for sexual favors, and other verbal or physical conduct of a sexual nature constitute sexual harassment when (1) submission to such conduct is made either explicitly or implicitly a term or condition of an individual's employment; (2) submission to or rejection of such conduct by an individual is used as the basis for employment decisions affecting such individual; or (3) such conduct has the purpose or effect of interfering with an individual's work performance or creating an intimidating, hostile, or offensive working environment.

Sexual harassment is generally divided into three distinct but interwoven categories: coercive, non-coercive, and gender harassment. We will consider these in order.

COERCIVE SEXUAL HARASSMENT

Cases of coercive sexual harassment are the easiest to determine, as both men and women seem to agree that sexual favors should not be made a condition of employment, advancement, or maintaining a professional position. In other words, we find less disagreement when the circumstances include an explicit proposition.

Coercive sexual harassment is sexual misconduct that offers a benefit (*quid pro quo*) or threatens some harm to the person to whom it is directed. An example of *quid pro quo*, which basically means "some-thing for something," would be a situation in which a supervisor offers an employee a promotion for sexual favors. An example of sexual misconduct threatening harm would be that of an instructor stating that a student will receive a lesser grade than deserved unless she performs a sexual favor. John Hughes and Larry May provide two tests to facilitate a determination of coercion: Would the woman have freely chosen to change her situation after the broaching of the offer or threat; and, would the woman be made "worse off" than she otherwise would be by not complying with the offer? If a woman answers no and yes respectively, then the harasser's offer would be deemed coercive. Moreover, they argue, convincingly, that sexual harassment is inherently coercive, regardless of whether it takes the form of a threat for noncompliance or of a reward for compliance.[9]

NON-COERCIVE SEXUAL HARASSMENT

Non-coercive sexual harassment, although it can be just as damaging as coercive harassment, has a different look. This kind of harassment is meant more to demean and annoy, than to get the harassed to perform sexual favors in order to keep her job or obtain promotion. Non-coercive harassers often use verbal intimidation to make the harassed feel upset or angry in the workplace or to undermine her authority. Because non-coercive harassment is generally considered a lesser offense than coercive harassment, it is not taken seriously. Another criticism of non-coercive sexual harassment is that it does not take the intention of the harasser into account: For example, some people had this problem with the Anita Hill/Clarence Thomas issue. If we believe what Hill said, then she was not harassed in the eyes of those who consider coercive harassment to be the only legitimate category (see appendix A). Hill testified that she was never told that she had to perform sexual favors in order to keep her job or obtain promotions.[10] In fact, when Clarence Thomas changed jobs, she moved with him to his new position as head of the Equal Employment Opportunity Commission, and he wrote her favorable recommendation letters, when she did leave. However, Hill could claim a hostile work environment in which she felt demeaned by unsolicited comments and stories. The fact that she depended on Thomas for professional support put her in a position in which she was forced to compromise her dignity and level of comfort.

Camille Paglia has been quite verbal regarding this issue. Paglia is appalled at the notion that Thomas was asked to recall conversations that took place ten years prior.[11] She feels, and she is not alone, that non-coercive harassment can be handled by a strong woman who lets it be known that she will not take this kind of treatment: an in-your-face response. Anita Hill's testimony that she filed no formal complaint, or only informed close associates of the offensive behavior, clearly hurt her case. In addition, being a minority woman with an Ivy League law degree made it ludicrous for some to believe that she actually felt she could not get employment outside of the EEOC. But, the question still remains, What if the harassment continues despite protest and thus causes a hostile work environment? Furthermore, what if the supervisor to whom one is required to report incidents of sexual harassment is the harasser—or worse, heads the federal office whose job it is to deal with such cases? What we have here is a fine line that is getting finer between coercive and non-coercive harassment with the landmark case being *Meritor Bank v. Vinson*. Here the U.S. Supreme Court states that a hostile work environment can constitute sexual harassment. This decision casts a wider net than previously thought and, insofar as it encompasses all three forms, it would put Anita Hill's testimony within the definition of harassment. So let us take a brief, but closer, look at the Meritor case and its implications.

<u>Meritor Savings Bank, FSB v. Vinson, et al.</u>[12]

Starting in 1974, Ms. Vinson (Respondent) worked at the same branch office of Meritor Savings Bank for four years. During her tenure, she was consistently promoted from teller to branch manager. Testimony validated that these promotions were motivated by merit. Ms. Vinson asked her supervisor, Sidney Taylor, for sick leave for an indefinite period. She was dismissed from her job at the bank on November 1, 1978 for excessive use of sick leave.

After being discharged Ms. Vinson filed an action against her supervisor, Mr. Taylor, and the bank, and asked that her attorney's fees be paid. She claimed that during her four years at the bank she had been continually sexually harassed by Mr. Taylor in violation of Title VII, justifying injunctive relief and compensation.

At the trial each side presented conflicting accounts regarding Mr. Taylor's behavior towards Ms. Vinson. Respondent painted a picture of a relationship that began as "fatherly" concern for a beginning worker to full-blown sexual harassment. Concern turned to requests for socializing outside of work. Ms. Vinson described a dinner engagement where during the course of the meal she was clearly propositioned. These first requests for sexual favors were refused, but eventually the respondent complied because she feared losing her job. These sexual requests were made both on the job and outside the workplace— she estimated that she had sexual relations with Mr. Taylor 40–50 times. Mr. Taylor followed her around at work, fondled her in front of other employees, exposed himself to her and forcibly raped her several times.

In addition, respondent offered to produce other employees that could testify to being fondled and harassed by Mr. Taylor, setting a history of a pattern of harassment. While some supporting testimony was admitted without objection, the District Court did not allow her "to present wholesale evidence of a pattern and practice relating to sexual advances to other female employees in her case-in-chief but advised her that she might well be able to present such evidence in rebuttal to the defendant's case—which did not take place.

Out of a fear of Taylor, Ms. Vinson stated that she never reported the incidences of sexual harassment to his supervisors, nor did she use the bank's complaint procedure.

Mr. Taylor denied all charges of sexual harassment and stated that respondent was making the charges as a response to a work-related dispute. The bank's attorney argued that Meritor Bank could not be held responsible for employee behavior that they did not know existed. Bank officials had no idea that Mr. Taylor was accused of impropriety, and no official complaint had been filed.

The District Court denied relief to Ms. Vinson and stated that she "was not the victim of sexual harassment and was not the victim of sexual discrimination" while employed by the Meritor Bank. Furthermore, the court found that the bank was not liable because it was not aware that there was a problem and, thus, had no opportunity to respond.

The Court of Appeals for the District of Columbia Circuit reversed the District Court's decision: the Appeals Court stated that a violation of Title VII may be predicated on either of two types of sexual harassment: harassment that involves the conditioning of concrete employment benefits on sexual favors, and harassment that, while not affecting economic benefits, creates a hostile or offensive working environment. The Court clearly decided that a violation had occurred and Vinson's grievance was of the hostile environment type. As to the bank's liability, the Court of Appeals held that an employer is absolutely liable for sexual harassment practiced by supervisory personnel, whether or not the employer knew or should have known about the misconduct. The court relied chiefly on Title VII's definition of "employer" to include "any agent of such a person," 42 U.S.C. 2000e(b), as well as on the EEOC Guidelines. The court held that a supervisor is an "agent" of his employer for Title VII purposes, even if he lacks the authority to hire and fire.

The Supreme Court upheld the decision of the Court of Appeals for the District of Columbia and the claim of "hostile work environment" as actionable under Title VII. The District Court's findings were insufficient to dismiss the respondent's hostile environment claim. As to employer liability, the Supreme Court concluded the Court of Appeals was wrong to entirely disregard agency principles and impose absolute liability on employers for the acts of their supervisors, regardless of the circumstances of a particular case. In conclusion, the Supreme Court states in Meritor Bank v. Vinson that a hostile work environment does constitute sexual harassment and Ms. Vinson was a victim of sexual harassment.

There are implications to this case that close the gap on distinguishing categories of sexual harassment, for both coercive and non-coercive harassment can result in a hostile environment. Even gender harassment, if taken to an unreasonable extreme can create an environment that causes mental anguish. To those who feel that only coercive harassment should be taken seriously, the Meritor Bank v. Vinson case "let the genie out of the bottle," so to speak. Opponents argue—some convincingly—that by considering all three categories of sexual harassment with the same weight, you "water down" the more serious cases of coercion and throw them into the same category as, for example, an insensitive joke. Others feel strongly that non-coercive harassment can be very damaging depending on the circumstances and we cannot dismiss it as unworthy of serious action.

A growing criticism of non-coercive sexual harassment is that it does not take into account the *intention* of the harasser. Possibly the harasser was only trying to be friendly and his intentions were misconstrued? While this may be true in a few cases, in most instances the fact that the harasser does not know appropriate from inappropriate behavior can be excused by the same kind of language that Watson cites in her research. A sort of "friendliness gone wrong," which was misinterpreted by the woman as harm when the man's intention was just the opposite. Still, we might then ask, to what extent are we justified in holding someone responsible despite such ignorance? That is, can we legitimately say that he "should have known better"? If the consequence of an action causes emotional stress and a hostile work environment, then the "intent" pales in its significance. Ethical theory might help us here if we look to Aristotle's *Nicomachean Ethics* and what it says about this issue of intentionality, as it is so often tied to the question of culpability. That is, to what degree or under what circumstances can one legitimately evade blame by claiming that his actions were not intended to cause offense?

ARISTOTLE ON INTENTION

We need to look more closely at the question of intentionality, because it is so often tied to that of accountability. Again, as the question above asks, is it ever justifiable for one to claim that an action was not intended to be offensive and that, therefore, he should not be held responsible? This is a claim that is heard quite often in cases of sexual harassment; namely, that the offender did not *mean* to cause any harm and was unaware that his actions would be perceived as hostile, aggressive or inappropriate. Aristotle makes some illuminating distinctions in book 3, chapter 1.[13]

To claim that one had no intention of offending another person, when in fact offense was taken, is tantamount to claiming that the act was committed in ignorance, that is, that one was unaware of some relevant factor or set of factors and thus could not have known in advance that his behavior would be found offensive. For Aristotle, another way of describing the act would be to say that the sexual harassment was "involuntary." If this type of justification is to be accepted and the behavior excused, several conditions must be fulfilled. First, actions can be regarded as genuinely involuntary when, and only when, "they bring sorrow and regret in their train: a man who has acted due to ignorance and feels no compunction whatsoever for what he has done was not a voluntary agent, since he did not know what he was doing, nor yet was he involuntary inasmuch as he feels no sorrow."[14]

Thus, for Aristotle, there are two kinds of acts "due to ignorance"—the involuntary and the nonvoluntary. In both cases, the person lacks some relevant circumstantial knowledge (see below) that would enable him to be conscious of what he is doing, the consequences that might follow, and so forth. However, once the agent does become aware that his act was offensive, or at least questionable, then some form of regret would be expected if, indeed, no harm was intended. To fail to express this, or apologize in some manner, would mean that the act was merely nonvoluntary, and this should not entirely divest someone of responsibility or place him beyond reproach. For it would appear then that the offender has no desire to become informed or sensitized to the situation in order to alter his behavior, and we might then have cause for concern that similar acts would occur in the future. At best, claims of involuntary or nonvoluntary acts could be made only once. For once the relevant information is received or knowledge obtained, one can no longer rationalize one's actions by pleading ignorance. In effect, Aristotle seems to be validating many commonly held intuitions about what is entailed in acting responsibly. Namely, that individuals do err and behave badly when they are uninformed or misinformed, and that this should be taken into consideration when we attribute blame. However, even when one unintentionally causes harm to another, we do expect him to express regret and amend his ways. Still, what kinds of factors or bits of information are relevant to legitimate claims of ignorance?

First, Aristotle claims, one can only be excused for being ignorant of certain "particulars." For example, Aristotle would find it nonsensical for someone to maintain that he was ignorant of the *general* truth that sexual harassment itself is wrong. In other words, there are certain "universals," or basic moral principles, of which no one may be blamelessly ignorant. Aristotle can say, that is, that there are situations where one *should know better*, since he takes it as given that all adult human beings have some knowledge of the good (and, thus, conversely of evil.)

Ignorance in moral choice does not make an act involuntary—it makes it wicked; nor does ignorance of the universal, for that invites reproach; rather, it is ignorance of the particulars which constitute the circumstances and the issues involved in the action. It is on these that pity and pardon depend, for a person who acts in ignorance of a particular circumstance acts involuntarily.[15]

Aristotle expects individuals to take some responsibility for making informed choices, and he believes that there are certain basic ethical presuppositions ("universals") that may be found in the traditionally accepted beliefs of the community. Thus, it is only particulars of which one may be excusably ignorant. He also takes it as given that there are "some actions whose very names connote baseness"—e.g., "adultery, theft, and murder."[16]   It is therefore the application of basic ethical precepts, applying universals to particular situations, that Aristotle is addressing. What this requires is *phronesis* (the practical moral faculty discussed in chapter one of this book), but his kind of practical wisdom cannot be taught or measured: it requires time and experience to cultivate, can only be operative in concrete contexts, and cannot be reduced to any one simple formula. What may be of assistance, though, in explicating and developing this practical faculty of judgment are actual examples. What follows, then, are some of the particulars that Aristotle enumerates, which may serve to determine what kinds of ignorance would constitute an involuntary or nonvoluntary action, and how they might be applicable in cases of sexual harassment.

1. If someone is ignorant of *who the agent is*, his action would be involuntary. However, cases like these are very rare, as it means being ignorant of one's own identity, which could be true only for those who are mentally ill or delusional.

2. If one is ignorant of *who or what is affected* by the act, it would not be voluntary. For example, if a man places sexually explicit literature or photographs in plain view in his workplace and does not realize that the women who come into this space are made uncomfortable by its presence, we could say he acted in ignorance of who might be affected by his act. And, in such a case, the best remedy would be a direct approach: he should simply be informed by the offended party or parties that they find it so. And, ultimately, reasonable and sensitive individuals should be able to work out what is best to insure a comfortable working environment for all concerned.

3. If someone is not aware of *what* he is doing, he would be acting in ignorance. Aristotle himself uses the example of a slip-of-the-tongue—as when one "divulges a secret" without knowing it was a secret. This seems to be a relatively common occurrence in communication between the sexes where something is unthinkingly blurted out that a woman finds personally offensive.

4. If one *intends a different result* than the one which actually follows, the act would not be voluntary. This can occur when one is genuinely ignorant of the consequences that might, or are even likely to, ensue. For example, in attempting to stroke a female employee's confidence or put her at ease, a male employer may compliment her on her appearance or manner of dress. Yet, many women find this demeaning or see it simply as a way of reminding women of their sexuality. Again, the best way to address this, as with most cases of ignorance, is to be direct and inform the person of the uncomfortable atmosphere his words are causing. These misunderstandings are often due to the way in which men and women interpret linguistic meaning differently, as Deborah Tannen has shown.[17]

5. Lastly, one may be excused for his ignorance of the *manner* of the action. That is, Aristotle says that one may act either "gently or violently." In other

words, how something is said or done can be as important as what is said or done. And again, very often people differ as to what constitutes an aggressive or seductive manner, so opening the lines of communication is key here as it is in so many areas of life.

If these concrete examples still seem somewhat vague, it is because no account can ever be exhaustive, and judgments can only be effectively made in concrete contexts. The particular personalities and specific circumstances involved in human relations are always unique and complex. What is offensive to some may not be to others. For instance, the words used by one person in one particular situation and deemed hostile may not be found so if uttered by another person in a different context. This should not be taken as hypocritical, a "cop-out," or inconsistent; it's merely an acknowledgment of the complicated realities of members of the opposite sex working together. And, if we add to these differences of sexuality, age, culture, and religious faith, then things can get even more problematic. Moreover, as noted before, practical wisdom is not something that can be statically defined, quantified, or definitively determined. It can only be developed through practice.

What is also important to recognize is what Aristotle explicitly eliminates from the realm of involuntary action, namely, acts that are committed "due to passion or appetite." For Aristotle, it is absurd to claim that passions are less a part of us than is our reasoning capacity. And it is hypocritical to accept credit for our accomplishments or acts of benevolence that also spring partly from our emotional states, while also attempting to avoid blame for wrongs that are committed under similar affective conditions. Aristotle asks us to ask ourselves, "Do we perform none of the actions that are motivated by appetite and passion voluntarily? Or do we perform noble acts voluntarily and base acts involuntarily?" For Aristotle, the latter is clearly not the case, "since the cause in both cases is one and the same."[18] Such a position dispenses with claims like those of Camille Paglia, who asserts that women who dress or act seductively must accept responsibility for any sexual act forced upon them by a man who is simply reacting from desire. If this were the case, then the women whose great beauty inspired acts of heroism or poetic literature should be credited with these good works rather than the men to whom such is usually attributed. Again, "it is absurd to blame *external circumstances* rather than oneself for falling an easy prey to such attractions, and to hold oneself responsible for noble deeds" (emphasis mine).[19]

GENDER HARASSMENT

Gender harassment is about power over others and manifesting this power by discriminating against them on the basis of gender. This can sometimes take the form of sexual harassment. This subordination is critically tied to sexuality as it applies to anatomy or reproductive capacities. Examples of gender harassment run the spectrum from a supervisor passing someone over for advancement because he really believes that women lack the decision making capacities that men possess, to a teacher telling a student that girls are not as good at math as boys. Making comments on the job about a person's anatomy and drawing graffiti that humiliates or embarrasses fall into the category of gender harassment. If we define sexual harassment as not only coercive (*quid pro quo*) but also using the hostile work environment criteria, then gender harassment could be considered sexual harassment in some instances if it is extreme, especially when we recognize that for many women sexual references carry an implicit threat of sexual aggression or even violence. Certainly, there are no hard and fast rules here when it comes to determining what is or is not appropriate professional behavior. Furthermore, differences exist not only in how men and women interpret the same scenario but among women too. Some women, even while acknowledging that they have been "harassed," aren't bothered by it and feel capable of dealing with it on their own. That is, they do not feel victimized or diminished but merely annoyed and may even have a sense of humor about it. On the other hand, we can imagine that a woman who has previously been a victim of rape or violent assault would be much more sensitive to sexual references, gestures, or innuendoes, and could easily feel threatened. The bottom line is that it is imperative to foster greater awareness and sensitivity to these issues in the workplace, encouraging men and women to educate themselves.

Critics of considering non-coercive and gender harassment as sexual harassment believe that gender harassment is something that women need to learn to control. If women are to function well in the workplace, they need to develop a tougher skin and a tougher attitude about dealing with harassment that appears to be in the nuisance category. But it becomes clear that the lines drawn are osmotic, and we really have to look at each case independently in order to draw conclusions as to whether the work environment is, indeed, a hostile one. With so many women entering the work force and taking jobs previously held only by males, this problem is not simply going to fade away.

QUESTIONS FOR REFLECTION

1. What are the distinctions between coercive, non-coercive, and gender harassment? Do you think that these distinctions are helpful in assessing or evaluating acts of sexual harassment and how one should attempt to redress them?

2. To what extent is our view of women, or conception of femininity shaped by the media? Or, to what degree are such the products of mass marketing and business objectives (i.e., based on the goals of sales, profit margins, and the like)?

3. Should businesses be held legally responsible for the actions of their employees if one charges another with sexual harassment?

4. Do victims of sexual harassment bear any responsibility for their victimization (either initially or if the situation is ongoing)? Should women pay particular attention to how they dress or to the "messages" that their appearance may be projecting?

5. Is flirting a form of sexual harassment? Is a flirtatious person "asking" to be harassed?

6. Can men be victims? Can women be perpetrators?

7. Should the intentions of the harasser be a factor in attributing blame or responsibility? Do you think that the distinction between involuntary and non-voluntary actions is valid or helpful here?

8. What, if anything, can be done to curb the amount of sexual harassment grievances?

9. If we take Anita Hill's testimony as truthful, does her account constitute sexual harassment? Why or why not?

10. Read Appendix A, Anita Hill's statement to the Senate Judiciary Committee. Is there anything she could have done differently to protect herself against unwanted advances and the fallout that ensued during and after the confirmation hearings?

11. In what kinds of cases might one be excused for acting in ignorance?

12. Is it always the case that the harasser is in a position of power and that the victim is a subordinate?

13. Can you think of an example of what you might consider sexual harassment that has not been addressed here? Could it be characterized in one of the three ways: coercive, non-coercive, or gender harassment?

EMPOWERMENT: SUGGESTIONS FOR HOW VICTIMS CAN PROTECT OR EMPOWER THEMSELVES

Confrontation

If possible, this direct approach may be the best way to put an immediate end to the harassment. Be diplomatic but resolute when informing the harasser that you have been offended. Be very clear and precise in the discussion and make sure someone is near enough to witness the confrontation.

Documentation

Without editing yourself in any way, write down all relevant or seemingly relevant information pertaining to the harassment. Be sure to include everything regardless of how trivial it may seem, as such can always be evaluated later. This will help to jog your memory and keep facts in order.

Times and dates are important if a grievance needs to be filed.

Confide

Confide in a coworker and/or seek out other victims if possible. There is a greater likelihood that your grievances will be taken seriously if you have the support and corroboration of others who have information or knowledge that is relevant to your situation.

Elicit outside support

Don't allow feelings of shame to force you into silence. By telling those you trust you will not feel alone, nor will you unwittingly protect the harasser. This action complements *Documentation* and *Confide* above, as all are likely to protect you, and perhaps others, from further victimization

NOTES

1. Jean Kilbourne, *Still Killing Us Softly* [videocassette], Cambridge, Mass.: Cambridge Documentary Films, 1987. See also, Kilbourne, *Slim Hopes* [videocassette], Northampton, Mass.: Media Education Foundation, 1995.

2. Ibid.

3. See also Jean Kilbourne, *Still Killing Us Softly* [videocassette], (Cambridge, Mass.: Cambridge Documentary Films), 1987.

4. Ellen Frankel Paul, "Bared Buttocks and Federal Cases," *Society* 4, 1991, Transaction Periodical Consortium.

5. See Deborah Tannen's books, *Talking from 9–5* (New York: William Morrow and Co., 1994) and *You Just Don't Understand* (New York: William Morrow, 1990), for in-depth discussion of gender and language use.

6. Tom L. Beauchamp and Norman E. Bowie, eds., *Ethical Theory and Business* (Englewood Cliffs, N.J.: Prentice Hall, 1993), p. 371.

7. Peggy Crull, "The Impact of Sexual Harassment on the Job: A Profile of the Experiences of 92 Women," *Sexuality in Organizations*, ed. by D.A. Neugarten and J. M. Shafritz (Oak Park, Ill.: Moore Publishing Co., 1980), pp. 67–72.

8. Helen Watson, "Red Herrings and Mystifications: Conflicting Perceptions of Sexual Harassment," *Rethinking Sexual Harassment*, ed. by Clare de Beauvoir and Yen Lee Too (London: Pluto Press, 1994), pp. 66–67.

9. Larry May and John C. Hughes, "Is Sexual Harassment Coercive?,"

Ethical Theory and Business, ed. by Tom Beauchamp and Norman Bowie (Englewood Cliffs, N.J.: Prentice Hall, 1993), p. 415.

10. Senate Hearing 102–1084, part 4. Washington, D.C., Government Printing Office, 1993.

11. Camille Paglia, Interview with Roger Ailes, *Straight Forward*, CNBC, January 1996.

12. Extracted from the Supreme Court of the United States, *Meritor Savings Bank, FSB v Vinson, et. al.*, 477 US 84 (1986).

13. Aristotle, *Nicomachean Ethics*, Book III, Chap. 1 (New York: Macmillan Publishing Co., 1962).

14. Ibid., p. 55.

15. Ibid., p. 55.

16. Ibid., p. 44.

17. Deborah Tannen, *Talking from 9–5*.

18. Aristotle, *Nicomachean Ethics*, p. 57.

19. Ibid., p. 54.

4

COMPARABLE WORTH AND VALUE

Virginia Woolf said it beautifully: "Every woman must have a room of her own." I like to carry this one step further. To my way of thinking, every woman must be financially independent, with a nice bank account of her own. Then she can have as many rooms as she likes.

—Suzanne Brangham

INTRODUCTION

On the surface, the issue of comparable worth, or equal pay for equal work, is simple. (Most of us would agree that fairness dictates equal compensation for equal work.) However, when we peel back the first layer of the onion, we see a much more complex issue. How we as a society value individuals and their particular work skills has much to do with gender roles and how these roles have been established (see chapter 2 on the construction of gender). We will show here how religion, in particular, often dictates moral behavior, especially in relation to gender. Our biases, however subtle they may seem, are informed by a culture that is based on certain religious beliefs and principles. Once we establish how traditional views (historically informed by a Judeo-Christian position) influence our conception of "family" and the accepted roles within this construct, a closer look will help us see how these attitudes affect the workplace. Moreover, as previously discussed, the concept of equality itself, or what constitutes "equal" treatment, is not easily determined.

Comparable worth is a fairly cut-and-dry issue as long as we are speaking about equal pay for identical work. But, how do we begin to find a system to compare dissimilar jobs, and should we even try? Human behavior and motivation cannot be quantified easily for it is both unpredictable and complicated with too many variables. For example, someone may have a great deal of responsibility in his or her job and a high level of education and experience, yet may still be unreliable or lazy. We can hardly begin to figure out a system that would fairly scale such human, subjective qualities: this would be like nailing jelly to a tree. There are strong feelings on both sides of the debate—our view being that any attempt to create a system for making such comparisons is futile and a magnet for economic, social and legal problems. There are many intricacies involved in legislating a comparable worth policy which we will attempt to address in greater depth later.

As with the other chapters in this book, various perspectives can be used to analyze the issues. As authors, we bring our own interests and values based on who we are as women and educators and where we see the need for further research and dialogue. Consequently, the way we approach the issue of comparable worth will center around four themes: women and the family, religious identification of family and gender roles, the workplace, and Marxist views on value. We hope this four-pronged approach will both enrich the debate and encourage others to analyze these areas for themselves within the constantly evolving environment of the business world.

RELIGION AND WORTH

It should be noted from the outset that when religion is referred to in a contemporary sense, we mean the Religious Right movement typified by Christian fundamentalism and its role as a strong political entity in the United States. While some Catholic groups are included, we are mainly targeting the views held by the Christian Coalition, the Moral Majority, and other groups on the Religious Right which have been growing in influence and political clout.

Comparable worth cannot be separated from how a society determines what is valuable, and values cannot be separated from religion, at least not historically speaking. Our moral framework is based primarily on a Judeo-Christian foundation, as it is woven throughout our nation's history. With the growing influence of the Religious Right lobbyists, religion is playing a starring role in contemporary society, especially in the backlash against the feminist agenda for women's emancipation. Many religious conservatives have strong opinions regarding the role of women within the family and society, and these views have become part of the political base of many politicians who seek the support of this vocal, well organized political constituency. We have seen this influence most recently in the renewed debate on abortion.

The idea of religion affecting norms, values and laws is not new. In 1965 the sociologist Emile Durkheim stated that it was religion that formed the intellect. He goes on to say that religion is so woven into our societal fabric that we often are oblivious to the areas influenced by religious thought, especially the Judeo-Christian tradition. In Durkheim's own words:

If philosophy and the sciences were born of religion, it is because religion began by taking the place of the sciences and philosophy. But it has been less frequently noticed that religion has not confined itself to enriching the human intellect, formed beforehand, with a certain amount of ideas; it has contributed to forming the intellect itself. Men owe to it not only a good part of the substance of their knowledge, but also the *form* in which this knowledge has been elaborated [emphasis mine].[1]

The "form" that this knowledge takes is of interest in this discussion, for the form the family takes is most often influenced by a religious perspective. A woman's place in the family and the world at large is and has been defined within a religious context. She is the caretaker, nurturer, and provider of emotional support for her husband and children. Families are only sanctioned if they conform to the narrow ideals of literal Biblical interpretation. It cannot be overemphasized that women's place within this family, although spiritually valued, is not valued materially.

In a capitalistic society, which measures value in terms of monetary income and in which women are paid less than men, women are seen as less worthy than men, not only in the job market, but in other areas of life. Wages are all too frequently used not only as a means of acquiring objects but also as a means of acquiring intangibles such as status or power. Because housework has not traditionally been considered wage labor and has primarily been the women's burden, "women's work" has tended to be devalued or regarded as inessential to a healthy market economy. This devaluation has followed women into the public sphere, resulting in lower wages, particularly for those jobs designated as "helping professions" (for example, nursing) where women outnumber men. Rousseau, the "father" of the French Revolution, in his *Discourse on the Origins of Inequality* notes four kinds of inequality: wealth, social status, political power, and individual merit. All of these are ultimately reducible to wealth, as wealth is the most immediately useful and easiest to measure. As a natural consequence, women's lower wages have significant effects on women and society. Women living in poverty far outnumber men, and families headed by women are four times as likely to be living in poverty. Almost 30 percent of White female-headed households and over 50 percent of Black and Hispanic female-headed households, live in poverty. Almost 67 percent of all children living in a female-headed household are impoverished.[2] The impact of women's wages is far reaching: money translates into power. Those who have it, have influence; those who do not, have little, if any. Women's lack of power and the devaluation of their work extend beyond the political: this is a moral problem as well.

Historically speaking, U.S. society has depended on a strong separation between the public and private domains to maintain itself, and there is no room in the marketplace for nonacquisitive traits. Certain traits that are defined as "feminine" are devalued in the public sector whether they are found in men or women. In general, skills involving cooperation, selflessness, and intuition have no place in business but are invaluable when it comes to raising and nurturing children. Yet, these nonacquisitive traits that tend to be altruistic are important. Affection, love, and human kindness can still be enjoyed in the private environment of home and family. Free-market conservatives are pleased with a competitive public arena, but they do not want to abandon these altruistic qualities completely. In order to have the self-interested and competitive as well the selfless and cooperative represented in society, women *must* be seen as different from men. Embodying the gentler sex, selfless women can remain in the private arena, while acquisitive men can maintain control over the public arena. In most cases, in order for a woman to succeed in the "man's" public domain, she must emulate male behavior and traits (see chapter 6 on leadership). It should also be noted that this was the position taken by Modern feminists, like Wollstonecraft, who sought political equality for women. They believed that women must cultivate their rational capacities, as men presumably had, in order to prove that they, too, could be good citizens. The prevailing belief among conservatives is that these "masculine" traits (such as rationality, autonomy, and competitiveness) are indispensable to the free market system and necessary for maintaining a leading edge. Whether or not this is true is still a subject of contention. All arguments aside, there is no reason why several qualities cannot be valued for what they are and what they achieve. If we agree that there is no job more important than raising the young, then it seems appropriate to start honoring and fostering inclusive qualities for successive generations. So, as many feminists have argued, perhaps we need to broaden our conception of what it means to be human and include these traditionally devalued traits in both the public and private spheres.

The fear among many religious traditionalists is that any change in the separation between the workplace and home could severely destabilize the status quo, and that instituting comparable worth policies will weaken the family structure. Changes in gender roles alter the very definition of family. If women are not in the home, there is a serious gap in the well-oiled system in which the woman is the caretaker and provides support to the breadwinner. The claim is that when changes in the social order occur, the family starts to lose ground, setting the stage for a domino effect of problems. In fact, there is ample evidence of the negative consequences of the dissolution of family all around us. However, the solutions offered by the Religious Right are no solution at all, for they are relying on "ideals" which are inherently unjust and unrealistic today. In the name of religion, these groups also oppose abortion, and rights for homosexuals. Allowing people autonomy on these issues threatens the status quo and their traditional conception of the family and "family values." Both wage gap and abortion, for example, are tied to a static view of the family structure and the woman's place within this structure. These issues are not unrelated and cannot be treated as such, for both concern women's autonomy and status as something other than wives and mothers.

Clearly, religious traditionalists oppose comparable worth policies because they pertain to women outside the home and because they demand equal treatment. These organizations are concerned with keeping women in the home as wives and mothers, so they are opposed to any policy that might in any way encourage women to leave this domestic domain. Their arguments are based on a very literal and narrow interpretation of Scripture. Because the public arena is viewed as a place for men, a patriarchal family, with the male as sole breadwinner, a patriarchal model is considered most suitable for building a public order. Under these circumstances it is no wonder that many women learn to be subservient to men, at least publicly (though they may be granted authority in the home). This version of the Christian home is validated by Bible passages such as Ephesians 5:21–25, which points to the necessity of wives' subordination and dependence. "Wives be subject to your husband," is hardly a call for female emancipation or independence. Biblical validation for the roles of men and women can also be bolstered by the Adam and Eve story in Genesis 3:12. After eating the forbidden fruit, Adam, Eve, and the snake receive three curses from Yahweh: The snake is forever condemned to crawl on his belly; Adam is told that he shall work "in the sweat of his face" and will decompose after death. To Eve Yahweh says: "I will greatly multiply thy sorrow and thy conception and thy desire shall be to thy husband, and he shall rule over thee" (Genesis 3:19). So here we have it. The distinct differences between men and women are God-given. This sanctioned form of "family" roles is scriptural. Work segregation is a consequence of God's response to Adam and Eve's folly. Along with growing concern about America's moral fiber, we see these Biblical justifications used in a modern context in order to preserve the divinely ordained, "natural" hierarchy.

George Gilder gives us an example of job segregation as necessity in his book *Men and Marriage*:

The women's place is in the home, and she does her best when she can get the man there too, inducing him to submit most human activities to the domestic values of civilization. Thus in a sense she also brings the home into the society. Like the legendary Mafiosi, they try to please their women by elaborate submission to domestic values in the household, while scrupulously keeping the women out of the male realm of work.[3]

Gilder's words do not fall far from the tree of forbidden fruit; the translation is literal. This strict separation of power maintains the family order that is validated in selective interpretations of Scripture. Men are kept from their natural tendency to seek out sexual gratification from partners other than their spouses by their family responsibilities to wife and children. Women handle the domestic and child rearing responsibilities in return for financial stability and a monogamous relationship.[4] The claim that women and men are different, and that this division of labor is "natural," strengthens the position against instituting comparable worth policies. For if women are distinct from men, and even biblically directed to perform certain tasks, then it would stand to reason that if they entered the marketplace they would choose jobs that were in harmony with their domestic duties. If jobs dominated by women pay less than jobs dominated by men, this could be explained, as market economy advocates claim, by factors relating to free choice rather than of discrimination. In other words, women are "choosing" to pursue vocations that are lower paying as a trade off for having greater flexibility and access to the job they presumably value most: taking care of the home and children. If the family is the core value that must be maintained—whether because it is biblically required or because it is the necessary cornerstone of society, or both—then women's equality in the workplace would have to be secondary to familial obligations.[5] But, as noted previously, although women may choose some professions over others, they do not *choose* to be paid less. Perhaps they feel that their caretaking skills (if they have been wives or mothers) better equip them to take on particular kinds of responsibilities. For instance, women who have been accustomed to playing the roles of helpmate and nurturer may be inclined to choose a subordinate position, such as secretary or nurse instead of corporate executive or doctor; but this should not diminish the value of their work, nor should it be seen as any less essential to the proper functioning of a corporation or hospital.

If one agrees that religion has played a large part constituting what a family is, and that the roles within it are biblically ordained, then it is not hard to understand why female independence and work outside the home would be viewed as a threat to the social order. However, one might also think that strictly defining family relations in this way is archaic and unrealistic today. Nonetheless, due to the profound influence of religion, it is clear that this traditional family ideal still holds much psychological power in our culture. If we stick to the concrete realities of the present, even a brief polling of the workplace shows that most women work out of economic necessity and the single income family is the exception rather than the rule. Women work to supplement their husbands' income, to make ends meet, or because they are single parents who function without support from a man. The family unit has changed because the forces that once supported it have altered. For example, two-parent families, with the male as sole breadwinner and the female at home represented only 18 percent of all families in 1992 (fig. 4.1). It thus serves no functional purpose to aspire to a structure that does not, and probably cannot, exist. We need to deal with the real life circumstances of most families living in the present and how women's roles are currently changing, despite the strong psychological appeal of an outdated "ideal" model.

WOMEN AND FAMILY TODAY

Despite reports from different politically motivated factions, we have to concede that having a strong parent figure within the home taking time and care to raise the next generation is necessary and vital. What to do about the weakening of this important structure and the aftershocks it produces is constantly under scrutiny from many fields of thought and research. Notwithstanding the different approaches and theories, these distinct political factions often come together when it comes to acknowledging that some form of family unity must be maintained and supported. Even controversial figures such as Louis Farrakhan, leader of the Nation of Islam, has received a favorable response for his insistence that African-American men must support their children, family, and communities because the trend of abandonment weakens the heart and blood of the future.[6]

If women are working outside the home for economic reasons as well as for personal independence and self-esteem, we must envision creative new methods for restructuring the family unit in order to accommodate changing economic needs and social relations. As fig. 4.2 shows graph-ically, this trend of women entering the work force in large numbers has been increasing steadily for the past 120 years. Energy spent on a nostal-

Figure 4.1
Work Patterns of Families, 1940 to 1992

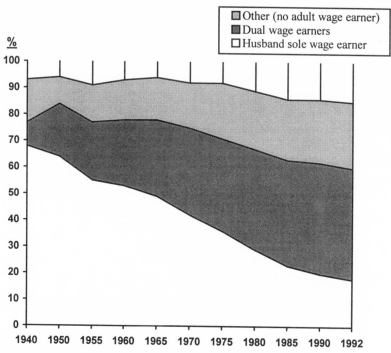

Adapted from: Reskin and Padavic, Women and Men at Work, 1994.

gic yearning for the "ideal" family of yesterday is a depleting effort. Flexible work schedules for men and women who wish to maintain continuity within the family and still take on outside employment is an avenue that needs more attention. Another challenge is to find a way to make the vocation of homemaker one that has value both socially as well as economically. In the face of the high cost of family breakdown, it may be both ethical and economical to find a means of compensating home-makers monetarily thereby affording them some degree of financial security. Not only would women benefit from such an arrangement but so too would their children. What might be considered is a "divorce" between marital dependency and economic security. By enabling home-makers to be financially solvent, we would be immunizing women and children against paternal abandonment, abuse, and poverty. The disso-lution of marriages (almost 50 percent today) leaves many women and children with a severely diminished quality of life. This idea of compensation for homemaking may seem alien at first, but it is worth serious consideration. When compared with the costs of the welfare and prison systems, drug rehabilitation, foster care, and other state and federally funded "systems" that support families in trouble, it would appear to make ethical as well as economic sense. For when value and support is given to the parent in the home, we are helping children and the community at large.

Figure 4.2
Percentage of each Gender in the Labor Force over 122 Years

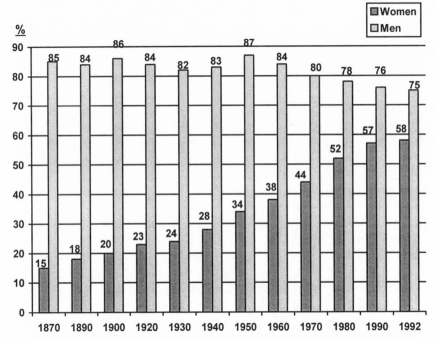

Source: U.S. Bureau of Census 1975: U.S. Bureau of Census 1992d: Table 609; U. S. Women's Bureau 1993: 1.

Despite increasing numbers, women's work outside the home is still seen as secondary or supplemental, even when they inhabit highly skilled, professional, or management positions. Women are often seen as being less committed to their jobs than men. Part-time work is considered especially advantageous for women with family responsibilities, even though part-time employment is generally low salaried and usually offers no health benefits. Researchers who support the free market economy point to the well documented pattern of women fading in and out of the workplace (primarily to attend to family commitments) as one of the hindrances to their entering higher paying vocations. For these are positions that expect and demand a greater amount of uninterrupted job tenure. When women take leave to meet domestic responsibilities, these absences hurt them in terms of their marketability for higher paying positions and advancement. Thus, lower paying jobs for women appear to be the direct result of personal choice, not gender discrimination, in business. However, if women continue to work without stopping for family concerns, they are often branded as uncaring or overly ambitious and risk the consequences of handing their duties over to child care providers, nannies, or other family members. They also have the option of remaining childless, though for many this is yet another situation that may be due more to unavoidable circumstances than to any genuinely "free" choice. Children's advocates and medical professionals have watched this delegation of parenting with a cautious eye, and most experts agree that even the very best of outside care is no substitute for parental love and attention. The dilemma, it appears, is that no one is going to treat a child the way a truly devoted parent would.

Few societal structures are more psychologically loaded than "family," for it is this unit that stands as the foundation for many others. When it is weakened, many experts predict a domino effect: illiteracy, drug abuse, crime, teen pregnancy, and gang identification, for instance. One can hardly watch the evening news or open a newspaper without seeing some indictment of the dwindling family structure's effects on our social ills. Suggestions for remedies run the gamut. On one extreme are liberals looking to spend on social justice programs to help break the cycle of poverty and despair. At the other extreme, some conservatives have come out in favor of bringing back orphanages, for they would surely do a better job of raising children than the presumably inadequate single-parent family. The implication here is that it is better for children to be raised in a public institution than to live in the crime infested inner city with a parent who may have a multitude of problems besides poverty. We do not need to consult statistics to see that the ghetto environment puts children at risk with respect to drugs, gangs, and poor schooling. Simply take a tour of New York City, Los Angeles, South Chicago, or any poverty stricken community to see both the consequences of familial dissolution and the futility of many of our social programs. Or, better still, speak to an inner-city teacher and listen to the frustration that he or she experiences on a daily basis. Although various theories have tried to shed some light on the causes and remedies of family disintegration, there is little argument that would deny its existence. The solution cannot be to reinstate the family of the past— mother at home, father working outside—for today's problems and concerns are not the same. Moreover, there is much historical evidence to suggest that such an ideal structure has only been a concrete reality in a thriving economy or for the privileged few. Regardless, this is not economically feasible today and is fundamentally unfair to women. Many politicians continue to deny this reality or are too out-of-touch with the average citizen to see that there has already been a transformation.

Evidence reveals that the family "ideal" many wish to bring back was actually rare historically, and is, in fact, a piece of mythology. Only in times of peace and economic prosperity have we come close to seeing the so-called perfect family structure. During periods of war or economic instability, the model for family life has had to adapt in order to meet the immediate needs of the time. For example, during World War II, women worked in factories manufacturing the products needed both for domestic survival and maintaining the war effort. Women rose to meet the need by stepping into male-defined jobs which, in times of peace, had been considered beyond their capabilities and physical strength (see chapter 7). All historical debates aside, the conditions that would allow for the average family to live on only one income do not exist in today's economy.

If the women's movement of the 1960s has taught us anything, it is the perils of embracing a domestic role that society does not honor in terms of financial security. This leaves us with the dilemma of women entering the work force in record numbers, while being consistently paid less than their male counterparts. Most women are still concentrated in female dominated vocations that are traditionally underpaid regardless of supply and demand. This history of underpayment is well documented and cannot be totally explained away as a natural function of a "gender-blind" free market system. For, as feminist theorists have pointed out, presumed gender neutrality often translates concretely into gender bias or discrimination. There is much more involved here; what and how much more are the deeper questions.[7] Female dominated positions, such as teaching and nursing, are relatively low paying despite the ongoing demand for both. This consistent underpayment is devastating in the face of economic realities. In March 1988, 59 percent of all women were either the sole support of their families or had spouses who earned $15,000 or less per year.[8]

Furthermore, divorce usually does not leave women in a better or equal financial situation, but it does tend to enhance the position of men. This may be partly the result of percentages: one half of a couple's net assets does not really equal one half for the woman if she is dividing her share among children. For example, one study cites that the standard of living for ex-husbands was found to have risen by 42 percent a year after divorce, while that of ex-wives experienced a decline of 73 percent.[9]

Without education and tenure in the workplace, these caretakers will have to overcome many obstacles if they are left to raise and support children on their own. If they need to work and cannot afford to pay the caretaking costs, they must look to jobs that let them work around the home schedule: fields like nursing, teaching, or other "helping" professions that are female dominated and historically underpaid. However, this assumes a best case scenario—that is, that a woman has the resources necessary to train for these fields. Women who do not face an even dimmer outlook: working in child care centers, taking other's children into their own homes, or performing domestic chores in other's households, for example. Besides paying low wages, these jobs normally do not provide health care for the worker or her children. It is easy to see how working in these areas without adequate pay and benefits can result in one's "slipping" into the welfare system, which at least offers some health care security and allows for time at home with children.

Everyone enters into the discussion of comparable worth at some level. Some economists warn us of its perils and the sheer impossibility of balancing something as elusive as worth on the job. We cannot, they say, compare apples with oranges and any attempt to do so is a waste of time and energy. Moreover, devising a universal rating system for job value by attempting to weigh dissimilar jobs against one another and assigning monetary value to them would lead us into a maze of problems. It could entrap us in a web of government mandated policies and leave open the potential for litigation brought on by disgruntled employees. Furthermore, the cost of implementing equal pay would bankrupt many small businesses or force them to lay off employees in order to absorb the cost. Policies like this, we are warned, could wind up hurting the very people that they were designed to protect. If businesses downsize to make up for the cost of comparable worth, women especially could be worse off than they are now: for it is likely that they would be among the first to be let go, as their value in the work place is in doubt to begin with. Critics of federally mandated and funded social programs caution us about instituting more programs monitored by the government without carefully weighing the long-term ramifications. Did anyone really predict the kinds of problems the welfare system has seen, for instance? Surely giving assistance to the needy was never meant to become a way of life, leaving people dependent and despairing. Legislating comparable worth shows similar signs of being equally problematic.

Philosophers urge a definition of terms before a genuine dialogue can ensue. Specifically, what do we mean by the terms "value" and "worth" within the context of this issue? Although these are commonly used terms, how one understands them at the conceptual level may be a matter of interpretation. For example, if we as a society agree that we value the committed inner-city teacher more than a defense attorney or investment banker, for example, does it follow that the teacher should be the higher paid individual? In a capitalistic society it may be that job "value" does not carry a moral component at all; or, that how much someone is paid is in no way indicative of how much they are worth and vice-versa. Some economists say that it is supply and demand that drives value, but this does not explain why some professions are underpaid despite a high demand. In the United States, how we define worth is a confusing issue because there is often no relationship between respect and monetary compensation, reflecting an unfortunate contradiction. A century ago, Karl Marx claimed that in a capitalist economy "price" replaces "value," which would suggest that we no longer have any sense of what this truly is or any concrete way of determining the meaning of the term. In other words, the skewed view of value and worth is foundational, or endemic to an economic system that is amoral. The question may arise as to why we seldom see capitalism criticized in business ethics textbooks. The answer is that most business texts begin with the assumption that a capitalist economy is the best or only viable system available. This is analogous to the doctor whose sole focus is treating the patient's symptoms while ignoring the root causes of the disease. We have to be willing to critique the foundations behind social and economic issues for the sake of intellectual honesty, if nothing else. Thus, a brief look at Karl Marx's conception of value should be beneficial here, for the devaluation of labor is at the heart of the discussion of comparable worth.

KARL MARX ON VALUE

As discussed above, value is hard to define. Besides being an abstract philosophical concept that can have various meanings in different contexts, there is something particular about our capitalist economy that may render it even more complex. Karl Marx was one of the first to see inherent problems and contradictions in capitalism.

Both Marx, who is known as the father of socialism, and John Locke, who is considered the father of liberal democracy, argue for a labor theory of value. That is, they maintain that there is no inherent worth to anything except insofar as it is made useful through the work or labor of human beings. For instance, land can be of value only to the extent that someone cultivates it, plants crops on it and harvest its fruits, or improves it in some manner. Nature provides the raw material that human beings, through their activities, can transform into something of value. In addition, if one has added her sweat and toil to this land, she can rightfully claim ownership to it as well as entitlement to the products of her labor that grow out of this relation between herself and the soil. Human activity—sweat and work—is therefore the fundamental or "natural" source of value and wealth according to this view. But something happens to this picture in a capitalist economy: there is a shift in the relationship between the worker and the product of her work. In his early writings, Karl Marx analyzes the specific activity of wage labor and its relation to capital. What follows is an attempt to distill some of the most important claims of Marx's critique and to show how questions of value and comparable worth become increasingly complex because of the nature of capitalism.

In brief, labor is the source of all wealth according to Marx; but in a capitalist society where one works for a wage, the worker receives only a small portion of that wealth, with the bulk of it going to the capitalist. Capital is defined by Marx as *"stored-up labor"* and is manifested as "the *power of command* over labor and its products."[10] Simply put, the capitalist is the exclusive owner of capital (wealth and profit), which means that the natural relation between the worker and the product of her labor is severed because she no longer owns or is entitled to what she has produced. The worker is being paid for her time and for what she manufactures, which is appropriated by the capitalist. Both the worker and the capitalist need each other; however, this is not a dependent relation determined by mutual interest. Rather, the relation between worker and capitalist inevitably leads to a conflict in which the capitalist, as owner, has all the advantages. Wages are determined by this struggle insofar as it is in the interest of the capitalist to keep wages to a minimum, thereby allowing for a greater return on the capital that is invested. The worker, on the other hand, is relatively powerless as all she effectively "owns" is her labor power, which can be bought and sold according to the laws of supply and demand. Marx claims that "the existence of the worker is reduced to the same conditions as the existence of any other commodity. The worker has become a commodity and he is fortunate to find a buyer. And the demand, upon which the worker's life depends, is determined by the caprice of the wealthy and the capitalists."[11]

What has occurred in such a system is that all human activities and relations have been conceived solely in terms of money relations and competition. What this implies is that value, which is fundamentally or "naturally" construed in terms of use or exchange and is determined by the laborer herself in relation to that labor, is now replaced by "price." Price is defined as a single equation in which all commodities are compared with one specific commodity (in our case this is money).[12] Certainly it would seem that a system like this makes life easier: when everything can be reduced to a single, quantifiable feature, some of the complexities and difficulties of human existence and relationships can be circumvented. But, then, how is this existence itself conceived? How are human relationships to be understood in such a context? Do we really want to put a price on everything, including human beings themselves? Is it no wonder that workers often feel degraded, alienated, and hate their lives and jobs, as well as their employers, when they are reduced to the status of mere wage earners and placed in this kind of competitive struggle. In a system in which there is an interdependency of worker and capitalist coupled with an unequal distribution of power, conflicts are inevitable. Loss to one necessarily means gain to the other: low wages for the worker allows for a greater accumulation of capital for the owner and vice versa. The interests of the two are working at cross purposes with apparently no room for a sense of commonality or shared objectives.

In an even more absurd twist, consider what happens when the worker is also the owner of capital, which is currently the case for some businesses. Under certain circumstances, corporations have encouraged their employees to become stockholders, which allows them to share in the profits and accumulation of wealth. But this means that the workers will find themselves in a lose-lose situation. For example, if an employee seeks fair compensation for herself in the form of higher wages, the over-all profit to her company will be reduced and her stocks will decrease in value, which means she too will be "worth" less. On the other hand, if she settles for barely adequate compensation, the company will be strengthened by the increase in capital, the value of her stocks will reflect this, and her financial net worth will be greater. How can one maintain any integrity in a system so weighted against workers?

When all questions of worth and value are measured in quantitative terms, matters become more, not less, vague and befuddling, even to the extent of throwing us back to the most basic question of human existence and relations. Treating individuals as commodities certainly goes against the moral grain, but this distaste has often failed to lead to the logical next step: questioning the ethics of our free market system. We need to begin by pondering whether there is something unique and irreducible about human existence that should be preserved over and against claims of financial gain or corporate interest. Furthermore, is competition always to be seen as a good thing? Once again, it appears that whenever we attempt to consider the practical issues of doing business, we are led back to some of the most fundamental and universal questions of ethics and philosophy. This is where we get into the real areas of critical thought and meaningful discussion. What we define as good and valuable, and what kind of creatures human beings are, stand at the heart of the matter. We get to this all important core by critically assessing the foundation behind the theory. We have done so here using Marx's thought, but one could certainly take other avenues or consider other thinkers to achieve this end. No scholar speaks more clearly and disparagingly of capitalism than Karl Marx; and one need not be a socialist to appreciate his critique. In his examination of capitalism, he has given us a better understanding of what is involved and what is at stake when we address issues like comparable worth. Let us now turn to the reality of today's workplace and women's place in it.

THE CONTEMPORARY WORKPLACE

The question of comparable worth becomes relevant because most jobs in America are segregated by sex. As fig. 4.3 illustrates, 1995 statistics show that 70 percent of women working full-time were in occupations with over 60 percent female employees. Women working part-time were even more likely to be in female-dominated occupations, such as sales or clerical work. According to the U.S. Department of Labor, of the 57 million women in the work force, 72 percent work full time, while 28 percent do so on a part-time basis. Many part-time workers are multiple job holders. In 1993, 3.3 million women held more than one job (see appendix B). Conflicting data makes this issue even harder to discern, for no clear vision emerges except the knowledge that something needs to change. Precisely what should be done, when, and how, will be the challenge of the next few years. Political commentators, such as Tony Brown of *Tony Brown's Journal*, an issue-based public interest program broadcast on PBS, contend that changes for working women will inevitably occur by virtue of their record numbers in the job market—the theory being that the global economy cannot afford to exclude any human resource in the face of growing competition. Because women and minorities will continue to make up an increasing percentage of the work force, businesses will have nothing to gain by discriminating and everything to lose. Eventually, what is good for women and minorities will be good for business and vice-versa. According to Brown, there will be no such thing as a "glass ceiling" in the future, for it will be women who own the glass.[13]   Others knowledgeable about comparable worth feel that such programs must be legislated into action—the theory being that the marketplace will not allow for fair compensation unless they are mandated by law to do so. Closing the gender gap in wages by legislation is extremely problematic, for there is no agreement as to what factors contribute most to the significant differences in pay between women and men.   Several explanations for this salary gap show up in various literature. Here are a few:

- Women do not possess the education, skill levels, and experience needed to put them at the same salary level as men. Even if they are holding similar positions, women still lag behind in vocational training and job tenure that accounts for wage differentials.
- Women choose jobs that are lower salaried as a trade-off for the other positives these jobs offer: working at home, flexible schedules, and part-time work that can be balanced with domestic duties.

Figure 4.3
Percentage of Women Workers in Different Areas of the Work Force

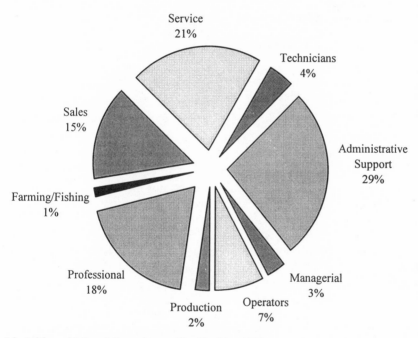

Adapted from: National Committee on Pay Equities, 1996.

- The commitment to the job is different for women. They are more likely to take breaks in their careers in order to tend to family concerns. These interruptions hurt them in terms of job advancement, although interruptions of six months or more do not appear to explain the wage gap (see fig. 4.4).
- Advocates for the free market system believe strongly that the system functions in a blind, neutral fashion and is not discriminatory. If there is a wage discrepancy between men and women, it is because women have gravitated to jobs that do not take advantage of the principle of supply and demand—for it is this that regulates wages. Clerical jobs, for instance, do

not pay a particularly high wage because there are ample people in the
system to do such work—this kind of work is not at a premium.

• Women are discriminated against in the workplace and are paid less for the
same work as men because our culture is fundamentally sexist. Female-
dominated fields, like nursing and primary teaching, have always been
under-paid despite supply and demand factors. Salaries only tend to go up
when men enter the field.

Figure 4.4
Effect of Work Interruptions of Full Time Workers, Ages 21-64

	All Workers	Workers No Interruption
All Occupations	69.5¢*	70.5¢*
Managerial or Professional	67.4¢	67.9¢
Technical, Sales and		
Administrative Support	66.4¢	67.2¢
Service Occupations	69.3¢	70.4¢
Precision Production, Craft or Repair	69.4¢	69.3¢
Operators, Laborers	70.0¢	70.0¢

* Average Women's Wage Compared to $1.00 for Men
Adapted from: Current Population Reports, Series P-70, No. 10.

Competing explanations aside, a few general comments can be made
to draw this information into perspective. The wage gap is closing, but
women are still lagging behind men in salaries. As fig. 4.5 indicates,
between 1960 and 1995, the annual female-male earning ratio increased
from 60.8 to 72.0—things are getting better, but there is still a 30 percent
gap. Again, the more that vocations are female-dominated, the lower the
pay, yet women still tend to gravitate to these fields. This tendency has
to be a factor, though to what degree remains a matter of debate. Free
market advocates are not entirely correct when they say that the system
is neutral and nondiscriminatory, for years of research indicate otherwise. However, the extent of the market's responsibility is a constant
point of disagreement among different factions. *Laissez-faire* advocates
put out caution flags when discussing any policy, such as comparable
worth, that would manipulate a self-regulating system. Tampering with
the "natural" wage-setting mechanism of supply and demand would
threaten the entire economic structure, they argue. If a person is in emi-
nent demand because of a special expertise, he or she will command a
high wage: for example, a heart transplant surgeon will be in greater
demand and, consequently, make more money at a time when there are
numerous patients waiting for such transplants. On a blue-collar level, if
there are few plumbers in an area where plumbing services are at a
premium, plumbers are naturally going to receive a good wage.

There are, however, some obvious glitches in this "hands-off" theory,
the most obvious being truth and fairness. In fact, government has

stepped in at certain points in history to establish limits on the free market system's autonomy, one example being Child Labor Laws and Title VII of the Civil Rights Act of 1964.[14] Most people consider this intervention a good thing and necessary for human justice, as it protects children against exploitation and makes blatant job discrimination illegal. A less popular form of market manipulation is practiced by the federal government when it acts to bail out corporations that are on the brink of bankruptcy, as happened in recent years with Chrysler and Amtrak (a practice commonly referred to as "welfare for the rich"). By acting in this

Figure 4.5
The Wage Gap since 1960: Women Still Earn 29% Less than Men

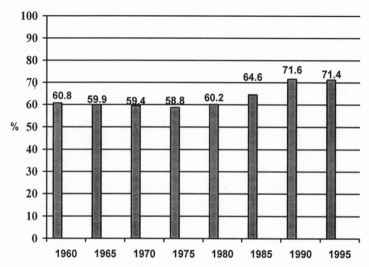

Adapted from: The National Committee on Pay Equity.

manner, the state has sought to shield the market and economy from the fall-out that would result if these corporations should fail, including the large numbers of layoffs that would inevitably follow. These cases alone should be enough to justify abandoning the language of "free" and "neutral" markets "untainted" by intervention.

BEYOND CATEGORIES

The last problem that will be addressed in this chapter pertains to methodology. Must we find a comprehensive method or put a system in place that would allow determinations to be made concerning a particular job's value in comparison to others? From there, ideally, fair wages could be calculated in accordance with this rating system. It should be obvious by now why this would be difficult to do. For example, even if we agree that qualities like loyalty and commitment are important in the workplace, will we ever discover a means of quantifying such qualities? Some workers perform adequately but at a merely average or satisfactory level, while others maximize their potential every day. Many of these variables seem far too subjective to be measured with any degree of accuracy. Moreover, many jobs have no points of comparison at all—how might one even begin to weigh the work of a clerical worker against that of a landscaper, for instance? These two occupations involve an entirely different work environment, distinct skills, and completely dissimilar objectives. Whether this is considered a plus or a minus on a rating system would be a matter of interpretation. Some workers may prefer to work outside all day as opposed to being in an office, while other people may consider working out in the elements a hardship that merits extra compensation. Further adding to the complexity, geographic location would play into this variable, as working outside in Maine or Vermont could be a hardship, while working outside in Southern California or Florida might be seen as a pleasure. Nevertheless, proponents of comparable worth policy are quick to point out—and rightfully so—that in many cases there are variables that can easily be compared, such as the years of education and training that a specific job requires or the number of employees a person supervises in his or her position. Helen Remick and Ronnie Steinberg are two researchers who feel that comparing dissimilar jobs may not be all that difficult. Even if we are talking "apples to oranges," these two fruits do have certain similarities: calorie content, vitamin and mineral composition, and freshness. Besides, Remick and Steinberg go on to say that some large corporations already use some type of evaluation system to classify disparate tasks or positions, especially at the management level.[15] The fact that some businesses have rating systems for management positions can shed light on comparable worth research in general, but it cannot tell us specifically how this might work for all sorts of jobs in all kinds of work.

As stated above, finding a comprehensive comparable worth policy is too riddled with problems to be federally legislated at this time. Employer advocacy groups have presented estimates that range from $2 billion to $150 billion as the cost of adjusting female wages to the standard of men's. Although expenditures could be temporarily defrayed or implemented in stages, the financial burden could ultimately prove catastrophic, especially for small businesses. Besides this cost and the problem of finding a way of measuring dissimilar jobs, what about the disgruntled employee who is not happy with how his or her job was measured? In a country where filing grievances, which turn into lawsuits, is common, are we not setting the stage for litigation "grid-lock"?

We hope that Tony Brown is right and, that with the increasing numbers of women entering the workplace, wages will gradually become equitable since this will simply prove to be "good business." Just as many corporations have continued to implement affirmative action policies (even though it has become a hotly contentious issue in both the legislature and many social circles) because maintaining diversity in today's global market is in their interest, so too can the same argument be made for comparable worth: It may be seen as good for business that women workers feel they are being fairly compensated. Women, sheerly by virtue of their growing numbers in the workplace, will surely gain more voice and power though it likely to be a slow process—perhaps too slow for many.

QUESTIONS FOR REFLECTION

1. How is value defined within a capitalistic economy?
2. Is there a clear-cut means to compare dissimilar jobs?
3. How does our Judeo-Christian tradition determine women's roles in or out of the family structure?
4. What is the relationship between power and money in our country?
5. Should a distinction be made between the public and private realms? How do these spheres influence and limit one another?
6. Do you agree with Marx that a capitalistic economy, by definition, is amoral and inhumane?
7. Should women be paid for domestic work in their own homes? How would this alter our understanding of work itself?
8. Why do you think women continue to concentrate in fields that are low paying and already female-dominated?

NOTES

1. Emile Durkheim, *The Elementary Forms of the Religious Life* (New York: The Free Press, 1965), p. 21.

2. Fredelle Zaiman Spiegel, *Women's Wages, Women's Worth* (New York: Continuum Publishing Co., 1994), p. 53.

3. George Gilder, *Men and Marriage* (Gretna, La.: Pelican Publishing Co., Inc., 1986), p. 176.

4. Ibid., pp. 5–6.

5. Spiegel., p. 14.

6. The "Million Man March" organized by Louis Farrakhan and the Nation of Islam had as its focus African-American men taking responsibility for the care and nurturing of their children in order to stop the ongoing downward spiral of neglect and absenteeism. Many American religious leaders felt this message was

a necessary and positive one, despite their personal concerns regarding the content of some of Farrakhan's teaching.

7. See Elaine Johansen, *Comparable Worth* (Boulder, Colo.: Westview Press, 19-84), pp. 11–13 for a more detailed discussion of studies on the persistence of pay differentials.

8. National Committee on Pay Equity, "The Wage Gap: Myths and Facts," Washington, D.C.

9. Alison M. Jagger, "Feminist Ethics: Some Issues for the Nineties," *Contemporary Moral Problems*, ed. by James E. White (Minneapolis/St. Paul, Minnesota: West Publishing, 1985), p. 62.

10. Karl Marx, *Early Writings*, trans. and ed. by T.B. Bottomore (New York: McGraw Hill, 1964), p. 85 [italics, his].

11. Ibid., pp. 69–70.

12. See chapter 2 of *A Contribution to the Critique of Political Economy* by Karl Marx, ed. by Maurice Dobb (New York: International Publishers, 1970).

13. Tony Brown, taken from a speech given at the Black Human Resources Network Conference, Washington, D.C., August 16, 1993.

14. Helen Remick and Ronnie Steinberg, "Comparable Worth and Wage Discrimination," *Ethical Theory and Business*, ed. by Tom L. Beauchamp and Norman E. Bowie (Englewood Cliffs, N.J.: Prentice-Hall, 1993), p. 398.

15. Ibid., pp. 397–398.

5

ADVERTISING

"I was born for this, I came into the world for this: to bear witness to the truth; and all who are on the side of truth listen to my voice." "Truth?" said Pilate, "what is that?"

—John 18:37

INTRODUCTION

A logical place to begin discussing advertising is to look at how it is treated in traditional business texts. For a critique of advertising is incomplete without also discussing the economic umbrella under which business functions, yet these texts seldom critique the capitalistic system. Rather, they speak of peripheral issues, such as the ethics of gamesmanship, or to what extent advertising can be manipulative without being coercive. It is sometimes easier to understand the limits and possibilities of a topic if we first have a base from which to launch our critique. For example, in this book we start with basic ethical theory (see chapters 1 and 2) to provide a foundation on which to build and to apply later to specific issues, such as sexual harassment and comparable worth. We then have a perspective from which to connect theory to practices in affecting the workplace. We can find a groundwork for advertising by examining what it means to tell the truth, what lying entails, and to what extent businesses have a duty to present the public with honest claims concerning their products.

When dealing with the topic of advertising the least common denominator is the virtue of truth. The business world defines this term differently from the way we generally do in our personal lives, and metaphysical truths are often distinguished from practical or scientific truths. Also, criteria for determining what is true differ from context to context, as do methods for arriving at various kinds of truths. Much as we have seen difficulties in defining value in the chapter on comparable worth, we meet the same kind of obstacles when it comes to defining truth within the context of capitalism: If profit is the sole objective and competition the motivating factor, can we satisfy both yet remain honest? It appears, from reading articles on business ethics, that the word "truth" has a dual meaning: one for the private arena, one for the public.

This is a difficult distinction in practice and is even harder to justify morally. We all face this dilemma in public life: how to balance truth and honesty within the competitive realities of survival in the workplace, unless we are brought up in a subculture or group that sees no such distinction (such as the Amish in the United States or in a theocratic state like today's Iran). In these religious societies, moral activities are woven into everyday life during the week as well as on holy days. Under these circumstances, there is no division between private and public behavior and contact with the outside world of nonbelievers is minimal. While there are apparent shortcomings in this way of life, moral ambiguity is not one of them. For most of us, who must function in the environment of capitalism and a pluralistic society, moral distinctions are much more complicated. Frequently, we are left to the limits of our own conscience to resolve ethical ambiguity in dealing with others.

It should come as no surprise that truth in advertising is flexible or often "molded" in order to appeal to consumers. Manipulation is used to create demand—that is, to influence us to feel that we need a certain product because it will make us young, sexy, desirable, or in some way "better" as human beings. Contrary to commonly held assumptions, most products do not merely supply "natural" demands. Rather, they too are often "manufactured." Specifically, needs and wants are manipulated by advertisers in order to *establish* a market for their products. The only limit imposed on advertising, outside of blatantly breaking federal regulations, is public opinion. Thus, there seems to be a vicious cycle here: public opinion being the ultimate judge of what can or should be said in advertisement and advertisers shaping public opinion.

This leads us to a situation where advertising functions as an amoral agent that has as its goal maximum profit to shareholders. In order to realize this objective, the public has to be persuaded to buy products and this is done through devices that hook the consumer psychologically, whether they are truthful or not. If this view has any validity, then one of the most effective psychological hooks consumers respond to is sex. Sexual allusions are seen throughout almost every area of advertising and, because our society sees sexiness as tied to youthfulness, remaining "young" has also become an American "ideal" (no matter how impossible it is to actually attain). Advertisements are full of childlike though sexually appealing models. However, this amoral, "give them what they want" approach to advertising can cut both ways. If a certain advertising campaign is unpopular, and hurting profit, companies will be forced to change their images in order to become more appealing to the consumer. For example, consider the controversy surrounding Calvin Klein's posters which depicted immature models in provocative poses. This group of ads garnered unfavorable responses from many consumers who felt that they bordered on child pornography. As a consequence, these ads were dropped or toned-down. On a much grander scale, the Nestle Corporation had to back down when faced with ongoing boycotts over its practice of selling infant formula in third-world countries. The product was demarketed when the negative press got to be too damaging. Let us take a closer look at what happened in this case as an indication of how a corporation changes its focus and practices when pressured by outside forces. It also provides a good illustration of how a demand can be created through aggressive advertising campaigns.

THE NESTLE CASE

Nestle Corporation, a large international conglomerate, was attacked by many individuals and groups who claimed that the rising infant mortality rate in third-world nations was due to the aggressive sales promotions of the infant formula companies, which influenced women to switch from traditional breast-feeding methods to the more "modern" idea of bottle feeding. Their primary target was the Nestle Company of Switzerland, which accounted for 50 percent of their world sales of infant formula.

The declining birthrate in industrialized countries, which began in the 1960s caused all the infant formula companies concern. They had seen the popularity of formula feeding expand their sales tremendously during and after World War II, but in the 1960s their sales began to diminish as the market became saturated. They viewed the developing countries as potential sources of new markets to restore declining sales.

As reports began to appear about women in the third-world who were abandoning breast feeding, many health professionals became alarmed because of the widespread lack of basic nutritional knowledge and adequate sanitation in the third world, two conditions that were necessary for using infant formula safely. It was estimated that only 29 percent of the rural areas and 72 percent of the urban areas in the third world had potable water for mixing formula or for sanitizing feeding equipment. The lack of sanitation facilities and the absence of clean water would only be remedied with further development. The lack of education in underdeveloped countries often meant that people did not properly mix formulas or did not follow correct sanitary procedures. Sometimes a poor family would also stretch the formula by adding extra water.

Despite these problems, the infant formula companies mounted aggressive marketing and promotional campaigns in third-world countries. These marketing and promotional practices included extensive mass media advertising, large quantities of free promotional samples to doctors and maternity wards, gifts of equipment, trips and conferences for medical personnel, and the use of company representatives called "milk nurses" whose jobs entailed promoting and explaining formula feeding to new mothers. Billboards and posters prominently displayed pictures of fat, rosy cheeked babies, subtly suggesting that the healthiest babies were those fed formula.

By 1977, an organization called the Infant Formula Action Coalition (INFACT) had been formed in Minneapolis to address the problem. This organization attempted to create public awareness and economic pressure through a nationwide boycott of all Nestle products. Nestle was chosen because it had the largest share of the world market and also because it was based in Switzerland and could not be pressured through shareholder resolutions in the United States. The boycott, which has the support of the National Council of Churches, had little effect on Nestle's business, but the antiformula movement did get the attention of some very powerful groups.

Despite Nestle's initial reluctance to go along with an International Code of Breast Feeding and Infant Formula Marketing adopted by the World Health Organization in 1981, in March 1982   the company announced that it would observe the code. In a further step, Nestle set up the Infant Formula Audit Commission, composed of doctors, scientists, and church people under the direction of former Secretary of State Edmund Muskie, to monitor its own conduct. In general, the industry, responding to recommendations from the International Council of Infant Food Industries (ICIFI) and the World Health Organization, started to demarket its products. Demarketing means that efforts to sell a product are reduced or stopped completely because of risks to health or safety and is usually initiated because of management decisions, public pressure, or government regulation. Demarketing is ordinarily carried out in declining markets or markets in which a company can no longer compete successfully, but in the developing countries, demarketing decisions were made for growing markets and contrary to usual business practice. [Excerpt from *Business Environment and Public Policy* by Rogene Buchholz (Englewood Cliffs, N. J.: Prentice-Hall, Inc., 1995). Reprinted by permission of Prentice-Hall, Inc.]

When it became clear to social justice groups as well as to the general public what was going on, the company relented. Although the formula remained financially profitable, the tarnished image of the company led to a demarketing of the product. From this case, we can distinguish three possibilities that might be employed for deterring unethical advertising: government regulation, self-regulation, or regulation by public opinion. In general, the latter solution seems most favorable since public opinion can be informed or corrected by education which, in turn, often leads to social action and further political pressure.

We see evidence of this when we look to environmental issues. As people became aware of the consequences of certain manufacturing techniques on the atmosphere or their surroundings and what ignoring them will mean to successive generations, the step to social and political action was not far behind. Recent public support for limiting tobacco advertising targeted at young people is yet another case. Many examples exist that illustrate how this cycle—education leading to public awareness leading to political pressure—can function as a means of responding to, or mitigating the damage of, manipulative advertising campaigns. We will turn now to a brief look at how the business world critiques advertising or ignores the topic altogether.

WHAT THEY DON'T SAY

As a preface to "what they do say" we will consider "what they don't say." In most articles addressing the issue of advertising, the assumptions and values of a capitalist economy are not questioned or examined in any detail: it is a given, an *a priori* principle, that capitalism is a good thing, the best of all economic systems, and that profit is a worthy and ultimate objective. While behaviors influenced by a capitalist system, such as greed and exploitation, face close scrutiny and are often met with disfavor, the fundamental presumptions that serve as a foundation or justification for this undesirable behavior are usually ignored. The view that the media is adding to, or is in large part responsible for, a growing atmosphere of decadence is coming from both conservatives and liberals alike. The advertising media is seen as a cause, not a consequence, of a theory which is beyond critique. Many politicians feel that advertisers should be slapped with Congressional ordinances, or given incentives to regulate themselves, to force them into taking responsibility for the effect they have on young adults and children. However, does it even make sense to claim that business, and its outreach in advertising, has any moral liability in an amoral system such as capitalism? We need to start asking questions that scratch below the surface, deeper philosophical questions which are often ignored. For instance, is a capitalistic economy the inevitable expression of a greedy human nature? Or, does capitalism encourage otherwise unselfish human beings to be greedy? Perhaps capitalism and human nature are mutually determining or self-perpetuating but, we might still ask, to what degree?   Until questions like these are seriously and openly discussed, we cannot even begin to consider how changes or modifications should proceed.   Conservative and liberal groups that engage in blaming each other may find this to be politically advantageous, but it most certainly does not lead to any constructive dialogue.   Unpopular and, yes, "politically incorrect" ideas and solutions need to be examined or, at least, reflectively considered as possibilities.

WHAT THEY DO SAY

The two usual issues discussed in relation to advertising and media, in general, are manipulation and free will. Just how far an advertiser can push the truth without being coercive, without taking away a person's freedom of choice, is the question.   Understanding physical coercion is not difficult, but psychological coercion is a much thornier problem.   The latter can be a very powerful force and it is this that is the central or pivotal issue here.   How far the truth can be "stretched" is a matter of debate.   Unless an advertiser is blatantly coercive—that is, forcing people to make wrongful decisions and infringing on their free will—there is a large gray area which they often exploit or take advantage of.   "Truth" in its strictest definition is not at issue, insofar as it is defined as a "true or actual state of a matter" (*Random House College Dictionary*).   The ultimate goal of advertising is not to portray the truth to the best of one's ability. Rather, it is to persuade consumers to purchase a product by convincing them, subtly or directly, that they need this product in order to better their lives: your life will be easier, you will look better, feel better, have a better quality of life if you buy "X."   Truth here is a matter of interpretation.   We must decide for ourselves whether product "X" will have a positive impact on our lives; yet this decision is not made in a neutral environment.

In order to convince the buyer, the media manipulates the truth through language and the use of props that affect some psychological influence.   Advertisers hire experts to gauge what strategies will work best on the public.   Nothing is done by accident.   When a handsome man pulls up in an expensive red sports car in the company of a beautiful young woman, this is saying much more than "buy our toothpaste; it is good for your dental health."   What it says is that you will be attractive to young, beautiful women and be able to drive expensive cars if you use a certain brand of toothpaste.   Often the psychological hook is so important in an ad that it is hard to discern what is actually being promoted.   If one takes a few minutes to page through any popular magazine, this point will be validated: Is it the jeans, the jacket, the motorcycle, the sunglasses, or something we don't even see, like the deodorant or insurance company, that is being advertised? This obvious manipulation is seen by some business ethicists as moral because both the advertiser and the consumer are playing a game functioning according to certain rules that are understood by all. But, we might ask, is this really the case?

THE MORALITY OF GAMESMANSHIP

An article by Albert Z. Carr that appeared in the *Harvard Business Review* in 1968 is still being discussed and it can help us understand how advertising can be seen as ethical. According to Carr, business functions much like a poker game in that there are certain up-front suppositions that everyone, including both buyer and seller, knows when negotiations begin. Under this theory a certain amount of gamesmanship or manipulation is justified because all parties, implicitly, know the rules: "The justification rests on the fact that business, as practiced by individuals as well as by corporations, has the impersonal character of a game—a game that demands both special strategy and an understanding of its special ethics."[1]

An example of this "special ethics" is seen in the practice that realtors and car dealers use when representing home and car prices as much higher than any anticipated buying charge or fair market value. The cost is then negotiated between the parties involved. This is an "even playing field," so to speak, because everyone involved is supposed to know the game rules. This kind of negotiation carries its own special code and is therefore ethical, relatively speaking. Car dealerships list a "sticker price" on new automobiles, but do not expect that the buying public thinks this is the "real" price. Because both the salesman and the buyer know that they can negotiate, gamesmanship between the parties is fair and moral. Furthermore, no rational adult expects advertisements to be completely truthful. Inflation and exaggeration are expected; therefore these psychological techniques of influencing a buyer's behavior are in keeping with the ethical universe of business practice or "fair play." In theory, at least, no one is being coerced and a customer still has freedom of choice, for all players know the game rules. Certainly there are limits to how much bluffing or exaggeration can occur, but this line is fuzzy. Carr's theory on the morality of business has many variables that can be examined further. We will look at two: Can we compare the world of business with a game, and do we all come to the table from an even playing field?

When we play a game, even one that involves money, such as poker, we are aware that it is just that: a game. There is a certain whimsy or frivolity about the situation, a feeling of recreation. The business world is far more serious, and decisions made within this system can have profound consequences. We are mistaken if we believe that a system is fair because "everyone knows the rules of the game." How do we know this and how is it determined? Who decides what the rules are and what basis? Moreover we do not all enter into the gamesmanship of business and advertising with the same maturity, awareness, intellectual ability, and grasp of cultural conditioning. Recent immigrants from some countries would not necessarily know that the asking price of an automobile is not the price the seller expects to accept; so under the "poker theory," this would not be a fair negotiation. Young girls usually do not realize that images of beautiful women seen in advertisements are virtually unobtainable without "touchups," airbrushes, and, all to often, near starvation and invasive surgery. Eating disorders and poor body image are huge problems for young women in our country today, and the prevailing norm of what is viewed as "beautiful" is an ideal image developed by advertisers to sell products. Adults are better equipped to sift out hyperbole and misinformation due to the knowledge they have gained through life experience; children and young adults have yet to acquire such a "filter." Furthermore, we are living in such a technologically complex environment that we need, increasingly, to rely on the advice of the seller to make informed decisions. For example, we can do research on computers before entering the store. But, inevitably, we will have to rely on the computer "experts" to answer our questions as to the capabilities of a certain computer and how it compares with other similar products. The same can be said for many other goods and services: satellite dishes, home appliances, landscaping, roofing—all areas requiring specialized knowledge for which we may lack expertise and have to rely on the veracity of the seller. We need to rely on medical doctors in a similar manner. Certainly one can do research on a certain disease, but most of us must still trust the opinions of doctors who specialize in the field to inform our decision on treatment. If we do not possess the same knowledge and maturity as the expert, an even playing field does not exist.

By speaking of certain professions, such as business (in Carr's case), as allowing for a "special ethics," we are wading into treacherous waters. Special ethics is an oxymoron, for what is ethical must be applicable to all. For what is actually being implied here is that the ethical is being "suspended," or reinterpreted for certain people in order to meet their own interests. We cannot have it both ways. There is either a commitment to truthfulness as a moral ideal or there is untruth (including stretching the truth), but this is hardly "special." And, though allowances may be made for differences in interpretation, this does not mean that "anything goes" or that anything may be deemed "true" in order to maximize profits.

We can hardly begin to fathom the chaos that would result if every area of life and vocation had its own code of "special ethics," formed around particular circumstances (which is not to say that circumstances play no part in our moral choices, see chapter 1). Those who choose to follow such special ethics usually wind up feeling the sting of the loss of integrity and credibility in the eyes of the public. For example, many defense attorneys openly admit that they are amoral agents working as if getting their client the best possible deal is their only professional duty and the sole justification for their actions.[2] Even if the crime or individual involved is personally reprehensible, they see this as secondary to getting their client minimal punishment. They also admit that stretching the truth is common practice, but how many would maintain that it is "ethical"? But, how many would maintain that this a positive good? This kind of thinking incites public debate over revamping the criminal justice system. Victims' rights groups are particularly upset with the lack of justice they see within the system and the unethical behavior of professionals who work within it.

Although polls differ in exact numbers, it is clear that politicians are also seen as agents who avoid truthfulness by constituents who see empty promises and deception as part of "the game." The deceptions surrounding the Vietnam War and Watergate, for example, undermined public trust in government, and that distrust still lingers today. Manipulation and deception can be seen as the way to handle volatile situations efficiently in the short term but may serve as social grenades later on. Another example of this kind of "backlash" is being felt by the tobacco industry, as scientists within the system are currently coming forth to indict the highest management with hiding earlier research indicating that nicotine is addictive. The CEOs of the major tobacco companies had previously denied the nicotine/addiction connection when testifying in front of a senate subcommittee investigating the industry.

MANIPULATION AND LYING

Manipulation is a gray area in which people are led to certain responses without physical force or coercion. Still, the term "manipulation" implies some kind of psychological coercion. Skewing information is condoned, to a degree, as long as it does not infringe on freedom of choice. But, what does this mean? Does manipulation really differ significantly from lying? For purposes here we will define lying as intentional misrepresentation, whether written, spoken, or through sign language. As manipulation can certainly be "intentional misrepresentation," it can easily be equated with boldfaced lying. Decisions are only as good as the information one is given in order to decide. If a person is fed faulty information, then the decision cannot truly be "free." Sissela Bok says it best in her book *Lying*:

All our choices depend on our estimates of what is the case; these estimates must in turn often rely on information from others. Lies distort this information and therefore our structure as we perceive it, as well as our choice. To the extent that knowledge gives power, to that extent do lies affect the distribution of power; they add to that of the liar, and diminish that of the deceived, altering his choices at different levels.[3]

Consent must be "informed" to be genuine. Manipulation (lying) distorts one's perspective and undermines one's free will. For example, if someone votes for a candidate because of a campaign promise and, once elected, she does not fulfill it, one would naturally feel duped and angry. This individual might well have voted for another candidate had he or she known "the truth" about the other politician's position. The vote was blinded because of the untrue or false information offered. When this happens continually, distrust in the entire political profession begins to seep into the collective psyche. During the Vietnam War, when the public was told by cabinet members and presidential advisors that we were not bombing Cambodia, when in fact we were, and that American combat casualties were low, when they were not, public outrage ensued. Without going into the history or debates about the causes of this war, it is now a matter of record that many decisions were made without a sound factual basis. Yet, these were policy decisions that would affect many American lives. Thus, there can be no freedom of choice without trustworthy access to accurate information and a respect for truth.

TEST OF PUBLICITY

Bok suggests that we use the test of "publicity" as a moral "ruler" for whether a statement or action can be defended. It works something like this: The test of publicity refers to whether or not a group of reasonable people, from varied backgrounds, would agree with a particular resolution. Let us take the case of the government lying about the number of American battle casualties during the war which was used above. If a random sample of the population was listening to the administration's justification for lying to the public, they probably would have had serious reservations, the least of which would be the effect on the public when the truth was finally revealed. History tells us that people in power often lie because they feel that they (and their immediate advisors) have a privileged perspective on the situation and that they, not the public, are in a better position to deal with the problem. The Vietnam War was escalating during an election year when President Lyndon Johnson was running as the candidate for peace. Even though he won the election, the war continued to intensify. Members of his advising team felt that they knew what was best for the country, and that history would ultimately validate the wisdom of their choices whether or not they had acted deceptively. The decision-making process was contained within a very select group and was not put forward for public scrutiny. In other words, Bok's "test of publicity" was not used. For obvious reasons of self-deception and personal bias, we cannot be our own test of publicity. This kind of check guards against the problem of solipsism—that is, the position that oneself alone determines what is true or which arguments are sound. The fact that it was an insulated select group who made policy decisions is at the root of the problem according to Bok's standards. Moreover, this particular small assembly had a vested interest in the deception: reelection for their president and their party and job security for themselves. Important resolutions need to be made by people who have some capacity for distance, and moral principles or political policies must be capable of passing public scrutiny. Thus, it is not a good idea to form ethical committees consisting exclusively of members of the same profession they are designed to "police": doctors overseeing doctors or congressional members monitoring their peers, for example. The "reasonable person" on the street represents the true test of publicity or arbiter of truth:

The test of publicity asks which lies, if any, would survive the appeal for justification to reasonable persons. It requires us to seek concrete and open performance of an exercise crucial to others: the Golden Rule, basic to so many religious and moral traditions. We must share the perspective of those affected by our choices, and ask how we would react if the lies we are contemplating were told to us. We must formulate the excuses and the moral arguments used to defend the lies and ask how they would stand up under the public scrutiny of reasonable persons.[4]

The potential weakness in Bok's test of publicity is that she does not adequately define who the "reasonable" person is—that is, how do we define what constitutes reasonableness, and who does the defining? Many would argue, especially those who would like to see a professional jury system replace trial by one's "peers," that juries made up of so-called reasonable people have often made terrible prejudiced decisions. Such errors are often perpetuated by jury nullification, namely, ignoring the facts and instead using the ruling to make a social or political statement. An example of this misuse of the justice system is typified by the Rodney King and O.J. Simpson cases: Where "reasonable" Whites and "reasonable" African Americans succeeded only in further polarizing race relations and making justice arbitrary.[5] The weakness of Bok's position is similar to those we find in a Kantian approach to morality. For both rely on the belief that individuals can transcend their particular cultural, ethnic, and personal differences making decisions based solely on "reason." On the other hand, Bok's analysis of lying has an appeal similar to that of Kantian ethics. Both provide us with basic moral ideals and principles ("respect," "duty," and "truth") that appear to have universal validity. We cannot even conceive of living in a world without truth, or one in which respect for others is not a basic value. Still, the question remains as to how much truth or respect is required of us in our personal and professional lives, for none of us can lay claim to the "whole truth" on any topic.

THE WHOLE TRUTH

Another instance of a "suspension of the ethical" is the supposition that because no one can possibly know the whole truth, then speaking about truth at all is a moot issue. In the case of medicine, as no doctor can know everything about an ailment, then she cannot speak as if to know the entire truth. This position leads us into the debate of "truth" versus "truthfulness." The fact that no one can know all there is to know does not negate the responsibility to be truthful to the degree that one can. Being truthful involves telling what one does know or sincerely believes to be true. A doctor *is* speaking truthfully when she states that, given her experience with spinal cord injuries, a particular patient cannot expect to walk again. If the patient should walk again, this does not necessarily mean that the doctor was not speaking truthfully.

Truthfulness is important in our private and public lives, and depends on information gathered from sources other than ourselves. The excuse that the whole truth is unattainable is disingenuous when used to justify manipulation and lying. This "whole truth" (all or nothing) argument has brought us full circle: lying and manipulation hurts us as a society as well as individually because this renders us powerless and denies our freedom of choice.

MEDIA UNRESTRAINED

In a recent article in *The New Yorker*, David Denby discusses the effects of commercialism on children from the perspective of a concerned parent. Experts and parents alike share the fear that children, bombarded by media images from an early age, cannot separate fiction (manipulation, skewed messages, misleading information) from reality. They don't know it is a "game" in which everyone knows their roles and "all is fair."

For many of them, pop [culture] has become not just a piece of reality—a mass of diversions, either good or bad, brilliant or cruddy—but the very ground of reality. The danger is not mere exposure to occasional violent or prurient images but the acceptance of a degraded environment that devalues everything—a shadow world in which our kids are breathing an awful lot of poison without knowing that there's clean air and sunshine elsewhere. They are shaped by the media as consumers before they've had a chance to develop their souls.[6]

Media saturation is so insidious that preventing children from seeing and hearing what parents deem unacceptable is simply not possible. Strict government regulation is one solution suggested, but many people fear weakening our constitutional right to free speech. The argument is that denying or limiting the freedoms of some will result in the further erosion of rights for everyone. Moreover, most Americans are resistant to the idea of government acting as a moral police agency. Yet, by definition, self-regulation, too, has obvious problems. When companies "police" themselves, self interest or bias is always an important factor and can take precedence over all other considerations. For example, the function of the CEO is to increase profits for the stockholders as much as possible. So, the interests being served and protected are those of the owners and stockholders, for it is their money that is at stake. Upper management is not interested in social responsibility.

Too much time and energy is spent on symptoms, while ignoring the causes of the disease. For example, there is congressional concern, sparked by public outrage, over the amount of violence in movies and television. Television executives were told to clean up their programming or face government intervention which would force them to do so. This denies that the bigger issue is the economic system that encourages the maximization of profit over and above everything else. Violence and lewd language apparently are what television viewers want, for they watch such forms of entertainment. Movies and television alike are responding to what sells, and this is what business is designed to do: sell and maximize profit for shareholders. If we want media executives to act differently, we need to look to modifying or examining this system that perpetuates behavior the public indicts as irresponsible.

Conservatives and the conservative subgroup the Religious Right, openly blame the media for what they perceive as society's descent into decadence: an atmosphere of crudeness, lack of respect, and denial of basic values. While they are correct in this, they fail to see how they, too, are complicit. Specifically, when they unquestionably support political policies that assume that the capitalistic model is best, they are valuing profit over people. Herein lies the paradox: For these groups, while runaway consumerism is bad, capitalism is good. As an economic theory, capitalism may be efficient and the reason we prosper as a nation. Any criticism of it is almost always perceived as not only danger- ous but anti-American. Thus, they may disagree with the policies of Time Warner or Calvin Klein for acting out of avarice instead of moral responsibility, but not a word is said about where this "avarice" originates. Rarely do conservative critiques admit that:

Capitalism in its routine, healthy, rejuvenating rampage through our towns, cities and farmland forces parents to work at multiple jobs, substitutes malls for small-city commercial streets and neighborhoods, and dumps formerly employed groups (like Blacks in the inner cities) onto the street or into dead-end jobs.[7]

Conservative politicians celebrate unrestricted capitalism, or a *laissez-faire* attitude towards the marketplace, and frequently cite the evils of government regulation, by advocating a "government off our backs" attitude. Ironically, in areas of personal morality (for example, sexual activity and drug usage), they seek greater government involvement and stricter regulations. This is both inconsistent as well as naive, for how can one expect capitalists to self-regulate or possess a social conscience within an amoral system. We cannot have it both ways: If capitalism fosters behavior that wears away the moral fabric of our nation, then it is nonsensical to attack the behavior while supporting the cause of it. If it is just and ethical to monitor drug usage and sexual activity, then this same type of regulation should pertain to advertising and holding businesses responsible for their actions.

Turning to the opposite side of the spectrum, while conservatives sing the praises of unrestrained capitalism, liberals celebrate "free expression." For approximately the last thirty years, vulgarity and defi- ance have been defended under the umbrella of freedom of speech. When this same freedom of expression turns into something "ugly," liberals say we have to accept this as the price we pay for individual autonomy. There will always be those among us who will abuse a right or privilege, but that does not mean that censorship is the answer. They contend that an educated, critically minded public will sort out the good from the bad, the "wheat" from the "chaff." This will regulate expres- sion by allowing all to approve or disapprove of the concrete conse- quences of such. However, is this celebration of freedom a good thing when it comes to protecting children? This is a common dilemma that many baby-boomer parents now face: What can they do to mitigate the negative effects of unhealthy media images that assault their children from their early years onward without seeming like hypocrites? It is they, and their taste for the irreverent and their skeptical attitude toward authority, after all, that set the stage for the coarseness and lack of general respect we see on TV, in ads, on radio talk shows, and in music.

What is even more disturbing is that there are now marketing services that help the nation's largest advertisers to enter the preschool and day-care markets. The children amount to what is called a "captive audience," ripe for promotional strategies.[8] Day-care directors welcome the free products that companies like Kellogg provide. Magazines are distributed that are designed for small children, providing creative sales pitches, such as scratch-and-sniff ads and Kellogg's Pop-Tarts springing out of toasters. The tone of our common culture has turned into something base and disgraceful, and we cannot easily isolate or protect certain groups from exposure. Adults learn to screen out the crude, or the real from the fictional, but it is doubtful whether children can do the same. At the very least, we first need to allow children the chance to cultivate a refined sensibility or develop "good taste." Still, we also need to ask what prices are paid when this free speech umbrella is used to protect deception committed for the sake of financial profit? When issues of physical harm or life and death arise (like in the Nestle Case), then one cannot be so glib about individual rights.

PORTRAYAL OF WOMEN IN ADVERTISING

While all factions share similar concerns and worries regarding children's exposure to an unbridled media, young girls are a particularly vulnerable group, especially when speaking of the effects of advertising. In a sexist society where any trait labeled "feminine" tends to be devalued or exploited, young girls learn through the media how to behave and look if they want to obtain the beauty and character of the "ideal" woman.[9] Early in their lives, women have a sense that something about them isn't quite right, and appearance takes on monumental importance as the girl matures. Open a magazine, any magazine, or pass a string of billboards along a highway and you will see the image of the beautiful woman: extremely thin, large breasted, sexually available, with flawless skin. This prototypical "beauty" is seen everywhere; clothes and products are designed for her and those who aspire to be like her. This is quite a feat when we consider that thirty-three percent of American women wear a size sixteen or larger![10] What should one do when besieged with this paradigm if she does not measure up (speaking both literally and figuratively)? This archetypal figure represents a body type that only 5 percent of women actually possess. However, the beauty industry has come to the rescue: make-up; products to eliminate wrinkles, blemishes, cellulite or any other physical flaw; plastic surgery, exercise videos and dieting tips.

Because such products are aggressively advertised, eating disorders are all too common among young women who accept the myth of the "perfect" body. These disorders, which involve both physical and mental health issues, are on the rise in the United States; whereas thirty years ago, they were almost entirely unheard of. Today, they are being called "the socio-cultural epidemic of our time."[11] This is underscored when we consider that the revenues of the diet industry are $33 billion. Furthermore, 72 percent of women report that they will be on a diet in any given year[12]—despite the fact that 95 percent of people who look to the diet industry to lose weight gain it all (and then some) back again.[13]

Can we even imagine men following a similar path to meet such a narrowly defined ideal? Of course some men diet, but we cannot find examples of men looking like hunger posters or behaving childlike in order to be attractive to women. Nor does the average man pick at a salad or raw vegetables at dinner, instead of ordering a meal. Men are afforded the dignity of being able to age gracefully and still be considered attractive. Showing a few wrinkles and gray hair is even deemed sexy for men. Many actors are cast as a desirable leading man despite graying or the loss of hair and weathered skin. Newscasters can show evidence of their age if they are male; but we are hard-pressed to find women who can successfully look or act their age and remain employable on television or the big screen.

In her book *The Beauty Myth*, Naomi Wolf talks about how this obsession with perfection came into being.[14] In the 1950s, advertising revenues soared as manufacturers targeted the American housewife, who was often bored with the repetitive tasks of housekeeping. Household products were marketed to make her life easier and more efficient. However, with the advent of a 1960s style feminism and economic instability, many women entered the work force. Shrewd business people recognized that they needed a new "hook" that did not pertain only to the closed environment of the home. Advertisers sought an obsession that women could take with them to work, and this is how cosmetic/toiletries promotional campaigns began. By 1989 this strategy was well entrenched with beauty products offering $650 million in advertising revenues to magazines; while soaps, cleansers, and polishes yielded only one tenth that amount.[15]

Even certain gains coming out of the women's movement of the 1960s and 1970s have been given an ironic spin by advertisers. For example, the idea that a woman could be naturally beautiful without props has been co-opted, and entire lines of products have been developed to promote the "natural look." A look, however, that could only be obtained with the help of the beauty industry. Now women can wear make-up without it being apparent that they are doing so and seem instead to be blessed with "natural beauty." Even eye color can be changed with tinted contact lenses—the general preference being blue. Moreover, this obsession has created new categories of what counts as attractive, such as the over-forty-but-forever-young look.[16] Scientific approaches to skin care, cosmetic surgery and fitness programs promise to stave off the inevitable changes of maturing, and magazine articles relating to diet increased 70 percent from 1968 to 1972. Articles on diet continued to rise steadily from 60 percent in the year 1979 to 66 percent in the month of January 1980 alone.[17] One of the models of the "fit for life," eternally attractive yet over-forty woman, is the actress and fitness guru Jane Fonda. She is also a woman with a long, sad history of eating disorders—over twenty years of eating and purging. Openly speaking of her disorder she said: "Society says we have to be thin, and while most of us don't have much control over our lives, we can control our weight, either by starving to death or by eating all we want and not showing the effect.[18] In order to "not show the effect" yet still eat heartily a pattern of binge-and-purge must be routinely followed. Fonda speaks of her bulimia as the secret device she used to maintain the physical perfection that was expected of her. Now the publicly stated approach to control-ling her weight is physical fitness and "sensible eating."

It is ironic that the goal in each case is the same: control over one's body. Of course, physical fitness does not carry the health dangers of an eating disorder, but the message is no different: find a way to maintain this image of self-control and ideal beauty, regardless of whether or not this reflects a deeper truth and no matter what the cost. The unfortunate message remains that women need to find ways to reach these ideals of eternal youth and physical perfection, though perhaps through "health-ier" channels. Something is amiss here, for in either case the burden falls upon women alone. That is, few people question these ideal images or ask how they originated. Perhaps men, too, should wonder why they hold onto such a narrow definition of what is beautiful, and look at the damage it may be doing to their wives, lovers, daughters, mothers, and sisters.

One criticism is that women themselves have helped to create or, at least, perpetuate this false conception of beauty that is portrayed in the media and advertising. After all, it is they who buy the magazines that typecast them into an ideal that is so hopeless and debilitating (as Andy Rooney argued in a 60 Minutes episode). It is women who submit their bodies and themselves to diets, surgery, and whatever else it takes to remain young, attractive, and competitive. But what are they actually competing for? Is male attention the main goal or obtaining a husband?

Are these reasons sufficient for explaining why a woman would risk her health and happiness? If so, how can this account for the "lipstick lesbians" who also buy into the advertising ideal? Why *do* so many women buy into a view of themselves that is virtually impossible and ultimately self-defeating? These kinds of questions are rarely asked, except by self-proclaimed feminists, and answers can only be speculative at best. However, maybe the "why" queries—or search for causes—are ultimately less important than asking, what should we do now? Or, where does one go from here if she wants to overcome these fears of being less than "perfect"? Perhaps one can begin simply by becoming more aware.

Could it be that a commitment to understanding how the professional (advertisers) affects the personal (women's lives) merely reflects a prejudice of a small group of highly educated, professional women influenced by the feminist movement? And, that most are not even interested in how deeply advertising has effected them? This is a criticism leveled by Camille Paglia, the antifeminist writer and lecturer, who basically feels the women's movement is run by East Coast, elitist intellectuals who are making "much ado about nothing." This view supposes that there is something wrong with being educated or an intellectual, and that there is something wrong with this type of woman reflecting upon the position of women in general. It takes a combination of strength, financial resources, and independence to face and overcome the traditionally prevailing model of women's worth or lack thereof. If we accept this, then it is only the educated, financially independent woman who can afford to critically examine this media image and attempt to bring this awareness to others. Women already caught up in the cycle of emotional as well as financial dependency on men lack the resources which would enable them to think, let alone act, in ways that might put their already modest standard of living in jeopardy. Many women have to channel their energies on just surviving and caring for children; they have little time left for contemplating or challenging the pros and cons of constricting gender roles but they are nonetheless hurt by them. It takes time, confidence, and security to confront the status quo.

Regardless, what is wrong with one group of women fighting the battles for those who cannot? Wouldn't seeing yourself as "your sister's keeper" be consistent with a care ethics that values relationships? If financially independent women are in a better position to raise others' consciousness and effect change, doing so should be a virtue not a fault. Moreover, there is a long respected tradition in our country in which those who are privileged speak out and help those who are less fortunate. The Kennedy family has been such an example of this *noblesse oblige*—that is, the moral obligation that goes along with power, wealth and social standing.

The image of women in advertising and other media is so ingrained in society that people don't even recognize it as damaging. Even in college classes, it is only after researching advertising in depth that students start to look critically at advertisements that have long been viewed as benign or neutral. Educating the public facilitates heightened sensitivity to the fact that advertisers work extremely hard, with the help of experts, to have anything but a "neutral" effect on the consumer.

For advertisements to be effective they have to play on fears that are based, at least partly, in reality. And, in fact, many women are afraid of losing love and domestic stability as they age and become less youthful in appearance. Moreover, almost half of all marriages end in divorce and the old story of a man leaving his middle-aged wife for a younger woman is not a myth. Advertisers find easy prey in the very real anxiety many women feel. Men do not have this same kind or degree of concern. As stated before, men can have gray hair and wrinkles and still be considered sexy. And in movies when mature men are teamed with a love interest, the woman is usually much younger and this seems quite "normal." But, more importantly, men are not financially dependent on women the way women are on men, despite social and political advancements. As Wollstonecraft indicated so many years ago: women are prized for their physical beauty and this is one of the few sources of "power" granted them. This may also explain why even some lesbians, who do not look to men for emotional or financial support, continue to aspire to the same standards of beauty. Specifically, beautiful women tend to be valued in ways that the "average" woman is not. They are seen as more powerful, competent, or, simply, as overall better human beings. Women in Hollywood complain that there are fewer and fewer scripts for them as they mature, regardless of their talent or abilities. Even with all that plastic surgery can do for those who are wealthy enough to afford it, one cannot stay young eternally, and fighting the inevitable process of aging is depressing and time-consuming. It saps women's energy to such a degree that sometimes they have little left over for more productive activities. And perhaps this is the objective: keeping women on the defensive about how they look allows them to be taken less seriously making them less threatening to men.[19] Whether or not one agrees with this, it is still clear that women have to be convinced to enter into this futile chase for eternal youth and this impossible ideal of beauty for many businesses to realize profit.

It would not be fair to blame advertising alone for how women are portrayed in media images, but there can be no doubt that business and profit play a significant role and, at the very least, exacerbate sexist assumptions regarding what is feminine and attractive. It is hoped that the next generation of women will not be blindly led by the beauty industry. For transcending cultural conditions is no easy task when a society has been so saturated. Women and men working in the field of ethics can teach students to critically examine advertisements and consider their effects on themselves. Most importantly they need to be empowered to avoid the trap of thinking that media images are innocuous or that the beauty industry, in particular, is only giving the public what they want.

QUESTIONS FOR REFLECTION

1. Is there a difference between lying and manipulating the truth? If so, how do we make this distinction?
2. Does the concept of "fair play" in advertising apply to everyone equally, including children or those unfamiliar with American customs?
3. Is truth relative? Can one be truthful, yet not speak "the whole truth"?
4. What are some of the effects of advertising on young women? How do these influences follow them into adulthood?
5. Is there an ideal of "male beauty" or "masculinity"? If so, what is it and how does it affect men's self-image? If not, why is this?
6. Explain the dynamics between public opinion and advertising.
7. What are your thoughts on the problems raised in the Nestle case?
8. Does a lie have to be committed by explicitly distorting the truth? Or, is there such a thing as lying by omission in advertising? Is what is not said as important as what is said?
9. What happens to a society in which politicians, doctors, lawyers or business men and women can't be trusted to be truthful?
10. Do advertisements simply appeal to what we naturally want, or are they designed to create "needs" and demands?

NOTES

1. Albert Z. Carr, "Is Business Bluffing Ethical?" *Harvard Business Review*, January/February 1968.

2. An example of such admittance is a statement by Charles Antes: "The relationship between lawyer and his clients is one of the intimate relations. You would lie for your wife. You would lie for your child." See also "To Defend a Killer" [video], from the series *Ethics in America*, where it is clear that some defense attorney's lead or en-courage their clients to lie or manipulate the truth in order to minimize punishment.

3. Sissela Bok, *Lying*, New York: Vintage Books, 1989, p 19.

4. Ibid., p. 93.

5. In the Rodney King case, a predominantly White jury ignored or dismissed video tape evidence and acquitted police officers accused of beating a Black man, Rodney King. This decision resulted in rioting throughout the inner-

city area of Los Angeles. The opposite racial situation was found in the criminal case of O.J. Simpson in which a majority Black jury, found the famous Black defendant not guilty of murdering his ex-wife and her friend. Many people feel that the jury ignored the evidence in order to make a statement to society about the police and justice system's treatment of African Americans. Jury nullification, of course, is nothing new; however, these high-profile cases are what bring it into the light of public scrutiny.

6. David Denby, "Buried Alive," *The New Yorker Magazine*, July 15, 1996, p. 48.

7. Ibid., p. 56.

8. "Show and Tell: Advertisers Take Pitches to Preschools," *Wall Street Journal*, Monday, October 28, 1996, p. B1.

9. Jean Kilbourne, *Still Killing Us Softly*, [videocassette] (Cambridge, Mass.: Cambridge Documentary Films, 1987).

10. *People Magazine*, June 3, 1996.

11. Eva Szekely, *Never Too Thin* (Toronto: The Women's Press, 1988), p. 12.

12. Jean Kilbourne, *Slim Hopes*, [videocassette] (Northhampton, Mass.: Media Education Foundation, 1995).

13. Ibid.

14. Naomi Wolf in her book *The Beauty Myth*, offers a good historical explanation of how the beauty myth came into being and the ensuing beauty culture that has been built around this myth. She is an excellent source for further research on the relationship between feminism and this change of advertising focus.

15 Naomi Wolf, *The Beauty Myth* (New York: Anchor Books, 1991), p. 66.

16. For a good discussion of "over forty" beauty, see "Changing Landscapes," by Wendy Chapkis, *Women Images and Reality* (Mountain View, Calif. Mayfield Publishing Co., 1995), pp. 94–95.

17. Naomi Wolf, *The Beauty Myth*, p. 67.

18. Leo Janus, "Jane Fonda, Finding Her Golden Pond," *Cosmopolitan*, January 1985, p. 170.

19. See Susan Faludi, *Backlash* (New York: Doubleday Publishing, 1992).

6

LEADERSHIP

Implicitly adopting the male life as the norm, they have tried to fashion women out of a masculine cloth. It all goes back, of course, to Adam and Eve—a story which shows among other things that if you make a woman out of a man, you are bound to get into trouble.

—Carol Gilligan

INTRODUCTION

Despite the oft-cited changing demographics of the work force and the optimistic outlook proclaimed by many, women are still significantly underrepresented in top management positions. Presently, women comprise almost half of the U.S. labor force, more than half of the students earning bachelor's and master's degrees, 40 percent of law school graduates, and one-third of MBA recipients.[1] The number of women in senior management positions held steady over five years (1990 to 1995) at only five percent.[2] A 1986 article claimed that even though almost one-third of all management positions are filled by women, "most are stuck in jobs with little authority and relatively low pay."[3] Moreover, women don't seem to be doing much better in government or educational institutions. According to a 1989 study by the U.S. Office of Personnel Management, only 8.6 percent women in government service were found in positions at Senior Executive Service levels; and a 1986 Department of Labor report showed that colleges and universities employed only 1.1 women at the level of dean or above.[4] The question, then, is what is holding women back? Why does this "glass ceiling" remain for most women in business? And, what can be done about it?

THE "GLASS CEILING"

When Catalyst, a nonprofit research organization that works with business to effect change for women, surveyed 1,251 executive women who held titles of vice president or above in Fortune 1,000 companies, they received three basic responses to the first question above. Fifty-two percent said that "male stereotyping and preconceptions of women" prevented them from reaching the upper-rungs of management, 49 percent said that "exclusion from informal networks of communication" contributed to a lack of advancement, and 47 percent indicated that lack of experience was a factor.[5] But something unexpected that emerged from this study is perhaps even more important—namely, a significant difference between the perceptions of these women and their male counterparts. For instance, most male CEOs claim that lack of experience constitutes the main factor prohibiting women's advancement (82 percent); the second major barrier they cited was women not having been "in the pipeline" long enough (64 percent; see fig. 6.1).[6] One might ask what, precisely, does this mean? Certainly, some on-the-job experience is necessary, but if job tenure is rated a primary requirement, then women could be led into a "Catch-22." That is, not only length but breadth and depth of experience is needed in order to advance, yet, at the same time, one needs to be allowed to advance in order to gain more experience of this sort. Moreover, what should also be taken into account is the reason why many women may have less time in the pipeline—namely, because they have often had to interrupt or delay careers for the sake of children or family matters. But, being in the pipeline may also mean inclusion in the informal networks of communication cited above. That is, regardless of how long a woman has been in the field or on the job, if she is excluded from the pipeline because of stereotyping and thereby denied access to these avenues of networking, then her tenure is compromised or rendered insignificant. Perhaps this helps to explain why only 29 percent of the executive women surveyed agreed that length of tenure, or the amount of time actually spent in a particular environment, was a relevant factor and, as indicated above, were more likely to cite obstacles attributable to an "inhospitable work environment."[7]

Many women have complained that the deck is stacked against them from the beginning. An example of this being that whenever a top position is advertised, a "male resume" is expected—that is, a certain amount of tenure is insisted upon for each rung of the corporate ladder leading to a standard that women, especially those who have had to take time off for family responsibilities, cannot possibly meet. What this suggests is a very basic distinction between how men perceive the situation and how women themselves interpret their status in the corporate setting. What accounts for this difference? And, which group is correct when it comes to discerning the ultimate causes of the glass ceiling?

Figure 6.1
Barriers that Prevent Women from Advancing to Senior Positions (the CEO Level); CEO's Perception Compared to that of Executive Women

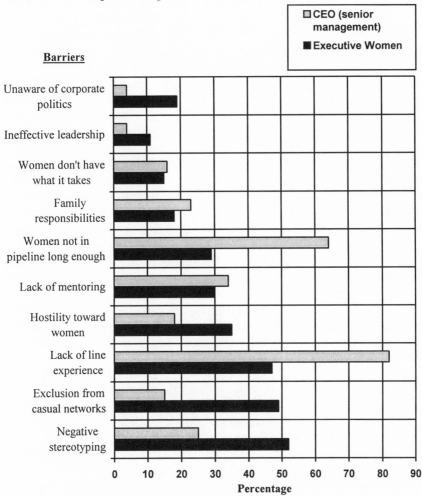

Adapted from: Catalyst, 1996.

Certainly, differences in perceptions can be attributed to differences in vantage points. When men still comprise a 95 percent majority at the level of senior management, it is their expectations, values, and ideals that constitute, and can therefore be expected to dominate, the corporate environment. Males are thus less likely to feel or actually be excluded; nor is it probable that such a milieu would be perceived by them as inhospitable. On the contrary, many men feel quite at home in an organization that has been structured, both formally and informally, according to their particular needs and interests. Until very recently, the traditional corporate model of success was a man "with a wife who was not employed outside the home and whose role was to support her husband's career by assuming responsibility for child rearing and all other domestic matters."[8] This would enable men to make career their top priority and to take advantage of those informal support systems—to conduct business over meals, during sporting events or activities, or in exclusive male clubs. But this is no longer the case (and perhaps was never a realistic family ideal to begin with), so new paradigms for success need to be sought out. Whether or not this model of success and family is historically accurate, the myth itself has had the kind of impact that could account for the differences in experiences and expectations of men and women. That men and women executives might see things differently based on their distinct experiences should be evident, but it is not clear which point of view is accurate in their assessment of the glass ceiling and its sources. It is probably safe to say that both are correct to some degree, but to what extent we won't even begin to surmise. When it comes to assigning ultimate causes to something, no one can ever say for sure what they are or to what degree they are responsible for effecting a particular outcome. In addition, the situation we are faced with here is unique and not all relevant data is in, so all we can do is speculate or draw inferences from the information that is presently available. It should suffice to say that the more important issue here is, what can be done about this resistant glass shield? Or, how can it be demolished once and for all? Rather than focus on questions of where blame may be placed or whose experiences and claims are more legitimate, our primary aim here is to understand where we are and in what direction we'd like to be moving.

BREAKING THE GLASS CEILING

One of the most important questions Catalyst asked the 1,251 women executives in its 1996 survey was, how did you do it?—that is, to what did these women attribute their unusual success in breaking the ceiling? Most women attributed their advancement to their own efforts and willingness to adapt to a corporate structure not of their own design, rather than to any initiative taken by the company or those who were already on the inside, for when these women entered the business world they became part of a working force in which the "rules of the game" had already been established. One common refrain was that they believed they had to overcome additional challenges not faced by men, such as putting in longer hours or being willing to work at undesirable hours, and being forced to "prove" themselves in various and seemingly arbitrary ways (Catalyst 1996: 14). When it came to understanding the concept of leadership, many had believed that it did not apply to them—that being female and a leader or authority figure were mutually incompatible roles and that the only avenue to advancement was to become "one of the boys."

However, what has often been overlooked is the fact that women have long been considered authority figures in the home. Certainly, there are extant remnants of the stereotypical ideal that "a man is king of his castle," and mothers have sometimes attempted to control an unruly child by warning "wait 'til you father gets home"; but no less traditional or typical is the nuclear family ideal in which the woman "calls the shots" at home—that is, she acts as an umpire or manager would by deciding how income is spent or by mediating among siblings or between father and child. Put simply, she is responsible for running the domestic sphere. We also see many situations in which women have been forced, or have chosen, to become single parents and have to play the role of "mother" as well as "father." Therefore, even if power and authority are identified with the male parent, women have already shown that they are capable of adapting to this ideal of leadership (whether on the home front or on the job). On the other hand, if leadership is differently construed, then perhaps a more "maternal" conception of authority is called for. (Note: This is the claim of feminists like Nancy Hartsock, discussed in chapter 2, who calls for a rethinking of the concept of power and power relation paradigms.)   It should not be surprising that books written on the topic of leadership in the early years of the women's movement counseled women to "become more like men" or to learn to play by "men's rules."[9] For despite any authority enjoyed in the home, women were still regarded, and tended to consider themselves, as outsiders with respect to the public realm of business. The prevailing belief was that they could only assume positions of power on the inside of corporate structures and be successful at it if they learned how to play by these preestablished rules, as well as follow an unwritten code of conduct. What then were these so-called rules or codes of the workplace? And what strategies did women use to accommodate them?

In three respects, the women in the Catalyst study were virtually unanimous. Ninety-nine percent claimed that "consistently exceeding performance expectations has been a critical or fairly important factor in their advancement"—one of the challenges that women faced that their male colleagues did not. Ninety-six percent said that "developing a style with which male managers are comfortable has been a critical or fairly important strategy"; and 94 percent credited "the importance of seeking out difficult or challenging assignments" (Catalyst 1996: 15). Other significant strategies were cited, such as the importance of having an influential mentor and impressive educational credentials, but only in the three areas above was there this kind of consensus. Two of these issues seem to be intimately linked. For exceeding expectations would most likely include taking on unusually difficult tasks and, in turn, succeeding at these tasks would mean going beyond what had been expected. But what does it mean to develop a style with which males are comfortable? Does it entail developing a style with which women are not comfortable? What must be sacrificed in order to attain such an end?

To some extent, luck must figure in here. For one may be lucky enough to work with men who are more open, or already educated about feminist issues, which would make things much easier. Or, one may be unlucky enough to encounter men who are hostile and have deeply entrenched sexist feelings. In the latter case, no matter what style a woman develops, it is unlikely that these kinds of men will ever be comfortable. And, we might ask, why should women be compelled to take men's comfort level into account at all? It is already apparent that different standards of employment or advancement exist for women than for men, as no evidence has been found where men have deemed it necessary to accommodate women's comfort needs. Let us turn, then, to an examination of each of these different styles of leadership in order to see what each entails.

MASCULINE VS. FEMININE STYLES

Nearly all of the available literature discusses a distinction between "masculine" and "feminine" styles of leadership. And, in order to clarify this difference, two pairs of metaphors are nearly always appealed to. For instance, when describing an organization and its leaders in "tradi-ional" or masculine terms, the two analogies that are almost universally invoked are team sports (like football with its coach, quarterback, and specialized players) or the military (with its ranking of officers, chain of command, and special units). However, there are two contrasting metaphors for a feminine conception of power and authority that are as prevalent as the masculine ones—namely, a "web," or network of relations, with a center or locus that resonates outward into various branches and subdivisions, or the family insofar as it is understood as an integrated whole involving interpersonal relations and intimate connections. Presumably, the masculine models evoke images of a rigid hierarchy emphasizing order and individual role identification and construe success as "winning" in the short-term according to what is measurable or quantifiable; while the feminine paradigms are designed to accentuate an essentially fluid structure with greater emphasis on relationships in which individuals play different roles and share power and in which success is more long-term oriented and includes intangibles like personal satisfaction or happiness. In war as in sports, individuals are said to thrive on "competition" with each aiming to achieve his personal "best"; while in a family or network, the whole is said to be "greater than the sum of its parts," "cooperation" is fostered and everyone shares credit as well as responsibility. But, one might ask, is this an accurate portrait of team sports or military activities? Isn't it instead true that both the feminine and masculine paradigms are dependent upon the cooperation, or personal sacrifices, of each and every member? Don't officers or coaches even go so far as to claim that one should regard his team or squad as he would his own family? Another problem with claiming that the sports and military metaphors are strictly masculine is the implication that women do not belong in these arenas—that is, that they are somehow inherently unsuited for the rigors of athletic competition or a soldier's life. This itself is a hotly debated ethical question that is far from being resolved.

Nonetheless, many women in the Catalyst survey said that they felt compelled to adopt a "masculine" attitude in order to succeed at higher levels of management, despite feeling that it threatened their own sense of personal identity. This included such things as demonstrating company loyalty, keeping their personal lives out of the office, and "not rocking the boat"(Catalyst 1996: 23). But what makes these traits particularly "masculine"? The presumption here is that a woman's sense of identity somehow depends upon *rocking* the boat, *bringing* her personal problems into the workplace, and *not* being loyal to the company or her coworkers. What is more remarkable is that it was the women themselves who made these claims. This indicates how deep certain sexist assumptions run and how so many men and women, regardless of educational background, still march to them, however unconsciously. Psychological researchers only add to this further and validate such presuppositions when they maintain that, "[w]omen's traits, behaviors, attitudes, and socialization are said to make them inappropriate or deficient as managers because of such factors as fear of success or their unwillingness to take risks."[10] Yet, claims such as these do not square with empirical evidence. For what could be more risky than bearing and raising children? What other endeavor is so fraught with uncertainty and has so unpredictable an outcome? On the other hand, there were also women who claimed that simply "being themselves" contributed to their success. This entailed leading by "recognition and encouragement" and seeking to "empower" others rather than commanding or controlling (Catalyst 1996: 23–24). So, the camp appears to be split between women who find it necessary to emulate a paradigm of leadership that is not their own and those who follow a model of their own making that fits their unique sense of self. In addition, while some corporations are actively adopting a more "female" approach to management, others remain resistant to any changes or innovations in the workplace.

Still, nearly all of the women quoted acknowledged having to "prove" themselves to their male coworkers, conceding that they were not afforded any benefit of doubt, as would have been the case if they were men. Whether they adapted to the masculine style of leadership, or maintained one with which they personally were more comfortable, the burden of proof remained on them to demonstrate that they, in fact, could be effective managers. This constitutes an incredible waste of time and energy that could surely be spent more productively—and may provide us with a hint as to why some women don't even want to get into "the corporate game" to begin with. But if women do break these barriers somehow, then what? What do women do once they have reached the upper rungs of the corporate ladder? And, is there one particular style of leadership which is favored above others?

Other studies have been done that asked women these questions—namely, what is their preferred style of management now that they are in a position to choose one for themselves? Again, according to these anecdotal accounts, a uniquely feminine approach emerged in contrast to a traditional or distinctly masculine style. What these studies concluded is that the feminine model is more "open" and flexible, reflecting a willingness to embrace ambiguity in situations where decisions are called for, whereas men look for a more rule-oriented, secure system that will enable them to make effective choices and ensure the best results.

This hearkens back to Carol Gilligan's distinction between an ethic of care and a justice orientation, which, in turn, presupposes a Kantian account of moral choice (see chapters 1 and 2). For Gilligan claims that women manifest a greater capacity for, or are better attuned to, evaluating matters that are ambiguous or unquantifiable and require some "reading between the lines." Moreover, if emphasis is placed primarily on relationships, which is what she claims women do, then clearly those are the kinds of connections that cannot possibly be measured or determined with mathematical precision (in either personal or professional contexts). Again, this is where an implicit appeal to a family metaphor comes in, for women who are wives and mothers must remain flexible and responsive to the individualized needs of different family members; there can be no single approach to dealing with all of the surprises and circumstances that may arise. These claims also bring us back to Nancy Hartsock, who insisted that a different notion of power and community is operative in the private realm of the household than in the public realm or marketplace. However, she believes, that justice and equality are more likely to be achieved if we bring some of these private values into the marketplace, just as Gilligan believes that men and women each have something to learn from the different emphases and attitudes of the other. So, what specifically are these "feminine" values that are manifested in a female conception of leadership? And, in what ways are they distinct from a "masculine" attitude or approach?

MASCULINE VS. FEMININE VALUES

The way in which most writers on leadership have distinguished between men's and women's styles is by appealing to a basic distinction in what each values. Where men are said to value individuality and the rewards of a competitive work environment, women, it is claimed, value cooperative enterprises that preserve or enhance relationships. As noted above, in the Catalyst survey, some female executives struggled to fit into the corporate structure and, at the same time, maintain their own unique sense of personal identity. Apparently, these women embodied the kind of care ethic described by Gilligan and felt uncomfortable having to suppress it, along with the values that it entails, in order to fit into a corporate structure. They believed that who they were in their private lives (mothers, wives, friends, lovers) was inappropriate for office relations or their professional circumstances if they wanted to succeed in this "alien" culture.[11] This separation of the personal and the professional was something they resented, but could not avoid if they wished to advance. However, upon reaching a top managerial position, it appeared that many of these women were able to develop a style with which they were comfortable, one that included a more personal or personable approach to doing business. In other words, they attempted to overcome this separation of their private and public lives by integrating the former into the latter.

In order to defend a specifically "feminine" style of leadership, most authors draw upon the work of Carol Gilligan. What Gilligan did with moral development in contradistinction to Lawrence Kohlberg, Sally Helgesen does with leadership contra Henry Mintzberg.[12] However, where Gilligan recorded responses from both male and female adolescents, Mintzberg limited his studies to five male managers and Helgesen, to four female executives or entrepreneurs. At this point, one might already suspect that the results of such studies would be similarly skewed, given the small number of participants and the fact that Mintzberg as well as Helgesen limited their studies to only one sex. Nonetheless, both researchers make claims that resonate with findings of many other surveys, studies, and psychological theories; so it might be worthwhile to consider what each has to say and assess their positions.

In 1968, Mintzberg studied the requirements for successful management successfully by observing what it was that top managers actually did in their daily activities. All of his subjects were men, and a basic pattern emerged: First, they worked at a very fast pace and took little time out for reflection and activities not directly related to the immediate tasks at hand. Secondly, the workday was characterized by discontinuity and fragmentation due to interruptions in the scheduled routine and/or unanticipated problems. Lastly, they had difficulty sharing information, delegating duties, and tended to tie their sense of personal identity to the position they held in the company—all of which reflects an inability to detach *who* they are as individuals from *what* they do as managers. In general, the portrait that was exhibited through this study was of a manager who focused on ends over means, had a "goal orientation" rather than a "process orientation," and thrived on the pressures endemic to competition and rapid decision making. When Hegelsen did her study on management, however, a different picture emerged.

While Mintzberg concentrated on five men, Helgesen interviewed and observed four women and discovered a style that stood in stark contrast from the one described above. First, the women she studied worked at a slower, steadier pace and took time for breaks and activities that were not necessarily work-related. Secondly, they maintained a sense of wholeness or "flow" by weaving surprises or interruptions into the work-day, indicating a more flexible sense of time and scheduling. And lastly, they saw themselves as playing many roles, sharing information, delegating tasks and, in general, being a part of a network of relation-ships. In sum, women appeared to be as concerned with means—*how* the job gets done or the process itself—as with the fact *that* it gets done or the ends and objectives. Again, we see how women are characterized as prone to creating a cooperative work environment where each employee is valued as an important part of a whole web of relations, whereas it is claimed that men thrive on the personal satisfaction that results from "winning" a competitive edge.

These two distinct styles are discussed in other literature as well, and the portraits are remarkably similar. For instance, Aburdene and Naisbitt provide us with a list of different attributes—one belonging to "traditional management," the other to "women's leadership."[13] The traditional style is characterized as hierarchical, controlling, and dependent upon a system of rank and order-giving. It seeks to limit and define individuals' roles within the corporate structure, demanding respect for certain positions but not others. And it is fundamentally mechanistic, taking an impersonal view towards the worker, who is simply a cog in the machinery designed to perform one specialized job. On the other hand, the feminine style supposedly relies upon strategies of empowering others, establishing and maintaining personal connections, and asking questions rather than disseminating "answers" or giving orders. In this way, it is claimed that consideration for all is facilitated, and workers are seen as persons whose creativity is encouraged by allowing them greater flexibility and latitude in the variety of tasks they might perform. For Aburdene and Naisbitt, this feminine approach is preferred and represents the trend in leadership style. According to their prognostications, it is women who now have the advantage and who will transform the corporate environment, as they "encourage participation, share power and information, enhance other people's self-worth, and get others excited about their work" (Aburdene and Naisbitt 1992: 101).

Thus, discipline and order is "out" and innovation and diversity is "in," making women the "natural" leaders of the future. But, one might ask, is this type of behavior really "natural" to women? And, whether it is or not, should it be encouraged as good for business or the best approach for women? What also strikes us as odd is the manner in which typical capitalist assumptions and values are being denigrated as not suited to the interior realm of the corporate structure, but are not questioned at all when it comes to the fundamental economic structure of our society. That is, "cooperation," among coworkers at least, is now being encouraged over and against "competition"; yet the socioeconomic system in which we live, and the basic paradigm for relations between corporations, is a competitive one. At this point, it would seem that certain critical questions must be raised. Before we do so in detail, however, there is one last text to consider that reflects on traditional approaches to conflict management and the ways in which masculine styles of leadership value reason.

MANAGING CONFLICT AND THE VALUE OF REASON

One final yet oft-cited criterion of sexual difference should be mentioned here and that is the degree of value placed on "rational" or "analytical" thinking. Marilyn Loden, in *Feminine Leadership, or How to Succeed in Business without Being One of the Boys,* claims that the ability to think analytically has been highly touted in traditionally masculine conceptions of leadership. Besides noting the value placed on rank, respect, and control as those discussed above do, Loden argues that the paradigm for intelligent thinking has typically been a "rational" one as opposed to an "intuitive" one. She further argues that intuition is not only natural to women, but represents an effective means of doing business despite its historical devaluation in our culture. But, it remains to be seen what she means by "intuition," how it is distinguished from rationality, and why it is peculiar to women.

Traditionally, Loden and others claim, there has been an over-reliance on quantitative analysis and deductive reasoning. We, too, maintain that this is the case in chapter 1 where the nature of moral reasoning is considered. What is assumed in deductive reasoning is some ultimate, universal, fixed standard of judgment that can be mechanically and uniformly applied to any particular case or ethical problem (an approach favored by the likes of Kant and Kohlberg). Loden argues that this form of reason no longer appears to be an "efficient" means of "problem solving" in business, even though solving problems is precisely what takes up the bulk of most managers' time.[14] According to her, the "intuitive" approach should be preferred, for it is primarily inductive in its orientation, a "more direct route to innova-tion," relies on emotion, and recognizes that "the whole is often greater than the sum of its parts" (Loden 1985: 186). Thus, intuition is essential-ly "induction"— that is, arriving at general conclusions on the basis of particular information or experiences. However, Loden also identifies it with creativity and a "holistic" approach to problem solving in addition to claiming that it "makes use of emotional as well as rational data" (Loden 1985: 186). Intuition, she claims, is particularly helpful when it comes to managing or negotiating complex, interpersonal relationships because it means staying attuned to what is not said, rather than merely focusing on what is said. Perhaps this may be better illustrated by those cases where one knows or senses that a coworker is struggling emotion-ally because of personal problems and is not acting like his or her usual self. (This validates many of Gilligan's conclusions regarding women's sensitivity to others feelings and human relations in general.)

As a trait said to be common to women (and traditionally devalued because of this identification), intuition reflects a capacity for reading between the lines and getting at the root of a problem in an immediate or direct manner. The women quoted in this context claim to rely on "gut feeling" or "instinct" and express a disdain for the "over-analysis" of issues. However, in her chapter on conflict management, Loden quotes a woman who claims that "men are likely to just go in and deal with the conflict without a lot of prior analysis. Whereas, I would be more inclined to analyze the situation in depth before acting" (Loden 198:

168). Thus, it is never entirely clear what she does or does not mean by "rational analysis," a problem not unfamiliar throughout the entire history of philosophy. For reason has never been a univocal concept with any obvious meaning nor is easily defined. Presumably, intuition is indicative of creativity and a willingness to take the risk of trying something new. All of this is said to add up to responsiveness and "openness," which represents the challenges that are now being posed to traditional corporate structures and which would, as some claim, render a feminine leadership style more conducive to good business in the future. This is the position taken by Aburdene and Naisbitt, who also claim that the value women place on "humility" provides a "basis for *openness*"[15] (italics, theirs). Furthermore, in discussing how women leaders tend to manage conflict, Loden cites "accommodation" as the practice most commonly chosen. And that, again, "we see the strong emphasis placed on relationships, even at the expense of achieving one's own goals" (Loden 1985: 170). Apparently, women are more likely to set aside their own self-interests and act altruistically if necessary, though "compromise" and "collaboration" are also seen as effective techniques.

As to why these traits are supposedly more prevalent among women, Loden and others primarily cite women's socialization as mothers or nurturers. Because it is this basic caretaking position from which so many women are said to draw their experiences, it is evident that the family metaphor would replace the military and team-sports analogies as the dominant ideal guiding the changes that we are told are beginning to occur in the corporate milieu. Women are said to be more inclined to think creatively, remaining open to surprises and input from others; to tolerate ambiguity, which allows time for problem solving, to accommodate the needs and interests of others, and are better able to handle several tasks at once by delegating and prioritizing. And, it is maintained, they can do all of this without becoming arrogant and by retaining an awareness of their limitations (i.e., the humility referred to above).

Until recently, these kinds of skills were only in demand for dealing with familial problems where mothers, as the primary caretakers, needed to remain flexible, open, responsive, and creative, as opposed to rigid and controlling (a description of wisdom not unlike that offered by Aristotle in chapter 1). Now, we are told that this will be the new model for leadership in business as well as in the home. And, that the old or traditionally masculine ways of leading have fallen into disrepute and are no longer conducive to success. This is where a closer, perhaps more critical, look is required. For why should we assume that a new leadership paradigm for business is best served by a feminine or familial perspective? Is the family model always preferable to sports or military metaphors? Are changing analogies an inevitable consequence of more and more women entering the work force, and is this type of paradigm shift enough to remedy the problem of conflicting leadership styles? Is success now measured or evaluated differently so that a new approach to leadership is warranted? Some (Helgesen, Aburdene, and Naisbitt) claim is that it is not only "the bottom line," or profits, with which business must be concerned today, but that matters such as personal job satisfaction and keeping employees happy are also crucial. They further claim that women leaders are best suited for leadership roles in the future because of their "natural" concern for others and the value that they place on relationships.

A CRITICAL LOOK

One of the first concerns that arises when considering these studies is a procedural one—namely, that nearly all of the women surveyed or quoted were White and upper-middle class and that leadership is only considered in a corporate or entrepreneurial context. What about women leaders in service industries or those who perform manual, "blue-collar" work? (for more on this see chapter 7). The problem with these paradigms is that they are too racially, ethnically, and culturally narrow, and they fail to take class distinctions into considera-tion—though, we must admit, corporate America still tends to look like this (i.e., White and middle-class) despite affirmative action or other diversification strategies. Moreover, in Helgesen's and Loden's studies, only women who have already "made it" were profiled. We have seen no formal studies dealing with women who have either abandoned the business world out of frustration or discovered their success at climbing the corporate ladder to be a hollow victory; yet, we frequently hear stories or anecdotes from friends and acquaintances that indicate that this too occurs.

Another thing with which we take issue is the family metaphor applied as an ideal structure for the corporate setting. Do we really expect or want managers to treat employees as they would family members? Besides, not all families are alike, nor should we assume that what works in one household will work in another. Healthy family dynamics depend on commitment, love, and support (among other things). But, we cannot expect coworkers to rely on such warm feelings and the kind of shared responsibilities that are part of what it means to be "a family." Can't individuals get along in the workplace, treating each other with mutual respect, without that having to entail shared affection or a sense of familial loyalty? Isn't there something to be said for maintaining some degree of separation between the personal and the professional? Some middle ground must be sought. For certainly there are positive benefits to be had by importing private values into the public sphere, if this means fostering a cooperative and less rigid environment. But, we have also seen the negative side when one operates from personal assumptions that are based exclusively on his or her own experience—namely, the tension and confusion that arise over the issue of sexual harassment (see chapter 3). For example, what one man's partner or friends may find complementary or funny, a coworker may find offensive or provocative.

Moreover, not only do we think that family is not a realistic or healthy paradigm for business in general, but we do not want to encourage women, in particular, to attempt to play maternal roles for which they may or may not be suited (after all, not all women are mothers, nor do they all desire to be). All too often we have seen that women who do not accommodate others by acting as nurturers or caretakers, but instead assume a tougher or more self-interested stance, are perceived as "bitchy" or overly aggressive and are criticized for this. In contrast, a man who acts in a tough manner or who regularly puts his interests first appears assertive and ambitious, and is praised for his strength and "leadership" skills. We do not expect men to behave in a "touchy-feely" manner (giving preference to relationships and showing consideration for others' feelings above their own), yet women who fail to exhibit these characteristics are regarded as lacking or denying their "feminine" side. In fact, Gilligan herself claims that this failure to act responsibly towards oneself, by focusing primarily on the needs of others, serves only to inhibit a woman's sense of self, which allows her to remain subordinate and collude in her own oppression. Why should it be any more "natural" for women to act altruistically than men? And, even if it were, is this tendency towards self-sacrifice something we would want young girls or women to cultivate?

An article in *The Christian Science Monitor* claims that "making all these distinctions between the ways men and women lead tends to support a sex segregation in the workplace that has typically worked against women."[16] This article quotes Robin Ely, an assistant professor of public policy at the Kennedy School of Government, who argues that such dichotomies merely preserve stereotypes that may lead to women being "professionally ghettoized" in female-dominated professions. Furthermore, she claims that "differences in the way people lead is often driven more by the work environment than by their gender," and that what companies need to do is to "root out elements not conducive to women" and to "get beyond tokenism." What women need to do is "be careful not to collude in or perpetuate stereotypes" and "to be able to translate not only your own behavior but other people's behavior, taking into account their gender, *race and culture*" (emphasis ours).

The term "translate" is helpful here, as it raises the issue of language differences as well.[17] That is, in order to adapt to a variety of situations, one can imagine having to cultivate a whole "wardrobe" or repertoire of communication styles. For example, many women claim that when talking to other women (especially those they know well), a more empathic, indirect approach in which certain things are simply understood and need not be stated explicitly may work very well. With children, however, another distinct tone or linguistic style may have to be adopted in order to communicate effectively; while in the working world, yet another approach might be called for: specifically, one in which a person strives to be as clear, direct, and concise as possible. This latter style is usually regarded as typically male insofar as men supposedly say exactly what they mean in as few words as possible. But, in everyday life, women, as well as men, seem to be well aware of the need to adapt their attitude or linguistic style in accordance with the circumstances of the situation at hand, and there is no reason why both could not do the same in the workplace. And, certainly a person's ethnicity and cultural background will have at least as much impact on how he or she speaks, understands others, and uses power as sex or gender does. In *The Christian Science Monitor* article cited above, Cynthia Fuchs Epstein's book, *Deceptive Distinctions,* is also referred to. In it, she says that "rather than focus on the small differences between the genders, we need to draw out the large similarities found in human behavior." If one agrees with this, the next logical question would be, what might these similarities consist in? How can we make sense of concepts such as power, authority, or leadership in a way that will enable us to discern what is best for business and meet ethical demands too?

What is striking in the discussion of distinct leadership styles are the ways in which these differences resonate with the fundamental dichotomies found in the feminist and ethical theory chapters. It is usually the case that in order to understand something at the conceptual level, we resort to making distinctions—that is, to understand x, we need to show how it is specifically *not* y or z. However, more often than not, such distinctions tend to become hardened into rigid either/or dichotomies: for instance, to be "female" is to be "non-male;" or to value reason entails the devaluation of emotions, and vice versa. Inevitably, then, the question arises as to how "opposite" these dualities really are, or whether, instead, they represent false dichotomies. Certainly, we notice differences of personal style in all endeavors, and these need not be reducible to masculine vs. feminine paradigms; yet that is what most of the literature on leadership appears to have done. Moreover, despite the various authors' disclaimers maintaining that neither style should be seen as superior to the other, this does seem to be what is going on in their evaluations. Aburdene and Naisbitt, Helgesen, and Loden all argue that it is women rather than men who are the "natural" leaders of the future due to their innate qualities and values, and that their way of leading is to be preferred. Again, even though these authors identify distinct styles of leadership and state that such should be seen as complementary, they still privilege the "feminine" over the "masculine," thereby preserving a separation. Thus, all that appears to have been done is to replace one stereotype with another and reverse the hierarchy. The problem with this is that we are no better off believing that "women are the wave of the future" than we were with traditional, "masculine" paradigms. One "box" in which the concept of leadership may be contained, has merely been dismantled and another has been substituted for it. And, whether the preferred model is the one described as feminine or masculine, those men and women who do not, or cannot, make themselves fit will be summarily excluded. Thus, some movement or balance between these distinguishable styles (without attributing any gender identity to them) would seem to be a more realistic and equitable ideal to aim for—what some recommend as a "middle-ground" model or "androgynous" paradigm of leadership."[18]

The "teaching archetype," which is invoked by Aburdene and Naisbitt also suggests an intermediate kind of position.[19] Still, no specifics as to what this might entail are offered, and there is certainly no single conception of what it means to be a good teacher. If this refers to a style of leadership that seeks to empower others by imparting information while remaining open to other perspectives or suggestions, yet also maintains a sense of control, insists on the value of mentoring and taking responsibility for decisions, as Naisbitt and Aburdene imply, then perhaps this is a worthy ideal to aim for. However, just as there is no uniform ideal for leading, neither is there simply one style of teaching; and being an effective leader or teacher often depends upon the context—that is, whom one is working with, what the objectives and priorities are, and how much time one has for meeting these demands. And, we often find good as well as bad teachers of both sexes—for some reason teaching archetypes have not traditionally been identified with one sex or the other—which is perhaps why such might serve as an effective androgynous model.

We would like to add here that one need not begin with the assumption that there must be only one paradigm of leadership appropriate for the future. Any question involving "the good"—or what is required to be a good leader, teacher, or human being—continues to come back to this key concept of flexibility. Specifically, the capacity to remain open and responsive to what a particular situation calls for and sensitive to what individual issues are at stake cannot be emphasized enough when it comes to ethical questions in any field or human endeavor. To proponents of "multiple intelligences," this ability represents just that—namely, a particular kind of practical intelligence or talent for making the specific adjustments necessary in order to get things done.[20]

Nevertheless, there are basic principles that must be adhered to in order to avoid the kind of situational ethics, or ethical relativism, that would justify almost any action or position. Other than this oft-repeated admonition that one ought to cultivate some sense of flexibility or receptivity, we might also add that integrity and maintaining the courage of one's convictions are of equal value. So, if women are said to exemplify the former and men, the latter, then both have something to learn from one another. But, can we find anything more concrete to say about women and leadership? Is there anything more specific in terms of policy that would assist in closing the gender gap in management? Time and again three things are cited in the literature which are said to function as effective means of breaking or "softening" the glass ceiling: the importance of mentors and networking, "flex time," and child care (see fig. 6.1). We will conclude by briefly considering the advantages of each.

MENTORING AND NETWORKING

Even though only 30 percent of the women in the 1996 Catalyst survey cited the lack of mentoring as an inhibiting factor in their advancement (see fig. 6.1), the value of having a role model should not be underestimated. A 1990 survey found that 74 percent of female executives at Fortune 2000 companies had a mentor. And a 1992 study by Catalyst found that mentoring helped women to adjust to a company's informal social structure and to feel more comfortable in general in the corporate culture.[21] The problem is that many women find it difficult to find appropriate mentors. Women mentors are few and far between due to the very existence of a glass ceiling; and in cases of cross-sex mentoring, women and men are often reluctant to seek each other out due to the possibility of sexual tensions or the concern that others would disapprove of the relationship for these same reasons. In addition, many women have reportedly been subjected to sexual innuendo or harassment by the very men they had trusted to mentor them.

When male senior executives were asked what factors had been critical to their success, many reported that having an influential mentor was second in importance only to their education.[22] So, it may seem odd that more women do not see mentoring as significant. However, as Catalyst's 1994 and 1996 reports indicate, this may be due to the particular gender-related challenges women face. Their research has found that, for women, there are both interpersonal and organizational barriers to effective mentoring. Not only is the potential for sexual innuendo or harassment ever present in cross-sex mentoring, but women have problems with mentoring for other reasons as well: the lack of access to informal networks of information, tokenism, stereotyping, the sheer absence of older or more experienced women available, and the apparent unwillingness of men to mentor younger women. We might ask why the latter would be a problem for men, and, most likely, the answer lies in the confusion surrounding the sexual harassment issue (see chapter 3). For whether a man is actually a harasser or not, there is always the fear of a lawsuit or concern with being informally charged. So, while the value of mentoring for women should not be underestimated, we still find ourselves in another Catch-22. For, in order to envision women in leadership roles, it would be helpful if there already were women in such positions to look to as role models. And yet, it is the glass ceiling itself that makes this nearly impossible.

Another strategy related to mentoring is that of women's networking or "women's councils." Just as groups for ethnic minorities have been formed to serve both their needs and the corporation's, so too have corporate women's groups been created in this manner. This may be especially useful as one of the other barriers cited above is the lack of access to informal networks, which have been traditionally male. Presumably, such groups could serve women's interests and accommodate the frequent demands made on their time. For the woman who has family responsibilities may be unable to take two-hour lunches with colleagues or play nine holes of golf, because her job is only one aspect of a very busy lifestyle. Perhaps this is also due to the fact that a woman's identity is generally not as tied to her vocation as a man's tends to be, especially when she is expected to fulfill the roles of dutiful daughter, wife, and/or mother. Catalyst's research shows that there is no typical corporate women's council, as they vary in terms of membership, structure and reason for origin.

However, most share the same basic goals of enhancing communication, identifying glass ceiling issues, testing pilot programs, boosting employee morale and company image, and developing leadership skills of members. Many groups examine corporate policy issues, such as work/family issues, diversity objectives and career paths, while others focus on career and skills development. Networks pursue their objectives through a variety of channels, including speaking engagements, works-hops, task forces and publications.[23]

This kind of networking has proved invaluable to the women who have had the opportunity to take advantage of it. For it may provide a "safe haven," in the context of a male-dominated work environment, where not only immediately job-related issues can be discussed but so too can personal or family problems be shared by those who wish to and are comfortable doing so with their coworkers. If the domestic sphere is to be brought into the professional world at all, then perhaps it should be in this limited way where one only cultivates personal relationships with those who have chosen to do likewise. These groups may also serve as "brainstorming" sessions in which various alternatives to the traditional corporate structure and innovations may be raised and hashed out by those who would be most likely to benefit from them. For instance, how can the demands placed on working mothers' time and need for child care be accommodated by the company in a way that is fair to both parties?

FLEX TIME AND CHILD CARE

As indicated above, one of the central dilemmas for working women who have families is how to strike a balance between their personal and professional lives. One way of enabling women to do this is for businesses to establish child care facilities in the workplace, and/or provide flexible working arrangements and hours. According to Catalyst, flex time, parental leave, telecommuting, job-sharing, and part-time work options are becoming increasingly common-place alternatives in many corporate settings. However, it is ironic that these strategies are among the least likely to have been used by women in the 1996 Catalyst study. One reason for this is that many women who have reached senior management positions have simply accepted the same intense time demands and have been willing to make personal sacrifices similar to those that men have previously made. In some cases, this may have meant postponing childbearing until later in life or forgoing it altogether. But most women, as well as many men, are no longer willing to pay this price for the sake of professional success. And why should they? What makes the rewards of work and career any more intrinsically satisfying than those of family life? Perhaps the most disturbing explanation that many women offered is that it would not have been "acceptable" for them to have taken advantage of options like those cited above. "Indeed, women spoke of going to great lengths to avert any perceptions that family responsibilities might affect their career commitment" (Catalyst 1996: 52). Moreover, this still seems to be the case today, as Catalyst found that most corporate environments are not supportive of those who require flexible working hours or arrangements. For example, women under 45 were no more likely to report that their companies offered such plans than those over 45 did. And that even those who only temporarily availed themselves of these alternatives were viewed as "less committed to their careers" (Catalyst 1996: 53).

So, despite the emphasis that is placed on women's experiences as mothers which supposedly serve to make them more effective managers, they are still regarded as incapable of playing both roles by the dominant corporate culture and no concrete means of accommodating motherhood are actually offered by most businesses. With all the talk about bringing the values of the private sphere or home life into the professional sphere, there still remains a resistance to such fundamental changes that runs even deeper. Finally, if mothers must go to work without their children, who will fill this domestic gap, and how will the demands of a household be met? We've already seen the proliferation of private nannies or *au pairs*, but they are a luxury only upper-middle class women can afford. Moreover, this situation has opened the door to an entire new set of problems. Just finding, and keeping, someone suitable for such an important and delicate job as child care, for example, can be a full-time endeavor itself (and is a responsibility that almost always falls on the woman). For that matter, nannies and housekeepers themselves are almost always women—usually women who are less educated, are considered "unskilled" in a market economy, or are undocumented or recent immigrants, making these women particularly vulnerable to economic exploitation or abuse by those who employ them. Traditionally, men with children were able to advance in their careers without facing these barriers because of the "free labor" provided by their wives. As this is no longer the case—65 percent of all American couples with children were dual-earner families in 1994 (*Bureau of Labor Statistics*, 1994)—other remedies must be sought. And there is no compelling reason why these kinds of solutions (i.e., corporate child care centers, mentoring programs, and so forth) would not be good for business and cost effective as well as ethical.

CONCLUSION

In sum, one of the conclusions Catalyst researchers have arrived at is "that in order for real change to occur, corporate leaders must develop the business case for dismantling the glass ceiling, then implement initiatives to eliminate the attitudinal, cultural and organizational biases that created it."[24] In other words, what must come first is the demolition of the invisible barriers that prevent women's advancement. Only then can the underlying issues be effectively dealt with; that is, the "symptoms" must be alleviated before we can begin to address the causes of the "disease." Perhaps these causes will simply fade away by themselves when they are no longer relevant. Or, changes in perception might occur over time solely because of the increasing diversity and number of women who are entering the marketplace and breaking barriers, which would render any attempts at stereotyping meaningless. Moreover, by proceeding in this way, we can avoid the kind of Catch-22s we've been witnessing all along. Discussion about why women are not promoted to the same degree and with the same frequency as men can go on *ad infinitum* without any real change ever taking place. The studies and theories could continue unabated without any action being taken or new practices established. Instead, what is needed are women workers in highly visible positions of leadership who can serve as role models, manifesting a manifold of different "styles," which would enable themselves as well as others to get comfortable with them at the top.

QUESTIONS FOR REFLECTION

1. How do men's and women's perceptions of the "glass ceiling" and its causes differ?
2. What characteristics are traditionally associated with leadership skills and in what ways are they typically "masculine"?
3. What qualities (other than those discussed) can you think of that are often attributed to men or women "by nature"?
4. What is to be gained by bringing personal or "family" values into the workplace? What are the costs or negative consequences of breaking down the barriers between the public and private realms?
5. In what ways might a woman's skills as a mother serve her well as a manager? Might these same skills work against her in any way?
6. Do you agree with the gender distinctions discussed here? If so, do you think they are in error due to how males and females are socialized in our culture?
7. Does feminist theory help us to understand the problem of the glass ceiling and find solutions to it? If so, in what respects? If not, why not?
8. In what ways are the different metaphors and analogies useful for illuminating leadership styles? In what respects do they break down?

NOTES

1. Catalyst, *Women in Corporate Leadership: Progress and Prospects*, New York, 1996.

2. See Catalyst, *Women in Corporate Management*, New York, 1990 and The Federal Glass Ceiling Commission, *Good for Business*, March 1995.

3. C. Hymowitz, and T.D. Schellhardt, "The Glass Ceiling," *The Wall Street Journal*, March 24, 1986, p. 1D.

4. Ann M. Morrison, and Maryann Von Glinow, "Women and Minorites in Management," *American Psychologist*, February 1990, p. 200.

5. Catalyst, *Women in Corporate Leadership: Progress and Prospects*, 1996, p. 37.

6. Ibid., p. 36. See also Figure 6.1.

7. Ibid., p. 39.

8. Ibid., p. 44.

9. Betty Lehan Harragan, *Games Mother Never Taught You* (New York: Warner Books, 1978) and Anne Jardim and Margaret Hennig, *The Managerial Woman* (Garden City, N.J.: Anchor Press/Doubleday, 1977).

10. Morrison and Von Glinow, p. 201.

11. Marilyn Loden, *Feminine Leadership, or How to Succeed in Business without Being One of the Boys* (New York: Times Books, 1985), claims that "much of what masculinism promotes is by definition alien to the majority of women in our society," p. 27. The validity of this claim will be considered towards the end of this chapter.

12. Sally Helgesen, *The Female Advantage: Women's Ways of Leadership* (New York: Doubleday/Currency, 1990), Chapter 1.

13. Patricia Aburdene and John Naisbitt, *Megatrends for Women: From Liberation to Leadership* (New York: Fawcett Columbine, 1992), pp. 100-101.

14. *Feminine Leadership or How To Succeed in Business Without Being One of The Boys*, pp. 184-85.

15. *Megatrends*, p. 103.

16. Susan Llewelyn Leach, "Success and Leadership Styles: Men and Women Seek Common Ground," *The Christian Science Monitor*, July 13, 1993, p. 9.

17. For more on linguistic gender differences, see Deborah Tannen's work or our discussion of this in Chapter 3, "Sexual Harassment."

18. James H. Davis, Alan B. Henkin, and Carol A. Singleton, "Conflict as an Asset: Perceptions and Dispositions of Executive Women in Higher Education and Business," *Education Research Quarterly*, 1994, Volume 17, Number 3. Without going into specifics, this article briefly identifies distinct styles of management by sex and then states that, "[a]lternative views commend a middle-ground model of androgynous leadership," p. 16.

19. Naisbitt and Aburdene, p. 105.

20. See Howard Gardner, *Frames of Mind* (New York: Basic Books, 1993). Gardner calls the particular intelligence that deals with communication skills "interpersonal" and insists that this is not merely a talent but an actual form of intelligence found particularly strong in certain politicians and religious leaders (like Jesse Jackson and Bill Clinton, for example).

21. *On the Line: Women's Career Advancement*, 1992.

22 *Korn/Ferry International's Executive Profile: A Decade of Change in Corporate Leadership*, New York: Korn/Ferry International and UCLA Anderson Graduate School of Management, 1990.

23. Catalyst, *Cracking the Glass Ceiling: Strategies for Success*, New York, 1992, pp. 49-50.

24. Catalyst, *The Year in Perspective*, New York, June 1994.

7

WORKING-CLASS WOMEN

Most of us are clerks, secretaries, salesgirls, social workers, nurses, and—if lucky enough to be working—teachers. For us, the superwoman who knits marriage, career, and motherhood into a satisfying life without dropping a stitch is as oppressive a role model as the airbrushed Bunny in the Playboy centerfold or that Cosmopolitan Girl.

—Sylvia Rabiner

INTRODUCTION

After discussing a "woman's place" at the high end of the economic ladder—as managers, corporate officers, and executives of the "white-collar" world (chapter 6)—we will now consider how women fare at the other end of the scale. That is, what particular issues and problems do low-income or working-class women face? And, how do traditional cultural assumptions operate against their interests while effectively serving those of employers and capitalists? In reality, most women do not find themselves in white-collar or professional positions, especially those that require a college degree. Rather, percentages indicate that the majority of women work in "unskilled" labor or service positions. However, there is also a significant number of women—though still a minority—breaking ground in blue-collar jobs, or trades that require some formal or technical training. And, despite the often extensive preparation required to obtain such jobs, they, like their sisters who are breaking barriers in the corporate world, are often victims of gender and sexual harassment or find themselves alienated or resented in various ways by the men they work with. Yet, women in traditional fields or pink-collar jobs, as well as those performing untraditional blue-collar work, are seldom mentioned in studies or surveys, leaving us with only a sketchy picture of their situation and forcing us to rely on individual voices or anecdotal evidence in order to discern it at all. Generally speaking, it is the women coming out of universities and graduate schools who write and speak about concerns in the workplace. Consequently, it is usually the concerns of middle- and upper-class women that are seen as primary, allowing us to lose sight of those in the majority who constitute the working-class.[1]

While there have been several articles available lately covering the experiences of professional women who break through the glass ceiling, there have been few which deal with women electricians, plumbers, waitresses, and homemakers. What we are attempting to do here is give these women a voice. As mentioned previously, in chapters 4 and 5, it takes a lot of time, energy, and education to enter into feminist debates or to engage in conversations about equality, social justice, and the possibilities for remedying gender discrimination. This is time, energy, and education that most women, especially those with young children, simply do not have, for they live too close to the precipice to think about much more than the next paycheck. Nonetheless, this majority should not be overlooked and studies reflecting their work experiences, allowing their voices to be heard, need to be done in order to avoid falling into the trap that academics and feminist scholars have often been criticized for— namely, creating or perpetuating an elitism that tends to throw a wide net over everyone by reducing all experience to fundamental categories and concepts that are gender, sex, race or class biased. Just as highly educated prosperous males cannot speak for all men, the academic or professional woman cannot claim to share the same experiences or ethical sensibilities with her working-class sisters. (Even the very notion of "sisterhood" is questionable, as not all women identify themselves in this way or share this sense of solidarity.)

What we can and should do, however, is seek these women out in order to listen to and record what they have to say, thereby allowing them a political "voice" that they otherwise might not have. Still, we must be careful to remind ourselves that we remain "on the outside looking in."[2] We also want to faithfully represent the concerns of single working mothers who, for whatever reason, have to function as the primary breadwinners as well as caretakers for their families. While the pundits sort out what to do about the rising problem of single parenting, the fact is that these women are not going away any time soon, so their needs must be addressed. As the heads of households, they have a right to work and raise their children according to some basic standards of decency. This is true both for their own sakes and for the sake of society as a whole, because the price we pay for ignoring the consequences of children brought up in poverty with a lack of adult attention is far too great.

Professor John DiIulio of Princeton University has studied the escalating juvenile crime rate and is disturbed by what he sees. He tells us that, "between 1985 and 1994, juvenile arrests for murder increased one hundred and fifty percent, while arrests for aggravated assault and weapons charges doubled." He concludes that, "in fifteen years there will be anywhere from one hundred and fifty thousand to two hundred thousand juveniles in confinement on any given day, almost three times the current figure."[3] The good news we have been hearing lately about the national decrease in crime is deceptive, for offenses committed by adolescents are increasing, especially in the inner city. These young criminals have, almost without exception, been raised in homes with single mothers. In years past it has been "politically incorrect" to speak of a correlation between single parenting, drugs, and crime, yet the statistics can no longer be ignored. Simply put, there is a link between disintegrating, poverty-stricken families and social problems such as adolescent criminal activity, drug usage, and gang identification. But this is not really news, for poverty and crime have always been connected. And, regardless of which comes first or what the ultimate causes are, this is everybody's problem.

It is not our contention that all single mothers are deficient parents or that single parenting alone is the source of our social ills. But, we cannot deny that there are problems plaguing the inner city and spreading to suburbia that are directly tied to the family and how well or poorly it functions. What we want to call attention to in particular is the fact that when poor women's or low-income families' needs are denied, the whole society suffers. And, while welfare, too, as we know it, is riddled with problems, some form of political and economic support is necessary. DiIulio suggests that the only institution capable of intervention and outreach is the community church, and that social services should be funneled through these traditional forms of association instead of govern-mental agencies. For inner-city churches are both relatively stable and have the trust of those living within the community where low-income families have a history of distrusting "outside" authorities.

While some of the issues already covered in previous chapters become relevant once again with this focus on working-class women, we also bear witness to a group that sees the world through a different lens. For example, when we listen to what these women have to say, we hear a distinct view of the power hierarchy and their relation to it. We also see a different conception of what it means to be a mother and what being a family entails or involves. Specifically, the notion that partnering with a man suggests security or support in a long-term sense is not part of the experience or expectations of most of these women. More often than not, they see men come and go, so it would be pure folly for these women to expect them to provide any kind of long-term safety net or support. On the contrary, in many cases these women have not only had to be the sole source of income and financial security for their children, but have had their men depend upon them for this as well. This same skeptical attitude or, perhaps, "pragmatism" is displayed when one is forced to count on governmental support. For this, too, implies a dependence on someone or something "outside" of oneself that may or may not be there when needed. Life is tough for these women, and yet they somehow manage to function within the contexts of the hard realities they see and, in addition, maintain a sense of dignity or self-worth.

Perhaps because their expectations are lower, these women realize that they are limited in what they can actually accomplish and don't allow their "reach" to exceed their "grasp." Rather than a hopeless or cynical vision of the world, their approach to life seems to be expressed in a matter-of-fact way that learns from experience and evaluates "what is" as opposed to "what should be." This represents both their greatest strength and, paradoxically, their greatest weakness. For this toughness may enable them to accept things they cannot change, but it may also lead to stagnation or resignation which prevents them from seeing any way out or potential avenues for change. For example, expecting and demanding that men take responsibility may go a long way toward affecting change for the better. If the community itself does not accept male abandonment, if it becomes a social taboo, probably less of it would happen. The acceptance of male irresponsibility and a willingness to have children without men's support is proving to be self-defeating. Perhaps this is why we see government taking the initiative once again to prosecute the growing number of "dead-beat dads." But, legislation should not be viewed as the only solution to such personal and social dilemmas.

Another difference between white-collar and lower-income women workers is the lack of "guilt" language. Working outside the home is a necessity and if this has a negative impact on being a good parent, it is not internalized as the "fault" of the working parent. This may be one reason why those who have children who turn to criminal activity or drugs appear to be at a loss as to what they might have done differently. We see that there is genuine concern about the children's well being, but not the idea that one can be a superwoman who "does it all." "[T]hese women recognize the clear limits of mothering both as their mothers practiced it and as they themselves practice it. They do not share the middle-class myth of maternal power."[4] Priorities are set in the order of necessity. Quality time with children is important, but it must come after the basic needs for food and shelter have been met. If working long, hard hours to insure that these fundamental requirements for physical survival means sacrificing time with children, then so be it. Care giving is not easy for these women—one woman joined the circus to feed and clothe her family of four; another performed arduous physical labor, such as hauling coal, even during her pregnancies to provide support for her children.[5] Perhaps because of sacrifices like these, lower-income women do not blame themselves if their children are not successful and know that they did the best they could with whatever limited resources they had.

In contrast, upper- and middle-class women do speak of feeling responsible if their children have problems, or turn out to be individuals they are not proud of, and resort to "should have, could have" language. Moreover, these mothers tend to trust outside support and are more inclined to seek it out. It is thus common for those who are more financially fortunate to rely on help from others outside the immediate family or community in the form of psychotherapy, drug and alcohol rehabilitation programs, private schools, and other such agencies. Unfortunately, these things are costly, so it is only those with "disposable" income who are capable of considering such options. This way of framing parenting is not found among many working-class women. Antidepressants and therapy, even the time for personal introspection or reflection upon family dynamics and problems, are luxuries they simply cannot afford. "The situation is what it is, so do your best and move on" is a typical refrain. This difference in perspective, and the means by which one deals with adversities, is also apparent when it comes to on-the-job difficulties like sexual- or gender-based harassment.

Pink- and blue-collar workers do not deny the reality of sexual or gender harassment in the workplace, but they are more likely to accept it as just another of life's problems that must be taken into one's own hands. These women do not readily turn to litigation or file grievances. However, it is hoped that with education and the support of laws prohibiting such behavior, standing up for one's "rights" will become a concrete option rather than a mere abstraction for these women—though presently there remains this lingering resistance to relying on management or support from those outside one's family or immediate social circle. A woman police officer tells of the time when she and her male partner were on duty and he pointed a gun at her saying that he just wanted "to see how fast you women cops can run."[6] She responded by reaching for her gun and demanding that he take her back to the station house immediately. When she reported the incident to her sergeant, he "laughed it off," leaving her alone to protest that she would never work with the officer again. Another woman, in an inner-city class of nursing students, talked about her tenure as a factory worker and the male coworker who had tried to touch her in an inappropriate manner. She waited for him outside the workplace, caught him by the shirt, and punched him so hard that he fell to the ground. The harassment stopped, and, from then on, she was treated with respect by other male coworkers, who had apparently gotten the message.[7] In this student's experience, there was no trust that there were "systems" in place to which "sophisticated" people could take work problems. The response from her fellow student nurses was unanimous insofar as they all expressed the sentiment that you cannot count on outside help in situations like these: you either handle it on your own or look for another job.

Perhaps this is one reason why many of these same students doubted the testimony of Anita Hill. For they see non-coercive and gender harassment (see chapter 3) as problems that can and should be dealt with by oneself alone. Hill's lack of immediate action and her failure to confront Thomas directly and forcefully seemed suspect. As an educated Black professional woman, they presumed that she could have easily gotten another position or she could have fought back. The prevailing attitude, especially among low-income working women, is "if someone sexually harasses you, only you can be effective in doing something about it." The same argument comes up when it is suggested that one call the police to assist in cases of domestic violence or marital abuse. Ironically, many of these women seem blind to the limits on their power or resourcefulness when it comes to fending off aggressive men, though they are painfully aware of their lack of control over their children. Still, in both cases, it is apparent that the trust that most upper- and middle-class women have in the various systems of protection is simply not there for their lower-income sisters. And, while we applaud their independence on the one hand, we cannot ignore the fact that these women are most often the ones who wind up victims of murder, rape, and other forms of violence and abuse. Thus, perhaps they need to learn to trust or rely on external powers that can step in and act on their behalf when they are unable to do so on their own. But this is a trust that must be earned by political authorities and, given the present state of our judicial system and government agencies that have a long history of bias against women, that is more easily said than done. So, once again, the burden of instituting change falls back on the shoulders of individuals, community leaders, social workers, and concerned business people.

Having indicated above how distinct perspectives among women can often be accounted for by examining class differences and pointed out the need for listening directly to the claims of women who may be unlike ourselves, we will proceed to divide the rest of this chapter into three parts. First, we will take an historical look at the underpayment of women as "policy" and explore how the "skilled/unskilled" distinction serves to perpetuate gender discrimination, as seen through the lens of the garment industry. Second, we will reflect upon the experiences of those who possess traditionally female jobs, such as waitressing and clerical, sales, and domestic work. These are positions that require little, if any, education and virtually no formal training, though we hesitate to say that they are "unskilled." And lastly, we will consider what women in nontraditional jobs or blue-collar positions that do demand some technical training have to say to us.

A HISTORY OF THE GARMENT INDUSTRY

The history of women in the garment industry is both fascinating and depressing. The invention of the sewing machine was at first seen to be liberating for women in the home, insofar as it freed them from tiresome hand sewing and gave them more time to devote to other matters. However, the sewing machine quickly became an instrument of oppression as women were hired to work in the garment industry for low wages. Early on, employers and capitalists realized that by defining sewing, or garment production, as an activity that is "natural" to women, they could avoid seeing the job as one requiring any special skills or training. If all women were seen as wives and mothers who "naturally" sew or make clothes for their families, then doing so outside the home could be construed simply as an extension of their domestic duties. This "naturalistic" conception of the task allowed employers to justify keeping it low paying and female dominated. As Cynthia Enloe writes:

Garment-company managers have drawn on various patriarchal assumptions to help them keep wages and benefits low in their factories. First, they have defined sewing as something that girls and women do "naturally" or "tradition- ally." An operation that a person does "naturally" is not a "skill," for a skill is something that one has to be trained to do, for which one could then be rewarded. Such thinking may be convenient and save money, but is it accurate? Many a schoolgirl has struggled through a home economics class trying to make the required skirt or apron without much success.[8]

Still the myth of women as natural-born sewers persists and serves to devalue the genuine skills involved in garment production. In a labor intensive and competitive industry like garment-making, the more the company holds down wages of "unskilled" workers, the greater the profit. In contrast, "skilled" positions and higher compensation can be limited to men who "naturally" possess the physical strength required for running specialized machinery, such as cutters, pressers, and zipper inserters. In factories across the globe as well as in the United States, such positions all pay more than sewing, though there is no plausible argument that could defend this kind of discrimination. Not only is it contradictory to assume that women's so-called "natural" capacities involve no acquired skills while men's "natural" strength does entail a capacity for performing skilled tasks, but many other realities must be ignored as well. For instance, many design options are available for this kind of technology that would make them usable by almost any able-bodied person. In addition, housework and farming place physical demands on women, which they have been capable of meeting quite effectively; and it cannot be denied that some men are in fact physically weaker than some women.

Another way that the wages of these women can be uniformly kept down is to regard the income they earn as supplementary rather than necessary. This is the case whether the woman is married, where the assumption is that she can depend upon her husband for support, or remains single and is assumed to have a wage-earning, financially solvent father to support her. Wives and mothers, it is claimed, will always put their domestic duties before their responsibilities as employees (which presumes the two are mutually exclusive). This denies the interdependence of the elements within the personal/occupational cycle: If it means providing subsistence for oneself and one's children or other family members, how can the responsibilities of the job be seen as secondary? Working women universally cite economic need as a reason for entering the work force, not recreation or the desire to earn their own "spending money." Thus, wage-earning women's vocational duties are inextricably linked to familial and domestic obligations. In the case of single women, the argument against paying them a decent wage is that their primary interest is to find a husband and start a family. It is claimed that work for them, too, is only of secondary importance, whereas for men it is essential. In sum, whether single or married, the labor activities that these women perform are not taken seriously. Consequently, they are treated accordingly, as the assumption is that they are in the work force only until they become wives and mothers or tire of such diversions. Many women themselves have bought into this myth, even though their own experiences tell them otherwise. Thus, they find it difficult, if not impossible, to question their employers' rationalizations and fight for better pay.

Lastly, there is the policy of assigning "piecework" and "homework" to women, which purportedly was implemented in order to allow for greater flexibility in working hours and conditions but instead has served as yet another justification for keeping wages down. In piecework, one does not get paid for making the whole shirt, for example, or for the amount of time it takes to complete such a task; rather, one is paid a minimal amount for each part produced. In addition to the economic hardship that this creates, the consequences of sitting and making pockets or sleeves all day long can be mind numbing and psychologically alienating. In piecework, the worker never has the satisfaction of seeing an entire product through from beginning to end. It is precisely this kind of scenario that Karl Marx criticized in his early writings.[9] When one is denied the valuable experience of acknowledging the end product of her labor as her own, because the capitalist severs the natural relationship that exists between worker and product, she is alienated not only from the product itself but from her work activities, herself, and her fellow human beings. This is because, for Marx, human beings are essentially laboring creatures and need to find themselves in and through their work. When this is restricted by separating the worker from the completed products of her labor, she is alienated from all other aspects of life. In addition, this kind of piecework can be done at home, further cutting manufacturers costs, justifying a low wage, and segregating women.

Ironically, it is precisely these kinds of "flex" plans, which corporate women are lobbying to put in place, that function against women in the garment industry. Those who are working mothers may find this kind of flexibility appealing, as it enables them to be at home with children and earn a living at the same time; however, for low-income mothers, working at home means that work never ends as one job feeds into another. In their situation, there are no support staffs of nannies and housekeepers to take care of the domestic chores while they perform their professional duties without interruption. This is one reason why flex plans may be more beneficial to white-collar, middle-class women who can afford a household staff and have the space for a home office. If a woman barely has enough living space for herself and her children to begin with and cannot afford to pay for outside help, where can she hide in order to complete her job tasks and how can she avoid the demands of her family? One minute she may be sewing sleeves, the next, folding the family's laundry, and the next, mediating a fight between siblings. It is clear that this kind of job flexibility may not serve these women's interests. It is more likely that they will end up working longer hours making less money, as they are paid by the piece and how much they produce rather then for their time.

This type of arrangement also allows the corporation to deny home workers other job benefits, such as training programs, promotions, and health coverage. In this way, exploitation is made to seem palatable to those who are being exploited, and they are prevented from seeing who really is profiting from flex plans. Thus, while white-collar, middle-class women are lobbying for greater flexibility in the upper rungs of the corporate culture (in terms of working hours, homework, and so forth), those who perform the labor (perhaps even for these very same companies) are being exploited by such "flexibility." For professional working women, homework does not consist of piecework. Like other corporate executives, they earn a salary and receive benefits that laborers can only dream of. And, salary and benefits do not depend on how many pages an executive produces for a financial report, for example, or for how many phone calls she makes. In sum, we can clearly see how the needs and responsibilities of working women differ depending on what kind of work they do or what types of tasks they perform. Thus, we cannot say, in general, whether "flex plans" are or are not a good thing for women in the work force. Like any ethical question, we first need to examine the details and the particulars of each concrete situation or case.

"THE BRIDGE CALLED MY BACK" [10]

As critics have pointed out for years, especially those with feminist sympathies, keeping wages low is not an accident of nature (in the garment industry or anywhere else). Rather, it reflects a calculated political and economic decision in which women's labor is used to maximize profit and remain viable in a competitive market. The few jobs within the garment industry that are considered skilled are given to men, whereas the bulk of the "unskilled" labor is placed squarely on the backs of women workers. Saying that a particular task requires skill or technical training directly correlates to salary scale, with the "skilled" workers typically making more than the "unskilled." Moreover, the argument that women earn less because their work is merely supplemental and temporary does not take into account the data that tells us that one-third of the world's households are headed by women.[11] This means that a decent wage is a serious matter of "sink-or-swim" for both them and their children. Yet, to maximize profit and stay competitive within a labor-intensive industry, those with the least power and the most to lose are sacrificed. For the shareholders and executives of a U.S. corporation, staying profitable may come down to a question of exploiting working-class women in this country or taking the work to "third world" countries where there are additional pools of laborers to be exploited and fewer labor regulations to contend with. The powerful metaphor of the "bridge called my back" reminds us that the road to wealth and prosperity is, indeed, built on the backs of those who are poor, could not afford an education, or have been denied other opportunities. These workers, often women and minorities, are forced into positions where the wages remain low because the value of their work is negated or the skilled aspects of their labor is ignored.

Finally, women's labor is kept cheap by preventing these workers from organizing or acquiring any political power or voice. As many of these women already distrust any kind of outside support or intervention and are accustomed to fending for themselves, it is not difficult to discourage their dependency on unions or some other form of collective activism. This is done by appealing to culturally entrenched notions of femininity and respectability and is further bolstered by a lack of governmental support or the drafting of laws that favor management and serve corporate interests at the expense of unions. The families of these women usually discourage them from being politically involved because it might threaten what little job security and income they do have. "Political activity seems to violate codes of feminine respectability by involving women in public conflict, conflict with men of authority."[12] Further, government officials do their part by passing laws banning unions, sanctioning only those friendly to management, or calling on police to break up strikes or demonstrations. Thus, both the personal and the political, in addition to the policies of the industry itself, work in concert to neutralize any collective power base and keep women's wages at a bare subsistence level.

In general, in order to adapt to changing styles and a demand for quality merchandise, labor costs must be kept as low as possible. By assigning piecework or homework, or subcontracting jobs out to small factories in depressed areas of the United States where cheap labor can be found and unions are weak or nonexistent, profits can still be attained without going overseas. To put it very simply, "if you can't move to the Third World, create a feminized Third World in your own backyard."[13] The formula for success in the garment industry (which can serve as a paradigm for business in general) has remained consistent from the Industrial Revolution to the present day: keep wages down, avoid strong union intervention, and, most importantly, keep the job female-identified and "unskilled." It is worth repeating that this devaluation would not be possible without labor laws that favor corporate officers and shareholders, and the cultural presumptions about marriage, women's work, family, and which kinds of activities are "naturally" feminine.

The postwar decades from 1970 to 1990 saw a dramatic increase in the numbers of women in the workplace, but their economic situation did not improve as one might have expected. Some scholars believe that this is because, with less unemployment and rising wages in the years after the Vietnam War, workers started to gain an edge on their employers and this eventually started to erode corporate profits.

Business had to find a way to slow down the economic boom (and worker advantages such as wage increases) in order to promote higher profits for themselves. This they did using a four- pronged strategy:

(1) to bolster profits by moving operations to lower cost regions of the United States or to other countries; (2) to diminish the power of the workers and their unions; (3) to reorganize the work process to use lower paid and part-time workers; and (4) to lobby the government to pass legislation that would favor their interests, such as changes in environmental laws.[14]

We have already seen each of these strategies manifested in the practices of the garment industry: One, taking jobs to areas where the cost of labor is low; second, exploiting social and cultural assumptions about women and family to prevent union involvement; third, taking advantage of flex plans in ways that will increase corporate profits rather than provide benefits to the worker; and four, exploiting the political power and access that corporations possess that are denied to most individuals.

In sum, the garment industry provides a good example of how sexism and gender discrimination is endemic to many corporate policies, and how radical the changes might be if some of our assumptions and attitudes towards women's work were reexamined.

RESEGREGATION

If we consider the statistics from a pragmatic perspective, it seems clear that women have made inroads into male dominated professions, but a word of caution needs to be invoked here. Two sociologists, Barbara Reskin and Patricia Roos, conducted research on twelve occupations in order to discern if women had truly gained "yardage" in the 1970s—and if they did, then by how much? Unfortunately, the outcome of their study paints an all too familiar picture: most women still worked in less than desirable settings, in "lower status" occupations, or in lower paid industries. This is a phenomenon for which Reskin and Roos coined the term "ghettoization."[15] So, despite, or in some cases perhaps because of, women's entrance into previously male-dominated professions, like baker or typesetter, these jobs lost whatever "skilled" status they may have had and turned into something else. Reskin and Roos give graphic examples:

[E]ven though women moved into the previously all-male occupation of baker, women's baking jobs tended to be inside grocery stores, "baking off" already-prepared baked foods and packaging them. The wages, benefits and skills of the "retail bakers" were relatively low. In other areas, such as typesetting, women made substantial gains in employment but technological changes in the field meant that the jobs required fewer skills and paid lower wages.[16]

The study also found there to be a resegregation of jobs, which crossed gender as well as racial lines. For example, practical nursing and low-paid clerical positions (such as keypunch operator) became dominated by African-American women. In all these areas, women did not make significant gains. Indeed, across-the-board in resegregated occupations, benefits, wages, and skill levels fell. This drop is often attributed to advances in technology which allowed machinery to take over the skilled portion of the job. In only a few cases did Reskin and Roos find genuine integration in previously male-dominated positions, and this was most likely due to pressure from women's groups or litigation.[17] Thus, it appears that most of the advances we have witnessed have been achieved primarily by women in white-collar professions who have access to avenues of litigation and/or support from women's groups. The majority of women, as this study indicates, did not make any real gains. For such progress clearly requires some political or social clout, if not direct government intervention, and most working women simply do not have this kind of power.

THE TWO SHIFTS

Working-class women claim they are working more hours, performing a multitude of tasks, and are basically feeling burnt-out. Unlike professional or most white-collar women, they seldom reap enough profit from the work-a-day salary to afford outside help. Without such resources, they are essentially working two shifts: one which is public and pays a wage, and one which is private (in the home) and non-paying. Women doctors, attorneys, and other highly paid professionals can, if they choose, hire others to do the house cleaning, laundry, meal preparation, and caretaking of young children. In other words, they can pay someone else to keep the "home front" going while they are at their salaried jobs, or even if they are performing their professional duties at home. If the workplace does not afford enough profit—and for the majority of women it does not—they get caught in the depleting circle of finishing one job only to begin the next, for which no compensation is offered. This has led many working-class women to ask the question, "what has feminism done for us besides giving us more work?" Or, "what have we gained other than longer hours and greater responsibility?" According to a 1993 study by the Family and Work Institute, "working women still do eighty-seven percent of the shopping, eighty-one percent of the cooking, seventy-eight percent of the cleaning and sixty-three percent of the bill paying."[18] So, until all kinds of work done by women is respected or valued, and salaried accordingly, we will have to admit that the feminist revolution has much farther to go.

PINK-COLLAR WORK

The term "pink-collar" has been used to describe occupations traditionally filled by women—jobs that are relatively low paying, require little formal education or training, and come with virtually no economic power or security. Women in fields such as waitressing, sales, office work, and homemaking are almost always regarded as replaceable, and the tasks they perform, though essential to the economy, are considered trivial or devalued. Not surprisingly, we find here yet another issue that cannot be examined without looking at the social and economic structure that perpetuates the situation of these women. Specifically, two things are operative here: the devaluation of "women's work" in general and the traditional definition of family that defines a "woman's place." Furthermore, when women make barely enough money to get by on, and have to survive from paycheck to paycheck, they have little power to alter the cycle of monotonous work and low pay as is often the case with factory and clerical jobs. The "ceiling" for them is barely in sight, glass or otherwise, in that most pink-collar jobs do not come with the prospect of upward mobility.

Advancement is not something that comes with the territory, and when promotions are given, they are relatively minor. For example, one may move, after a certain amount of tenure, from receptionist to clerk typist, but this does not constitute a significant jump in prestige, potential, or salary. Perhaps this is because the leaps are made within a female-identified vocation in which salaries are already low in comparison to the traditionally male-dominated positions. Often, experience or years on the job are irrelevant to advancement or salary increases. Waitresses and beauticians, for example, do not necessarily make more money simply because they have been on the job for twenty years. On the contrary, most of these women are dependent on both a healthy economy and the generosity of their customers. For it is only in times of economic prosperity that they can count on a steady clientele with disposable income or on increases in the minimum wage. Neither do homemakers have the assurance of pension plans or medical benefits, or any prospect of advancing to another level or type of work. Indeed, as we have discussed in chapter 4, the job of homemaker is one of the most vulnerable. As they do not even earn a bare subsistence wage, they are entirely dependent on the loyalty and good will of their husbands.

In pink-collar work, the employers who own these businesses (whether male or female themselves) rely on a cheap labor pool in order to remain competitive and realize maximum profits. Restaurant owners, for example, are usually required to pay no more than the minimum wage, again leaving those who wait tables to rely on tips or the graciousness of customers in order to earn a decent standard of living. Moreover, we find men holding waiter positions in gourmet restaurants, where meals are expensive and alcohol is served (making a 15 percent gratuity worth working for), while women are overrepresented in diners, and coffee shops where food is cheap and tips are low. As in the garment industry, men are hired as "skilled" workers and enjoy power status and economic compensation unknown to women despite the fact that they are performing virtually the same task. Many times women are turned away from the more lucrative restaurant jobs with the simple claim that, "we only hire waiters," or "we only employ skilled professionals." If pressed, the manager may argue that he is only looking for "experienced" workers, but the kind and degree of experience required is arbitrary enough to have the actual effect of excluding most women. For example, one can only obtain work in a "fine" restaurant provided that one has already worked in "fine" restaurants, with the employer alone determining what constitutes a "superior establishment"; and slinging hash in a coffee shop for five years certainly does not count.

Although such practices may smack of blatant sex discrimination, it is very difficult to prove cases like this against a proprietor, and most working women do not have the time or resources to make formal charges. Even when there are systems in place to combat such obvious sex discrimination, the process of bringing charges is time consuming and difficult, and the penalties faced by the proprietor are minimal. And, if an employer is forced to hire someone, the backlash against the employee will be far more likely to outweigh any benefit accorded to her.[19]

In sum, despite the fact that pink-collar jobs do require certain skills and these women should be regarded as trained workers, they do not have the social status or economic power and privileges that are afforded most men or white-collar women. Waiting tables means juggling the demands of several people at once as well as mediating between customers and cooks, managers, hosts, and busboys.[20] Office work requires knowing how to type, acting as a go-between, filing, answering phones, and, sometimes, doing several of these things at the same time. Similar claims can be made about homemaking skills, which must be learned, often on a trial and error basis, and are no more "natural" to women than to men. Thus, a change in our attitudes and priorities may be in order here. A space for dialogue needs to be opened up in order to collectively reflect upon our current values and traditions, where they may be leading us, and whether we are moving in the right direction. Only then can we expect government or public agencies to follow suit.

BLUE-COLLAR TRADES

Women have labored in skilled crafts alongside men since pre-revolutionary times when they worked as sawyers, loggers, grist mill operators, carpenters and printers. The first signed copies of the Declaration of Independence were printed by a woman, Mary Godard. The circular saw was invented by a Shaker woman. Its invention revolutionized the building industry because until then lumber had been sawed and hewn by hand.[21]

The past two hundred years have witnessed phases in "women's work" that have depended on changing economic and political circumstances. As mentioned previously, in times of war, jobs have been automatically allotted to women that were traditionally considered too strenuous or technical for them. When there is a shortage of manpower, whether due to a military draft or economic hardship, women are permitted to step in and pick up the slack in so-called male professions. However, when the war ends or the economy recovers, these women are expected to relinquish their training and job tenure and return to the domestic realm of the home. Unfortunately, in these fields, as in the garment industry, history has shown that unions fail to support women or have edged them out completely. For instance, "[w]omen made up a large percentage of printers until the early 1800's when the trade was unionized, and female typesetters also were driven out of their craft when a union was organized for the benefit of men."[22] During World War II, women saw a window open that allowed them into the industrial crafts, but it quickly slammed shut again after the war ended. One woman welder describes how employers' attitudes, wages, and working conditions changed dramatically from the period during the war to immediately after it ended:

There was such cooperation [then]. We got paid the same as men and got the same work and training. I was the first woman in New Jersey to be certified as an aircraft welder. I'd say half of the workers at Eastern during the war were women in all kinds of trades. We weren't trying to prove anything, just trying to win the war. We worked right up to the Hiroshima bomb and then they marched us out like cattle. They said I didn't want the war to end, but that wasn't true. I just wanted to keep my job. I was a damn good welder. But after the war nobody would hire us. Employers would look at me and say, "What are you, some kind of freak? A woman can't weld.[23]

In some cases, excluding women has even been built into a union's charter. And, in the early part of the twentieth century, most of the unions belonging to the American Federation of Labor refused to allow women members as a rule. Not until the Civil Rights Legislation of the 1960s and 1970s did women see another crack in the closed window open up for them in the trades, but they remain underrepresented, making up only eight percent of precision production, craft and repair workers, and comprising only 1.1 percent of construction workers as of 1988.[24] Still, access to skilled trades is crucial for working women, for these jobs pay at a rate of two to three times more than the traditional female vocations or pink-collar positions. Obtaining blue-collar work can thereby dramatically alter the quality of life for these women, especially those supporting children, as they often allow for flexible working hours, better pay, and greater job security, without the heavy investment of time and money that a college or graduate degree demands. Moreover, the benefits to a woman's own sense of self-worth should not be underestimated here, as so many "hard-hatted" women speak of the immense satisfaction that comes from seeing the finished product of their labor (the very thing that is denied to women in the garment industry, as was shown above).

Ironically, at a time when men are expressing more and more dissatisfaction with these types of jobs, women appear to be finding blue-collar work both refreshing and rewarding. Perhaps this is due to yet another difference in perspective. Often the very things that men are complaining about, that is, the "routine, tiresome, and alienating" aspects—women are praising. "Women may, in fact, value their apparently routine jobs because, in comparison to domestic work, they are stimulating, varied, and challenging!"[25] Besides, unlike the sometimes mind-numbing work found in the household or garment industry, these jobs actually offer good monetary compensation. Moreover, the skills that women in the garment industry possess are not valued as such, and garment workers are not inclined to see themselves as skilled professionals anymore than the homemaker or waitress is. This can do nothing but contribute further to their exploitation and the dehumanizing elements of their working conditions. Whereas, in the trades, blue-collar women are recognized as skilled or seriously trained workers, by themselves as well as by others, and thus they are accorded the respect and financial rewards that goes along with that perception.

Still, while there are advantages for women who venture into the trades or nontraditional jobs, they face many problems similar to those confronted by their corporate sisters, albeit from a different angle. For instance, because blue-collar women are moving into uncharted territory—like women in management or leadership positions—gender discrimination and sexual harassment tend to happen more often to them than it does to those who are not bucking tradition. Although these abuses are certainly not unheard of in pink-collar jobs, or anywhere one finds men and women working together, they may occur more frequently, perhaps due to the close proximity and sheer number of male coworkers, in executive and blue-collar work. It is also clear that executive women and women in blue-collar jobs present more of a threat to the male power structure than those laboring in factories or restaurants, for most men are not competing with women in these fields. However, the perspectives blue-collar women have and the means for addressing these concerns differ. So, in order to see how the same issue can be differently interpreted and dealt with, we will turn to some personal anecdotes of women in the trades and examine their strategies for success. As previously discussed in the introduction to this chapter, research and data on working-class women's experiences is so scarce that we must turn to the actual voices of the workers themselves.

Almost all of the women interviewed claimed that the hardest part of blue-collar work was the "attitudes" of their male coworkers.[26] Consider what Mary Ruggiero, the welder mentioned earlier, has to say:

Most men didn't want a woman around. They made fun of me, they'd sabotage my work bench and my tools. One guy said, "I got a woman at home, who needs one on the job?" Management is responsible for a lot of the harassment. They support the fellows' hostility rather than stick up for us. They have a lot of old-fashioned macho ideas about what kind of work women should do. They think we belong in the kitchen.[27]

Another woman who had followed in her father's footsteps and become a merchant sailor said:

My problems came not from the work, but from the men, especially after I gained equal or higher status with some of my shipmates. On my last ship, I worked with two ordinary seamen who would ignore me or turn and walk away when I spoke to them. Another shipmate told me that I had no respect for the male ego. "How do you think it makes us feel," he asked, "to have you go out and do the same job as us?"[28]

These are only two examples of gender harassment (though not necessarily of a sexual nature; see chapter 3 for more on this distinction), yet the sentiment expressed and experiences described here are typical. It is not just among blue-collar women that harassment exists; as we've indicated in previous chapters, we find this kind of harassment in the workplace in general. However, what is different is how or the particular ways in which the sexist assumptions about women and their "place" are manifested. For blue-collar women tend to experience a much more "in your face" type of harassment or more blatantly aggressive acts. Besides the obvious resentment expressed by the men in the cases above, many blue-collar women speak of overt forms of sexual aggression, for instance, being grabbed, fondled, or touched in a way that leaves little room for interpretation or misunderstanding.

Polly Jerome, a rural builder, represents a case in point.   She describes her ongoing experiences with a male coworker who became increasingly hostile and sexual towards her: "On one job, he decided that he had to hold onto my belt so I wouldn't fall as I leaned out the window to cut the metal siding away for the trim. Window after window, day after day, he began to put his hand farther and farther down in my underwear. Well, I was scared. Too scared to say anything."[29] Jerome had previously described another encounter in which this coworker grabbed her breast and she had reacted by trying to kick him but failed to "connect." Incidents like these are very disconcerting, leaving women not just psychologically vulnerable, but vulnerable to a very real and imminent physical threat in a manner in which other working women may not be. What this also means is that an "in your face" type of response is likely to be most effective or appropriate here, and many of these women speak of the satisfaction gained from directly facing and standing up for themselves against their harassers. Like most working-class women, they either do not or cannot trust outside intervention and tend to be quite self-reliant. However, in Jerome's case, her attacker was so aggressive that he did not get the message when she fought back and even seemed to enjoy her increasing frustration and sense of powerlessness. She describes him laughing at her, touching her in front of other male workers, and says that, in general, his behavior simply got "sicker." Moreover, being the foreman and her superior, he assumed that he could get away with it. It wasn't until some of the men she worked with, who had observed these incidents and were sympathetic to her, went above the foreman's head and complained to "the boss" on her behalf that she was placed under another foreman. So, despite the personal satisfaction of striking back for oneself, we cannot assume that this will always be sufficient, as some men may feel so much hatred and resentment towards their female coworkers that only intervention by others or a higher authority will have any efficacy.

There are other concerns that blue-collar women have voiced that are unique to their particular circumstances. One example is the problem of "ageism," which is a source of worry to them in a way it need not be for women in less physically demanding jobs. A female carpenter, for example, besides noting the pervasiveness of gender and sexual harassment on the job, tells of her additional worries about getting older and how she identified with some of her male counterparts who had been subjected to age-based harassment: "The young ones don't seem to realize that the old ones have forgotten more than they'll ever know, so they make cracks about "carrying" the old guy and doing his work, about how he's worth nothing and doesn't know anything. I see this and think—what are they going to do to a sixty-plus-year-old *woman* carpenter? That's why I worry."[30] This woman was well aware of how aging women are usually perceived in our culture, and recognized how much more problematic that would be for a woman performing manual labor. Specifically, once a woman has passed her prime childbearing years, she is often seen as less vital and physically diminished. When this perception is coupled with the view that women lack the capacity to meet the demands of physical labor to begin with, women in the trades have every reason to worry about how they will be treated as they age. Thus, for blue-collar women, the deadly combination of ageism and sexism can result in consequences that are not as likely to be faced by those in pink-collar or corporate jobs.

In sum, blue-collar women are alienated in various ways by their male coworkers, and their work can be quite lonely because of this. Still, many of these women find that they value their independence and solitude, and some flourish even more because of it. Whether this is due to their own inherent personality traits or is a coping mechanism learned in response to the particular difficulties of their situation, we cannot say. What we can say, however, is that women breaking barriers always have a tougher time; and this is true in the trades as well as in the corporate world. But, perhaps with an increase in their numbers, their own efforts, and the efforts of men who sympathize with or support them, conditions will improve. It is hoped that the next generation of women in these fields will not have to adapt to working alone or learn how to defend themselves against physical assault, but will be able to feel comfortable laboring alongside men.

WOMEN IN THE MILITARY

A final case involving yet another under-researched, almost invisible blue-collar category is that of the woman soldier. Moreover, it is another area that is experiencing growth in the representation of women. Women tend to join the military for some of the same reasons that they seek out employment in other formerly male-dominated professions: good benefits and salary, and personal independence. The use of the word "independence" here does not necessarily mean freedom from the constraints of a patriarchal institution; rather, it implies the freedom to leave one's limiting environment and enter a different milieu—one that offers financial independence, security, and the freedom (for some) not to marry. Although the armed forces is ambivalent about how women military personnel are to be trained and utilized, because of declining birthrates, they have been actively recruiting females. Reluctant to consider combat for women soldiers, the armed forces has still found a need for them in support categories such as computer technology. As the military becomes more sophisticated technologically, there will be an even greater demand for those who can function well in supportive services. And, the issue of combat may ultimately become moot, as warfare has already become more of a technical feat than one requiring brute strength.

Military recruiters are quite successful when they target areas where women have had the least opportunity for educational training and decent salaries. As a result, Black women have been choosing military life in large numbers. "While Black women are approximately only 11 percent of all American women, by June 1982 they comprised 25.7 percent of all women in the armed forces combined and 42.5 percent of all enlisted women in the U.S. army."[31]

Women in the military, like those in any untraditional field, face many obstacles, including sexual harassment and gender discrimination. However, once again, the particular form that such discrimination takes differs for women soldiers. For example, the otherwise innocuous fact that one is required to wear a uniform in military service can actually be used against women for the express purpose of humiliating or degrading them. Not only women in the armed forces but other blue-collar workers, such as train conductors, police officers, and security guards, complain of having to wear uniforms that have been specifically cut or designed for men. This is not an issue of vanity, but a practical one of fit and comfort. For how can these women be expected to perform their duties effectively, especially those involving physical exertion, if their clothing is constricting or does not fit properly? When these women formally or informally grieved about such matters, they were ridiculed or their concerns were dismissed as trivial. They were simply accused of being vain, shallow, or too preoccupied with fashion. This served to silence many of the women as their complaints were merely taken as "proof" that they "could not cut it in a man's world." Once again, we can see how many sexist assumptions about women's values and capacities are perpetuated, and how women in male-dominated fields often face difficulties that are unknown to those who remain in more traditional professions and roles.

Still, many military women claim that the positives seem to outweigh the negatives. Like women in the trades, they find their work challenging, value their independence and the security of a daily routine, and are usually well respected in their areas of expertise or are perceived as seriously trained professionals. Yet, there is a continuing discussion within the ranks of the military hierarchy as to what to do with women in times of war. Exclusionary points are debated, and the studies are still ongoing as to questions of physical strength, pregnancy, and the effects of menstruation. These issues are seen by many women as attempts to keep them from obtaining senior command positions that are only open to officers who have seen combat.[32] Like the rationalizations keeping women in "unskilled" positions in the garment industry, these "problems" are usually cast in terms of what is "natural" or "unnatural" to women. As we have seen in chapter 2, this distinction is often made arbitrarily or without any compelling evidence.

In conclusion, we need to rethink what women's work involves and, again, encourage discussion as to how women may be welcomed into untraditional areas without completely displacing the men who are already there. Most importantly, we need to seek out and research issues affecting working-class women so that they do not become a subgroup that loses its distinct identity by getting lumped into the mainstream feminist agenda.

QUESTIONS FOR REFLECTION

1. Do you agree that the women's movement has put too much emphasis on professional women to the exclusion of the majority who work in pink-collar jobs?
2. Has feminism ignored the concerns of working-class women in general, whether in traditional or untraditional fields?
3. What is the relationship between single parent-families living in poverty and social problems?
4. Is the inner-city church the best institution through which to funnel social services? Why or why not?
5. Many people feel that any real change in the inner-city family's plight must come from within the constructs of the inner city itself and the people who live and work there. Why has government and state intervention proved inadequate or ineffectual?
6. Discuss the "double shift" that working-class women say is leaving them depleted and tired. What possible solutions are there to this dilemma?
7. The underpayment of women is no accident; rather, it is a calculated method used by business to maintain maximum profit. Explain. Do you agree with this?
8. What problems are unique to blue-collar women? And, which issues do they share with their corporate sisters?
9. Why are many jobs considered "skilled" when dominated by men and "unskilled" when women enter in large numbers?

10. Should "homemaker" be a paid position and come with benefits? If so, how could such a system be instituted and who would compensate these women?

NOTES

1.   We do not wish to imply here that class lines can always be clearly or rigidly drawn.   Nonetheless, there are differences that cannot be ignored or denied.   Thus, we will be assuming that a "professional" or middle- to upper-class working woman is someone who has, at least, an undergraduate degree, potential for upward mobility, and greater economic power.

2. Louise Kapp Howe, author of *Pink-Collar Workers: Inside the World of Women's Work* (New York: Putnam, 1977), is herself careful to acknowledge that, even when she worked in a New York City department store, she had not "been there" in the same sense as her fellow sales clerks, who had been working there for years and would most likely continue to do so since they had virtually no other options available to them as she did (p. 23).

3. Quoted in James Traub, "The Criminal of Tomorrow," *The New Yorker*, November 4, 1996, p. 52. Note that Dr. DiIulio sees the problem as so intertwined with the disintegrating family that he suggests bringing back the "shotgun" wedding in an effort to "re-moralize" the inner-city culture where most of these juvenile offenders are brought up. (A "solution" we are not sympathetic to.) He is responsible for coining the term "super-predator," to describe the new breed of child criminals who manifest no remorse for their crimes, nor any sense of right and wrong, and appear to be completely indifferent to punishment.

4. Susan Contratto, "Introduction" to *Dignity: Lower-Income Women Tell of Their Lives and Struggles*, oral histories compiled by Fran Leeper Buss, (Ann Arbor: University of Michigan Press, 1985), p. 9.

5. Ibid.; see the stories of Irene and Darlene, respectively.

6. *Hard-Hatted Women: Stories of Struggle and Success in the Trades*, edited by Molly Martin (Seattle: Seal Press, 1988), p. 74.

7. This incident was relayed to Candice Fredrick during a discussion on sexual harassment in a 1996 ethics class. For purposes of confidentiality, we are leaving out names, dates, and locations.

8. Cynthia Enloe, *Bananas, Beaches and Bases: Making Feminist Sense of International Politics* (Berkeley: University of California Press, 1990), p. 162.

9. See chapter 5 for more on Marx's concept of alienation and labor theory of value.

10. This is a well-known saying or creed that came out of the feminist Marxist movement in the 1960s. It is a metaphor used to illustrate how women (especially minorities, immigrants, and those inhabiting "Third World" countries) are exploited so that capitalists can profit. Origin unknown.

11. Enloe, *Bananas, Beaches and Bases*, p. 166.

12. Ibid., p. 166.

13. Ibid., p. 155.

14. Teresa Amott, *Caught in the Crisis: Women and the U.S. Economy Today* (New York: Monthly Review Press, 1993), p. 30.

15. Ibid., p. 79.

16. Ibid., p. 79–80.

17. Ibid., p. 80.

18. Steven A. Holmes, "Is This What Women Want?" *The New York Times*, Sunday, December 15, 1996, Sec. 4, p. 5.

19. This is an account of one of the co-author's (Camille Atkinson's) own experiences, over a ten-year period, while working in restaurants during her college and graduate school years.

20. Again, Louise Kapp Howe states clearly, in *Pink-Collar Workers*, that she did not even attempt to "walk in the shoes" of a waitress (though she had tried doing so in other types of pink-collar work) because she immediately realized "how difficult and confusing the job can be" (p. 23). Instead, she spoke with those who were, or had been, waiting tables for many years.

21. Molly Martin, *Hard-Hatted Women*, "Introduction," pp. 5–6.

22. Ibid., p. 6.

23. Ibid., p. 34.

24. Martin, *Hard-Hatted Women*, p. 7.

25. Mary Lindenstein Walshok, *Blue-Collar Women: Pioneers on the Male Frontier* (New York: Anchor Press/Doubleday, 1981), p. xx.

26. See both Martin, *Hard-Hatted Women* and Walshok, *Blue-Collar Women*.

27. Martin, *Hard-Hatted Women*, p. 35.

28. Ibid., p. 183.

29. Ibid., p. 115.

30. Ibid., p. 47.

31. Cynthia Enloe, "Some of the Best Soldiers Wear Lipstick," in *Living with Contradictions*, edited by Alison M. Jagger (San Francisco: Westview Press, Inc., 1994) p. 602.

32. Ibid., p. 603.

CONCLUSION

We are living through difficult, confusing, and morally ambiguous times, especially in the United States where we find ethnic diversity, religious pluralism, and advances in technology and science proceeding at a rapid pace. These issues affect us all, whether we recognize it or not. And yet, the book of Ecclesiastes tells us there is nothing new under the sun. The problems of greed, cruelty, and indifference to others have always been with us. And every age and society has seen dilemmas that were trying or seemingly insurmountable. However, one way to test the strength of a culture is to see how it projects itself into the future and how well it can accommodate or adapt to change. Our lives as individuals, as well as members of a community, are precarious indeed: they can "turn on a dime." This is why we have maintained throughout this work that rigid systematic thinking will not suffice when it comes to negotiating the complex, human, existential issues of ethics. Just as people have been willing to seek, and have found, ways of adapting to radical technological developments, so too must we be open to change in the realm of ethics and morality.

If we cannot or will not make adjustments for women and minorities, we are in trouble. For it is they who will soon constitute a majority in the work force; thus, it is no longer advantageous for business to marginalize these groups. By the sheer force of their numbers, and increasingly through the power of their voices, it is women and people of color who will take us into the future. If we wish to remain competitive in the world marketplace, and also intend to preserve our democratic constitution in conjunction with a capitalist economy, then we cannot afford to waste human resources of any kind. Whether one is a worker, corporate officer, or philosopher, he or she has something to contribute to the culture, not only practically or materially but in terms of thought and discussion. Only through critical reflection, dialogue, concerted effort, and action can we look ahead with hope rather than with despair, for, to some extent, "we are all in this together."

Again, the precursor to solutions in any field is thoughtful deliberation. This is a process, sometimes without a clear end, which has to include an openness to all ideas and different experiences, as well as a willingness to question the foundations behind traditional theories and cultural norms. Otherwise, we merely learn by rote: that is, we simply memorize and reiterate what those before us have thought or said, and then act accordingly. What we hope to have offered here are some fresh insights, new ways to approach old problems, and a clarification of basic questions, instead of just a "book report" on what others have said or done. This is why we have resisted giving any hard and fast answers or coming to any definitive conclusions about any singular issue. Rather, our aim has been to stimulate others to discussion and to continue researching and pursuing further questions. In most cases, this comes from students, formally or informally, practicing dialectic—sharing and challenging one another and their ideas in order to engender insights and questions that the individual alone could not envision. Such may be a daring and daunting proposition, but, as teachers first and foremost, we believe that this is the only way to move beyond static thought and disabling prejudices. This is what we think should be meant by critical thinking, and nowhere do we thirst so much for this type of thought-provoking process than when dealing with ethical issues.

We have chosen to stress a few of the issues that women face in the workplace, but we wish to emphasize that many more topics of importance exist. We also have tried to show how one problem often slides over into another or may be manifested in various ways, thus requiring different approaches to resolution. For example, the question of women's capacity for leadership roles may be intimately related to the problem of comparable worth or wage gap. If women are seen as ineffective in powerful positions, they will undoubtedly be paid less; and, if they are paid less, this will be interpreted as an indication of their being less competent. In the case of gender or sexual harassment, it becomes clear that there is more than one way to deal with this issue, and that such depends upon the context and circumstances of the particular case. This is why we favor the methodology of introducing theory into practical situations, which allows for readers to get involved and see how otherwise abstract concepts and principles may have applications to contemporary life conditions. On the other hand, we believe that practical action without theory, or some prior reflection or deliberation, only creates further difficulties, as one is then acting blindly or thoughtlessly and often without regard for consequences. To paraphrase Kant, thoughts without content are empty, experiences without concepts are blind.[1] Or, as Socrates says, ultimately, the unexamined life is not worth living.

Thus, we have sought to show the importance and interdependence of theory and practice, the "universal" and the "particular," the abstract and the concrete, without valorizing one at the expense of the other. Philosophical ethics should be dynamic, vital, and available to all who ponder questions of life's meaning and value. If we had attempted to frame the discourse of our topics in terms that only other academics with similar backgrounds could understand, then we would have engaged in an exercise in futility as our aim was to encourage mass participation in dialogue. Philosophy in general, and ethics in particular, is an exciting, useful discipline that needs to be made available to all thoughtful individuals. Therefore, we proudly consider this book a work for anyone and everyone who cares about what it means to live the good life. We do not pretend, nor do we have any illusions, that our perspectives represent the only ways or best approaches. For, as we've said repeatedly, there can never be only one method, system or point of view when it comes to tackling complex existential issues. This is why we hope to stimulate more voices to enter into conversation, and we offer this work to serve as a springboard or catalyst for others to develop their own means of understanding and coping with both old and new dilemmas.

In many respects, this book feels like a contribution to "liberation ethics," in the way we have stressed personal responsibility and examined various theories (like capitalism) from a different perspective. The feminist theologian Dorothee Soelle speaks beautifully about the ways in which feminist liberation theology can revolutionize traditional theology, and, we believe, the same can be said for philosophy and ethics:

Preachers may tell of Mary and Joseph but do not know the particular homeless in our own cities. They expound on the story of the paralytic and his friends, but whether those suffering from AIDS have friends, they do not know. They mention the "Hungry," but the feminization of poverty remains outside of their horizon.[2]

Change the word "preacher" to "philosopher" or "ethicist" in the quote and it rings just as true. For too many centuries, theologians and scholars have remained in their "ivory towers" of abstract thought and academia, speaking eloquently of universal and timeless truths of human existence without actually descending into this realm of messy contingencies and uncertainties. We would like to think that we have avoided this trap and shown that everyone should feel that he or she has something of value to contribute. As moral beings, we should all care about dignity, fairness and respect and be willing to listen to the voices of those who have not yet been heard or to speak for those who have no voice, whether in the workplace or elsewhere. We hope that, in some small way, we have communicated this challenge to our readers.

NOTES

1. Immanuel Kant, *Critique of Pure Reason*, trans. Norman Kemp Smith (New York: St. Martin's Press, 1965), p. 93.

2. Dorothee Soelle, *Theology for Skeptics* (Minneapolis: Fortress Press, 1995), p. 39.

ANITA HILL TESTIMONY

"Statement of Professor Anita F. Hill To The Senate Judiciary Committee, October 11, 1991." Senate Hearing 102-1084, part 4. Washington, D.C.: Government Printing Office, 1993.

Mr. Chairman, Senator Thurmond, members of the Committee:

My name is Anita F. Hill, and I am a professor of law at the University of Oklahoma. I was born on a farm in Okmulgee County, Oklahoma, in 1956. I am the youngest of thirteen children. . . .

[Deleted is Ms. Hill's account of her early development.]

I graduated from the university with academic honors, and proceeded to Yale Law School, where I received my JD degree in 1980.

Upon graduation from law school, I became a practicing lawyer with the Washington, D.C. firm of Wald, Hardraker & Ross. In 1981 I was introduced to now Judge Thomas by a mutual friend.

Judge Thomas told me that he was anticipating a political appointment, and he asked if I would be interested in working with him.

He was in fact appointed as Assistant Secretary of Education for Civil Rights. After he was—after he had taken that post, he asked if I would become his assistant, and I accepted that position.

In my early period there, I had two major projects. The first was an article I wrote for Judge Thomas's signature on the education of minority students. The second was the organization of a seminar on high-risk students, which was abandoned because Judge Thomas transferred to the EEOC, where he became the chairman of that office.

During this period at the Department of Education my working relationship with Judge Thomas was positive. I had a good deal of responsibility and independence. I thought he respected my work, and that he trusted my judgment.

After approximately three months of working there, he asked me to go out socially with him. What happened next, and telling the world about it, are the two most difficult things—experiences of my life.

It is only after a great deal of agonizing consideration, and a great number of sleepless nights, that I am able to talk of these unpleasant matters to anyone but my close friends.

I declined the invitation to go out socially with him, and explained to him that I thought it would jeopardize—what at the time I considered to be—a very good working relationship. I had a normal social life with other men outside the office. I believe then, as now, that having a social relationship with a person who was supervising my work would be ill advised. I was very uncomfortable with the idea and told him so.

I thought that by saying no and explaining my reasons, my employer would abandon his social suggestions. However, to my regret, in the following few weeks, he continued to ask me out on several occasions.

He pressed me to justify my reasons for saying no to him. These incidents took place in his office, or mine. They were in the form of private conversations which not—would not have been overheard by anyone else.

My working relationship became even more strained when Judge Thomas began to use work situations to discuss sex. On these occasions he would call me into his office for a course on education issues and projects, or he might suggest that because of the time pressures of his schedule we go to lunch to a government cafeteria.

After a brief discussion of work, he would turn the conversation to discussion of sexual matters. His conversations were very vivid. He spoke about acts that he had seen in pornographic films involving such matters as women having sex with animals, and films showing group sex or rape scenes.

He talked about pornographic material depicting individuals with large penises or large breasts involving various sex acts.

On several occasions, Thomas told me graphically of his own sexual prowess.

Because I was extremely uncomfortable talking about sex with him at all, and particularly in such a graphic way, I told him that I did not want to talk about this subject. I would also try to change the subject to education matters or to nonsexual personal matters such as his background or his beliefs.

My efforts to change the subject were rarely successful.

Throughout the period of these conversations, he also from time to time asked me for social engagements. My reaction to these conversations was to avoid them by eliminating opportunities for us to engage in extended conversations.

This was difficult because, at the time, I was his only assistant at the Office of Education—or Office for Civil Rights. During the latter part of my time at the Department of Education, the social pressures, and any conversation of his offensive behavior, ended. I began both to believe and hope that our working relationship could be a proper, cordial, and professional one.

When Judge Thomas was made chair of the EEOC, I needed to face the questions of whether to go with him. I was asked to do so, and I did.

The work itself was interesting, and at that time it appeared that the sexual overtures which had so troubled me had ended.

I also faced the realistic fact that I had no alternative job. While I might have gone back to private practice, perhaps in my old firm or at another, I was dedicated to civil rights work and my first choice was to be in that field. Moreover, at the time, the Department of Education itself was a dubious venture. President Reagan was seeking to abolish the entire department.

For my first months at the EEOC where I continued to be an assistant to Judge Thomas, there were no sexual conversations or overtures. However, during the fall and winter of 1982 these began again. The comments were random and ranged from pressing me about why I didn't go out with him to remarks about my personal appearance. I remember his saying that some day I would have to tell him the real reason that I wouldn't go out with him.

He began to show displeasure in his tone and voice and his demeanor and his continued pressure for an explanation. He commented on what I was wearing in terms of whether it made me more or less sexually attractive. The incidents occurred in his inner office at the EEOC.

One of the oddest episodes I remember was an occasion in which Thomas was drinking a Coke in his office. He got up from the table at which we were working, went over to his desk to get the Coke, looked at the can and asked, "Who has put pubic hair on my Coke?"

On other occasions, he referred to the size of his own penis as being larger than normal, and he also spoke on some occasions of the pleasures he had given to women with oral sex. At this point, late 1982, I began to be concerned that Clarence Thomas might take out his anger with me by degrading me or not giving me important assignments. I also thought he might find an excuse for dismissing me.

In January of 1983, I began looking for another job. I was handicapped because I feared that if he found out, he might make it difficult for me to find other employment and I might be dismissed from the job I had. Another factor that made my search more difficult was that there was a period—this was during a period—of a hiring freeze in the government.

In the spring of 1983, an opportunity to teach at Oral Roberts University opened up. I participated in a seminar, taught an afternoon session in a seminar at Oral Roberts University. The dean of the university saw me teaching and inquired as to whether I would be interested in further pursuing a career in teaching beginning at Oral Roberts University.

I agreed to take the job, in large part because of my desire to escape the pressures I felt at the EEOC due to Judge Thomas.

When I informed him that I was leaving in July, I recall his response was that now I would no longer have an excuse for not going out with him. I told him that I still preferred not to do so. At some time after that meeting, he asked if he could take me to dinner at the end of the term. When I declined, he assured me that the dinner was a professional courtesy only and not a social invitation. I reluctantly agreed to accept that invitation but only if it was at the very end of a working day.

On, as I recall, the last day of my employment at the EEOC in the summer of 1983, I did have dinner with Clarence Thomas. We went directly from work to a restaurant near the office. We talked about the work I had done, both at Education and at the EEOC. He told me that he was pleased with all of it except for an article and speech that I had done for him while we were at the Office for Civil Rights. Finally he made a comment that I will vividly remember. He said that if I ever told anyone of his behavior that it would ruin his career. This was not an apology; nor was it an explanation. That was his last remark about the possibility of our going out or reference to his behavior.

In July of 1983 I left the Washington, D.C. area and I've had minimal contacts with Judge Clarence Thomas since. I am of course aware from the press that some questions have been raised about conversations I had with Judge Clarence Thomas after I left the EEOC. From 1983 until today, I have seen Judge Thomas only twice. On one occasion, I needed to get a reference from him and on another he made a public appearance in Tulsa. On one occasion he called me at home and we had an inconsequential conversation. On one occasion he called without reaching me and I returned the call without reaching him and nothing come of it.

It is only after a great deal of agonizing consideration that I am able to talk of these unpleasant matters to anyone except my closest friends. As I've said before, these last few days have been very trying and very hard for me and it hasn't just been the last few days this week.

It has actually been over a month now that I have been under the strain of this issue.

Telling the world is the most difficult experience of my life, but it is very close to having to live through the experience that occasioned this meeting.

I may have used poor judgment early on in my relationship with this issue. I was aware, however, that telling at any point in my career could adversely affect my future career, and I did not want, early on, to burn all the bridges to the EEOC.

As I said, I may have used poor judgment. Perhaps I should have taken angry or even militant steps, both when I was in the agency or after I left it. But I must confess to the world that the course that I took seemed the better as well as the easier approach.

I declined any comment to newspapers, but later, when Senate staff asked me about these matters, I felt I had a duty to report.

I have no personal vendetta against Clarence Thomas. I seek only to provide the committee with information which it may regard as relevant.

It would have been more comfortable to remain silent. I took no initiative to inform anyone. But when I was asked by a representative of this committee to report my experience, I felt that I had to tell the truth. I could not keep silent.

WOMEN, FAMILY, FUTURE TRENDS:
A SELECTIVE OVERVIEW

- Women comprise 46 percent of the work force, and will account for 48 percent of the labor force by 2005. Their wages have become an essential component of family income.
- According to the U.S. Department of Labor, of the 57 million women in the work force, 72 percent work full time, while 28 percent are part-time workers. Many part-time workers are multiple job holders. In 1993, 3.3 million women held multiple jobs.
- The U.S. Bureau of Labor Statistics indicates that only 20 percent of contingent workers have employer-provided health insurance, compared with 54 percent of those in permanent jobs.
- Most women work because they are the sole support of families. The declining value of men's wages over the last two decades has made it nearly impossible to support a family on one income alone.
- Forty percent of working women are mothers of children under the age of eighteen, and approximately nine million (16%) have children under the age of six.
- U.S. Census Bureau data from 1994 indicates that families maintained by women had a median income of $19,872, while families maintained by men had a median income of $30,472, $10,600 higher. Married couples' median income was $45,041.
- Collectively, women lose up to $130 billion in wages due to pay inequity. This lost income has a tremendously negative effect on families and on the economic health of local communities.
- Since 1970, the percentage of married working women with children under age six has more than doubled; yet family income has increased by only 10

percent, while costs for housing, education, and cars have risen at a higher rate than the increase in family income.

- Taken from "Women, Family, Future Trends: A Selective Research Overview," An Analysis by the National Committee on Pay Equity, Winter 1996.

BIBLIOGRAPHY

Aburdene, Patricia, and John Naisbitt. *Megatrends for Women: From Liberation to Leadership*. New York: Fawcett Columbine, 1992.

Amott, Teresa. *Caught in the Crisis: Women and the U.S. Economy Today*. New York: Monthly Review Press, 1993.

Aristotle. *Nicomachean Ethics*. Translated by Martin Ostwald. New York: Macmillan Publishing Co., 1962.

Beauchamp, Tom L., and Norman E. Bowie, eds. *Ethical Theory and Business*. Englewood Cliffs, N.J.: Prentice Hall, 1993.

Bernstein, Richard. *Beyond Objectivism and Relativism*. Philadelphia: University of Pennsylvania Press, 1983.

Bok, Sissela. *Lying: Moral Choice in Public and Private Life*. New York: Vintage Books, 1989.

Brant, Clare, and Yun Lee Too, eds. *Rethinking Sexual Harassment*. London: Pluto Press, 1994.

Brown, Tony. Address. Black Human Resources Network Conference. Washington D.C. August, 16 1993.

"Can Computers Think?" *Time Magazine*, March 25, 1996.

Carr, Albert Z. "Is Business Bluffing Ethical?" *Harvard Business Review*, January/February 1968.

Catalyst. *Cracking the Glass Ceiling: Strategies for Success*. New York, 1992.

———. *Women in Corporate Leadership: Progress and Prospects*. New York, 1996.

———. *Women in Corporate Management*. New York, 1990.

———. *The Year in Perspective*. New York, June 1994.

Chapkis, Wendy. "Changing Landscapes." *Women, Images and Reality*. Mountain View, Calif.: Mayfield Publishing Co., 1995.

Chodorow, Nancy. *The Reproduction of Mothering: Psychoanalysis and the Sociology of Gender*. Berkeley: University of California Press, 1978.

Collins, Patricia Hill. *Black Feminist Thought*. New York: Routledge, 1991.

Contratto, Susan. *Dignity: Lower Income Women Tell of Their Lives and Struggles*. Ann Arbor: University of Michigan Press, 1985.

Current Population Reports. Washington: Government Printing Office, Series P-70, No. 10.

Davis, James H., Alan B. Henkin, and Carol A. Singleton. "Conflict as an Asset: Perception and Dispositions of Executive Women in Higher Education and Business." *Education Research Quarterly*, 1994.

de Beauvoir, Simone. *The Second Sex*. Translated by H.M. Parshley. New York: Vintage Books-Random House, Inc., 1989.

Denby, David. "Buried Alive." *The New Yorker Magazine*. July, 15 1996.

Durkheim, Emile. *The Elementary Forms of the Religious Life*. New York: The Free Press, 1965.

Enloe, Cynthia. *Bananas, Beaches and Bases: Making Feminist Sense of International Politics*. Berkeley: University of California Press, 1990.

Faludi, Susan. *Backlash*. New York: Doubleday Publishing, 1992.

Federal Glass Ceiling Commission. *Good for Business*. Washington D.C.: Government Printing Office, March 1989.

Feinberg, Leslie. *Stone Butch Blues*. Ithaca, N.Y.: Firebrand Books, 1993.

Gardner, Howard. *Frames of Mind*. New York: Basic Books, 1993.

Gilder, George. *Men and Marriage*. Gretna, La.: Pelican Publishing Co., Inc., 1986.

Gilligan, Carol. *In a Different Voice*. Cambridge, Mass.: Harvard University Press, 1982.

Harragan, Betty Lehan. *Games Mother Never Taught You: Corporate Gamesmanship for Women*. New York: Warner Books, 1978.

Hartsock, Nancy. *Money, Sex, and Power: Toward a Feminist Historical Materialism*. New York: Longman, 1983.

Helgesen, Sally. *The Female Advantage: Women's Ways of Leadership*. New York: Doubleday/Currency, 1990.

Hill, Anita. Testimony before Senate Hearing 102-1084, Part 4. Washington, D.C.: Government Printing Office, 1993.

Holmes, Steven A. "Is This What Women Want?" *The New York Times*, December 15, 1996.

Howe, Louise Kapp. *Pink-Collar Workers: Inside the World of Women's Work*. New York: Putnam, 1977.

Hymowitz, C., and T.D. Schellhardt. "The Glass Ceiling." *Wall Street Journal*, March 24, 1986.

Jaggar, Alison M., ed. *Living with Contradictions: Controversies in Feminist Social Ethics*. San Francisco: Westview Press, 1994.

Janos, Leo. "Jane Fonda, Finding Her Golden Pond." *Cosmopolitan*, January 1985.

Jardim, Anne and Margaret Hennig. *The Managerial Woman*. Garden City, N.Y.: Anchor Press/Doubleday, 1977.

Johansen, Elaine. *Comparable Worth*. Boulder, Colo.: Westview Press, 1984.

Kant, Immanuel. *Critique of Pure Reason*. Translated by Norman Kemp Smith. New York: St. Martin's Press, 1965.

————. *Foundations of the Metaphysics of Morals.* Translated by Lewis White Beck. Indianapolis: The Bobbs-Merrill Co., Inc., 1959.

Kilbourne, Jean. *Slim Hopes.* Videocassette. Northampton, Mass.: Media Education Foundation, 1995.

————. *Still Killing Us Softly.* Videocassette. Cambridge, Mass.: Cambridge Documentary Films, 1987.

Korn/Ferry International. *Profile of Women Senior Executives.* New York, 1982.

Korn/Ferry International and UCLA Anderson Graduate School of Management. *Korn/Ferry International's Executive Profile: A Decade of Change in Corporate Leadership.* New York, 1990.

Leach, Susan Llewelyn. "Success and Leadership Styles: Men and Women Seek Common Ground." *The Christian Science Monitor,* July 13, 1993.

Littleton, Christine A. "Reconstructing Sexual Equality." *California Law Review.* Volume 75, No. 4, July 1987.

Loden, Marilyn. *Feminine Leadership, or How to Succeed in Business without Being One of the Boys.* New York: Times Books, 1985.

MacIntyre, Alasdair. *After Virtue: A Study in Moral Theory.* Nortre Dame, Ind.: University of Notre Dame Press, 1984.

Martin, Molly, ed. *Hard-Hatted Women: Stories of Struggle and Success in the Trades.* Seattle: Seal Press, 1988.

Marx, Karl. *A Contribution to the Critique of Political Economy.* Edited by Maurice Dobb. New York: International Publishers, 1970.

————. *Early Writings.* Translated and edited by T.B. Bottomore. New York: McGraw Hill, 1964.

Mill, J.S. *The Subjection of Women.* Indianapolis, Ind.: Hackett Publishing Co., 1988.

————. *Utilitarianism and Other Writings.* Edited by Mary Warnock. New York: New American Library, 1962.

Morrison, Ann M., and Maryann Von Glinow. "Women and Minorities in Management." *American Psychologist,* February 1990.

National Committee on Pay Equity. "Women, Family, Future Trends: A Selective Overview." Washington, D.C.: 1995.

Neugarten, D.A., and J.M. Shafritz, eds. *Sexuality in Organizations.* Oak Park, Ill.: Moore Publishing Co., 1980.

Nicholson, Linda, ed. *Feminism/Postmodernism.* New York: Routledge, 1990.

Nussbaum, Martha. *The Fragility of Goodness: Luck and Ethics in Greek Tragedy and Philosophy.* New York: Cambridge University Press, 1986.

Paglia, Camille. Interview with Roger Ailes. *Straight Forward.* CNBC. New York, January 1996.

Paul, Ellen Frankel. "Bared Buttocks and Federal Cases." *Society* 4. New Brunswick, N.J.: Transaction Periodical Consortium, 1991.

Rabiner, Sylvia. "How the Superwoman Puts Women Down." *The Village Voice,* May 24, 1976.

Ragins, Belle Rose and John L. Cotton. *Easier Said than Done: Gender Differences in Perceived Barriers to Gaining a Mentor.* 1991.

Reskin, Barbara F., and Irene Padavic. *Women and Men at Work.* Thousand Oaks, Calif.: Pine Forge Press, 1994.

Rousseau, Jean Jacques. *Emile*. Translated by Allan Bloom. New York: Basic Books, Inc., 1979.

————. *The Social Contract and Discourse on the Origin of Inequality*. Edited by Lester G. Crocker. New York: Washington Square Press, 1967.

Singleton, Carole A., James H. Davis, and Alan B. Henkin. "Conflict as an Asset: Perceptions and Dispositions of Executive Women in Higher Education and Business." *Educational Research Quarterly* 17.3, 1994.

Soelle, Dorothee. *Theology for Skeptics*. Minneapolis: Fortress Press, 1995.

Spiegel, Fredelle Zaiman. *Women's Wages, Women's Worth*. New York: Continuum Publishing Co., 1994.

Szekely, Eva. *Never Too Thin*. Toronto: The Women's Press, 1988.

Tannen, Deborah. *Talking from 9-5*. New York: William Morrow and Co., 1994.

————. *You Just Don't Understand: Women and Men in Conversation*. New York: Morrow, 1990.

Traub, James. "The Criminal of Tomorrow." *The New Yorker*, November 4, 1996.

United States Bureau of Census. Washington: Government Printing Office, 1975 and 1992.

United States Women's Bureau. Washington: Government Printing Office, 1993:1.

Walshok, Mary Lindenstein. *Blue-Collar Women: Pioneers on the Male Frontier*. New York: Anchor Press/Doubleday, 1981.

White, James E., ed. *Contemporary Moral Problems*. St. Paul, Minn.: West Publishing, 1985.

Whitehead, Alfred North. *The Function of Reason*. Boston: Beacon Hill, 1962.

Wolf, Naomi. *The Beauty Myth*. New York: Anchor Books, 1991.

Wollstonecraft, Mary. *A Vindication of the Rights of Women*. New York: Alfred A. Knopf, 1992.

Woolf, Virginia. *A Room of One's Own*. New York: Harcourt, Brace, and Jovanovich, 1929.

INDEX

Abolitionist Movement, 19
abortion, 33-34
absolutism:
  in Kant, 3
Aburdene, Patricia, 120-21, 123-24,
  127
Adam and Eve, 71, 111
adolescence:
  and crime, 136-37
advertising, 47-49, 89-109
affirmative action, 86, 124
ageism, 154
agency:
  in Aristotle, 60. *See also* intention
American Federation of Labor, 151
American Revolution, 19
Amish, 90
Amtrak, 85
androgyny:
  concept of, 43
  leadership model of, 127
Aristotle, 9-16, 21, 25, 29, 34, 123
  on intention, 59-62
artificial intelligence, 13
autonomy:
  in de Beauvoir, 31-32

beautician, 148. *See also* pink-collar
  work
beauty:
  ideals of, 90-91, 96, 103-108. *See
  also* diet industry
Bernstein, Richard, 12, 18
blue-collar work, 84, 124, 135, 150-
  54
bluffing in advertising, 95
Bok, Sissela, 98-100
Brangham, Suzanne, 67
Brown, Tony, 82, 86

Cambodia, 98
care ethics, 33-34, 118. *See also*
  Gilligan, Carol
Carr, Albert Z., 95, 96. *See also*
  gamesmanship
Catalyst, 111-19, 128-31
categorical imperative, 3, 7. *See also*
  Kant, Immanuel
character development, 15
child care, 128, 130-31
Child Labor Laws, 85
Chodorow, Nancy, 34, 38, 39, 40
Christian Coalition, 68
Christian Science Monitor, 125-26

Chrysler, 85
Civil Rights Act of 1964, 55, 85
Civil Rights Movement, 19
clerical work, 83, 148
community:
    models of, 27, 30, 34-39. *See also*
    Hartsock, Nancy
comparable worth, 67-87. *See also*
    value
conflict management, 121-24
corporate downsizing, 14
Cosmopolitan, 49, 135
crime:
    drugs and, 76-77, 137
    adolescence and, 137-38
Crull, Peggy, 52

De Beauvoir, Simone, 21, 26-32,
deception. *See* lying; manipulation
deliberation. *See* moral deliberation
demarketization, 91-93. *See also*
    Nestle
Denby, David, 100
deontological ethics, 1, 2-5, 7, 43
diet industry, 103-105. *See also*
    beauty, ideals of
DiIulio, John, 137
difference theory, 38-41. *See also*
    Young, Iris
divorce:
    effects of, 76-77
Dodson, Angela, 53
domestic work. *See* homemaking
drugs, 76
Durkheim, Emile, 69
duty:
    in Kant, 2-4, 7. *See also*
    good will

Early feminism, 21-26
eating disorders, 96-104
Ely, Robin, 125-26
employer advocacy groups, 86
empowerment for victims, 64-65
Enlightenment, 21, 24
Enloe, Cynthia, 141-45
Epstein, Cynthia Fuchs, 126

Equal Employment Opportunity
    Commission (EEOC), 55-56, 58,
    67, 163, 165
equality:
    concepts of, 42-44
    political, 21-25
essentialism, 26, 34, 38-40

family:
    dissolution of, 76-77, 136-39
    leadership paradigm of, 117, 124
    religious conceptions of, 69-73.
    See also religion, worth and
    women and, 73-79, 131
Family and Work Institute, The, 147
Farrakhan, Louis, 73
femininity:
    conceptions of, 23, 25, 26-31
feminism:
    conceptions of, 45
feminist movements, 19-21
Flax, Jane, 38-41
flex time, 74, 83, 128, 130-31
    exploitation of, 143-44, 146
Fraser, Nancy, 38-39
free market, 75, 81
free will, 94, 98 *See also* informed
    consent
French Revolution, 19, 69
Freud, Sigmund, 32
friendship, 4, 14, 16

gamesmanship, 95-97
gangs, 76, 137
Gardner, Howard, 128, 133
garment industry, 141-44
gender:
    concept of, 25-27, 40-41
    construction of, 25-27, 63
    gap in wages, 82
    harassment, 63, 135, 139. *See also*
    sexual harassment
ghettoization of women, 146
Gilder, George, 72
Gilligan, Carol, 27, 32-34, 38-40, 43,
    111, 118-19, 122
glass ceiling, xi, 82, 113-16
good will, 2-4, 8. *See also*

duty; Kant, Immanuel
goodness:
   in Aristotle, 9-10
Greatest Happiness Principle, 5-6.
   See also Mill, John Stuart
greed, 93

Hamad, Kay Keeshan, 19
happiness:
   in Kant, 3-4, 6
   in Mill, 5-8
Harragan, Betty Lehan, 133
Hartsock, Nancy, 27, 34-39, 43, 115,
   119
hedonism, 5
Helgesen, Sally, 119-20, 124, 127
Hennig, Margaret, 133
Hill, Anita, 47, 51, 56, 140
   testimony of, 163-67
homemaking, 74-75, 114, 131, 148-
   49
   advertising and, 104
homework. *See* piecework
hostile work environment, 56-58
housework, 35. *See also*
   labor
Howe, Louise Kapp, 149, 158
Hughes, John, 55

ignorance:
   in Aristotle, 56-57
   Socratic, 16
Industrial Revolution, 134
Infant Formula Action Coalition, 92
informed consent, 98
intention:
   Aristotle on, 56-59
   of harasser, 55
intuition. *See* rationality

Jaggar Allison M., 40-42
Jerome, Polly, 141
job-sharing, 120
Johnson, Lyndon B., 92
Judeo-Christian religions, 63-64
justice:
   friendship and, 13, 15, 110
justice orientation, 32-33. *See also*

Gilligan, Carol

Kant, Immanuel, 2-9, 12, 14, 32, 33,
   119, 122. *See also* deontological
   ethics
Kantian ethics, 2-5, 100, 118, 122
Kilbourne, Jean, 48
Klein, Calvin, 91-101
Kohlberg, Lawrence, 32-33, 91, 102,
   119, 122

labor:
   "free," 114, 131, 148
   skilled vs. unskilled, 131, 135,
   141-45
   stored-up, 80. *See also* Marx, Karl
   women's, 35
   unions, 145
labor movements, 19
laissez-faire, 84, 102. *See also* free
   market
leadership, 111-33
   styles of, 116-19, 126-28
lesbianism, 26, 49, 106
liberation ethics, 161
Littleton, Christine A., 42-44
Locke, John, 22, 79
Loden, Marilyn, 121-24, 127
lying, 8, 14
   government and, 97-99
   manipulation and, 97, 98

MacIntrye, Alasdair, 16
management. *See* leadership
manipulation:
   demand and, 90
   free will and, 94, 98
   lying and, 97-98
market economy, 35, 36. *See also*
   Hartsock, Nancy
Marx, Karl, 35-36, 40, 79-82, 143
May, Larry, 55
media:
   advertising and, 96, 100-103
mentoring, 128-30
Merit Systems Protection Board, 51
Meritor Bank v. Vinson, 57-58
military:

metaphor of, 116-17, 124
women and, 117, 154-56
Mill, John Stuart, 2, 5-10, 12, 22, 25
Mintzberg, Henry, 119-20
Modern feminism, 21-28, 70
moral character, 9, 14-16
moral choice:
  paradigms of, 2, 13-15, 118
moral conduct, 6-9
moral deliberation, 2, 4-16, 40
moral law, 2, 7. *See also* duty
moral luck, 12-15
Moral Majority, the, 68
moral values:
  communitarian, 34, 37-38
  incommensurability of, 16
  masculine v. feminine
  conceptions of, 119-21
multiple intelligences, 128. *See also*
  Gardner, Howard
music videos, 47-48
Muskie, Edmund, 92

Naisbitt, John, 120-21, 123-24
Nation of Islam, 73
National Committee on Pay Equity,
  170
National Council of Churches, 92
Nestle, 91-92, 103
networking, 112, 128-130
New York Times, 49, 53
New Yorker, 49, 100
Nicholson, Linda, 38-41
non-coercive sexual harassment, 56-
  59
nursing, 84
Nussbaum, Martha, 12-15

Office for Civil Rights, 166
Oral Roberts University, 166
"otherness," 28-30

Paglia, Camille, 56, 62, 106
parental leave, 130
particulars:
  in Aristotle, 11-15, 60
part-time work, 75, 82-83, 130. *See
  also* flex time

workers, 82
phronesis, 9-11, 34, 61. *See also*
  Aristotle
piecework, 142-43
pink-collar work, 136, 148-50
Plato, 9
pleasure, 5-7. *See also* utilitarianism
pornography, 37
  in advertising, 91
post modernism, 38, 41, 42
poverty:
  crime and, 76
  women and, 77-78, 136-40
power:
  conception of, 29, 36-37, 115, 119
  sex and, 37. *See also* leadership
practical wisdom, 9-15, 123. *See also*
  phronesis
price:
  value v., 80-81. *See also* Marx,
  Karl
proletariat, 35, 36
public opinion, 90, 91, 93
publicity:
  test of, 98-100 *See also* Bok,
  Sissela

quid pro quo, 55, 63. *See also* sexual
  harassment

Rabiner, Sylvia, 135
rap music, 49, 103, 101
rationality:
  intuition and, 122, 123
  in Wollstonecraft, 23-25
reason:
  in Aristotle, 9-11, 61
  emotion and, 3-4, 11, 14-15, 27,
  30, 33
  in Kant, 2-5
  leadership and, 121-24
reasonable person:
  in Bok, Sissela, 99
religion:
  ethics and, 3
  worth and, 68-73
Religious Right, 68, 71, 101
Remick, Helen, 86

resegregation:
  in workplace, 146-47
Reskin, Barbara, 146
Rooney, Andy, 49, 105
Roos, Patricia, 146
Rousseau, Jean-Jacques, 21-23, 30 69
Ruggiero, Mary, 150, 152

scientific objectivity, 7-10
Senate Judiciary Committee, 163.
  See also Hill, Anita
sex roles. *See* family
sexual harassment, xi, 47-65, 125,
  135
  coercive, 55
  conceptions of, 55-59, 63, 139
  gender, 53, 63, 135, 139
  non-coercive, 56-59
single-parent families, 76, 136-38
socialism, 79. *See also* Marx, Karl
Socrates, 17, 161
Soelle, Dorothee, 161
special ethics, 96, 97
Steinberg, Ronnie, 86
suffragist movement, 20

Tannen, Deborah, 52, 61
Third World, 145
Thomas, Clarence, 51, 56
Time, 13, 49
Time Warner, 102
tobacco industry, 93, 97
tokenism, 125
trades:
  women and, 150-54. *See also*
  blue-collar work
transcendence:
  in de Beauvoir, 31-32
Truth, Sojourner, 27
truth:
  advertiser's definition of, 94
truthfulness, 100
twentieth-century feminism, 21, 32-
  44

United Methodist Church:
  harassment study, 51
United States Bill of Rights, 6

United States Bureau of Labor
  Statistics, 169
United States Census Bureau, 169
United States Department of Labor,
  82, 111, 169
United States Office of Personnel
  Management, 111
universality, 3, 7, 8
universals:
  in Aristotle, 11-15, 60
utilitarianism, 5-9, 43. *See also* Mill,
  John Stuart

value:
  comparable worth and, 67-87
  Marx's conception of, 79-82
victim's rights, 97
Vietnam War, 50, 98, 99, 145
Village Voice, 53
violence:
  eroticization of, 37
vote. *See* suffragist movement

wage gap, 71, 82-85. *See also*
  comparable worth
wages:
  and gender, 82-85
waitressing, 148-49. *See also* pink-
  collar work
Watergate, 97
Watson, Helen, 53-54
white-collar, 135, 147. *See also*
  leadership
Whitehead, Alfred North, 1
Wolf, Naomi, 104, 105
Wollstonecraft, Mary, 20-26, 30-31,
  43, 70, 107
Woolf, Virginia, 29, 67
working class. *See* blue-collar work
  in Marx, 35
World Health Organization, 92
World War II, 150

Young, Iris, 38-39

About the Authors

CANDICE FREDRICK is Adjunct Professor at Mount St. Mary's College in Los Angeles.

CAMILLE ATKINSON is Adjunct Professor at Manhattan College.

ISBN 0-275-95643-1

HARDCOVER BAR CODE